The Insiders' Guide to Factual Filmmaking

Tony Stark

Routledge
Taylor & Francis Group

NEW YORK AND LONDON

First published 2021
by Routledge
52 Vanderbilt Avenue, New York, NY 10017

and by Routledge
2 Park Square, Milton Park, Abingdon, Oxon OX14 4RN

Routledge is an imprint of the Taylor & Francis Group, an informa business

This book contains material originally written by the author for the
Jordan-based Arab Reporters for Investigative Journalism for use in the
Arab world.

Library of Congress Cataloging-in-Publication Data
A catalog record for this title has been requested

ISBN: 978-0-8153-6977-6 (hbk)
ISBN: 978-0-8153-6978-3 (pbk)
ISBN: 978-1-351-25146-4 (ebk)

Typeset in Bembo
by Newgen Publishing UK

Visit the companion website: www.routledge.com/cw/stark

For Ingrid, Adam, Simon, Melina, my mum and in memory of my dad and my dear friend Steve Annett.

Contents

Acknowledgements

I would like to express my sincere thanks to the leading figures in British and American factual filmmaking who kindly contributed to this book. Their insights and thoughtful comments have added immeasurably to the contents of *The Insiders' Guide*. I am especially grateful to those contributors who went beyond the call of duty and whose expertise and co-operation helped me to complete certain sections of *The Insiders' Guide*. I'd specifically like to mention: director of photography **Jeremy Humphries** whose valuable suggestions enhanced the creative chapters on directing images and filming interviews. My thanks also for his skillful filming of the examples on *The Insiders' Guide* website; production manager **Lareine Shea**, who's experience helped me dot the 'is' and cross the 'ts' in the more technical sections of this book; archivist **Gerry Healy** for his informed advice on using stills and footage from copyrighted sources and royalty-free archives; sound recordist **Mike Williams** for his knowledgeable audio advice; and facilities house MD **Peter Zacaroli** who kept me on the right track about the processes of post-production. I'd particularly like to express my appreciation to media lawyers **Mike Cleaver** and **Prash Naik** for engaging in an extensive dialogue about crucial aspects of the law as it applies to factual filmmakers. And grateful thanks also to my wife **Ingrid Geser** for her valuable input into the contents and the format of the book. Finally, I'd like to acknowledge the advice and help of **Mandy Calder** and **Coral Williamson** at PRS, **Julia Nancarrow** at SoundMouse and **Noelle Britton**, Managing Editor at BBC News and Current Affairs.

Credits

The photo shown in the middle of the front cover and on page 72 – Lasse Jensen/Tony Stark

Figure 6.2 on pages 110–112 – Steve Phelps

Introduction

Today's factual filmmakers navigate a landscape that's changed – and is still changing – beyond all recognition. What was once a specialist profession requiring expensive film stock, a technically skilled team whose livelihoods depended on a small number of broadcast outlets has been democratized by digital technology and computer editing software. One person can now do what four or five used to do and factual filmmaking has been brought within reach of just about anyone with a smart phone and a desire to tell a visual story. In parallel with this growing accessibility, is a marketplace for factual films that's undergoing a complete revolution. The lure of the internet and social media platforms is gradually depleting television of its audiences, especially young audiences – and content creators who've understood this radical change are chasing audiences online. The once clear distinction between the written word, the spoken word and the moving image is blurring: quality newspapers and radio shows have opened online video documentary channels. Traditional TV has also sensed the winds of change – with most mainstream broadcasters now flying the flag on social media. And there are, of course, a dizzying number of other online upstarts providing further opportunities for those who wish to make factual films: Buzzfeed, Vice, Field of Vision, ProPublica, London 360 and countless others all offer accessible outlets of varying quality and content for wannabe filmmakers. And if you want to dispense with commissioners and go down the DIY route, YouTube, Vimeo and Instagram await enterprising filmmakers willing to self-fund their projects.

So factual filmmaking has never been easier. There's never been as many outlets for producers' work. But if you're a newcomer to the profession you must also take on board that there are very few staff jobs. Most producers and directors of documentaries and current affairs films work freelance, relying on the quality of their work and the relationships they build in the industry for their survival. And much more is expected from factual filmmakers than ever before. Budgets are lower than in the past and schedules tighter. It's tough out there in the filmmaking world! And that's why I've written *The Insiders' Guide to Factual Filmmaking*: a comprehensive introduction to the craft and to the skill-set producers and directors need to survive in today's very competitive world. This is an '*Insiders' Guide*' because the advice offered in these pages is the product of my long career as a factual programme-maker. I have produced and directed a wide range of internationally based factual films for high profile broadcasters in the UK and US. They have included short news features, long investigative documentaries, undercover current affairs films, major historically based documentary series, low budget self-shot films and well-funded drama docs. I have also seen factual filmmaking from the commissioner's seat, running a documentary department at the BBC, and from the independent sector – executive producing projects for my own production company. But the *'Insiders' Guide'* title is also justified by the collective wisdom of 19 top industry professionals based in Britain and America who were interviewed specially for this book and their informed comments appear throughout. You'll find short resumes of each at the end of this introduction.

Who will Benefit from this Guide?

The guide will be an invaluable resource for students on media courses with a passion to become the next generation of factual filmmakers. Whether you are based in the UK or in the US, the advice in these pages will be relevant. It will not tell you everything there is to know about the craft, but it's written without jargon, assumes little prior knowledge of the subject on the part of the reader and will tell newcomers who'd love to make short features, long documentaries or current affairs films all they need to know to get started. *The Insiders' Guide* will also benefit:

- Journalists who want to move their reportage from the written page to the online or broadcast televisual worlds by producing or directing films.
- Filmmakers with some on-the-ground experience who wish to learn key safety, ethical and legal issues of making investigative undercover films.
- More established filmmakers who wish to run a commission on their own and need advice on scheduling and budgeting a factual film – whether the film is well funded or being run on a shoe-string.

The Insiders' Guide has an accompanying online site (www.routledge.com/cw/stark) where readers can watch 24 videos that illustrate the chapter on directing images, sequences and reporters – along with a range of downloadable forms to aid the organization of a production.

What's Covered in this Book?

Part 1: Survival Skills for Newcomers to Factual Filmmaking

- *The factual filmmaker's skill-set* – the attitude and the abilities that put you in the best position to thrive in the industry. And why collaboration is a critical component of success.

Part 2: Creative Skills for Producers and Directors

Factual filmmakers trade in creativity and this section of *The Insiders' Guide* aims to inform the creative process from start to finish.

- *How to turn a good idea for a film into a strong treatment* – the craft of writing a compelling film proposal that will catch the eye of commissioners who have the money to fund them.
- *How to direct good looking images that will edit together* – whether you are shooting it yourself or directing a camera operator, this chapter will help you make the best of your locations and your reporter, and shoot images that can be cut into sequences.

- *How to direct interviews and question interviewees* – basic composition, sound and lighting techniques for directors and self-shooting filmmakers. Plus advice on interviewing technique.
- *The art of visual story telling* – the key differences between written stories and factual film stories. And suggestions on how to structure a film narrative and visualize your story.
- *Finding the story buried in your rushes* – the organization and the attitude needed to make the most of your edit.
- *Making factual films for online content creators* – what factual filmmakers need to know to interest online commissioners and survive in the online and social media world.

Part 3: Planning Skills for Newcomers to Factual Filmmaking

Creativity and imagination are just two of many skills that go into the crafting of a good film. Part 3 offers practical advice on handling the logistical, organizational, and risk assessing aspects of filmmaking.

- *How to take risks in a responsible way* – keeping crew and contributors safe on location.
- *How to create a space for creativity* – organizing yourself before, during and after a shoot

Part 4: Undercover Skills – Key Editorial, Ethical, Safety and Legal Issues of Secret Filming

Miniaturization combined with digital technology has ushered in a new age of revealing show-not-tell undercover investigative films. It can make compelling viewing – but secret filming is risker than the average shoot – and *The Insiders' Guide* addresses serious questions for more experienced filmmakers who want to make serious investigations:

- How do you convince a broadcaster to let you film undercover?
- How do you keep yourself, your team and your contributors safe – during production and after your film has been shown?
- How do you avoid accusations that you are acting unethically – or illegally?

Part 5: Financial Skills – For Experienced Producers with a Commission Who Need to Budget Their Production

This last chapter is about preparing a production budget that lets you respond to a crisis without plunging into the red.

- *Designing and working with a budget* – how to give yourself the financial room to respond to the unpredictable demands of filming and editing. Plus a look at the hidden costs that can make schedule changes more costly than you might expect
- *A production budget demystified* – a line-by-line breakdown of a factual film budget – with detailed explanations of the more complicated spending categories

Who's Contributed to this Book?

The thoughts that I express in *The Insiders' Guide* are complemented by the voices of the following 19 top professionals from the world of broadcast and online factual filmmaking in America and Britain. They were all interviewed specially for this book.

Barbara Ballow. An award-winning editor who has been telling compelling stories for over 30 years. She has edited films on diverse topics – from religious pilgrimages to spying, autism and oil spills. Her films have appeared on PBS, HBO, National Geographic and CBS, and in film festivals around the world.

Charlie Phillips – Head of Documentaries at *The Guardian*. Charlie created and has run *Guardian* documentaries since 2014. This is a documentary strand set in a journalistic context that relies on actuality, more than commentary, to tell stories. Before joining *The Guardian*, Charlie was director of the Meet Market and Deputy Director at Sheffield DocFest and editor of FourDocs, Channel 4's online documentary channel.

Charlotte Cook – Co-Creator and Executive Producer, Field of Vision. Field of Vision is an online international documentary platform that champions a more artistic approach to telling stories. Before co-founding Field of Vision, Charlotte was Director of Programming at Hot Docs, North America's largest documentary festival. She has also worked at The Frontline Club in London as Head of Film Programming.

Debbie Ramsay – Editor, BBC Newsbeat. Debbie has been working with young audiences for more than a decade. Newsbeat serves some of the youngest, most difficult-to-reach audiences across the UK reaching them through national radio, online, with filmed documentaries on the BBC's iPlayer and on social media. Before joining the BBC, Debbie worked for commercial radio in London, Birmingham and the North West of England. She started her career in local newspapers after studying a journalism degree.

Diana Martin – Executive Producer, BBC TV, *Panorama.* Diana runs the development and commissioning process for the BBC's flagship investigative strand. She oversees *Panorama*s made by both the BBC production team and those produced for the show by independent production companies. Diana has also edited the BBC international current affairs TV series *Our World*, commissioned films for *Newsnight* and been deputy editor of the BBC general election coverage.

Gerry Healy – Freelance Film Archivist. Gerry has been an archivist since graduating and now provides content and specialist copyright and ownership advice for television and online platforms. He's worked on a wide range of genres and his credits include the BBC, ITV, Channel 5, NBC, Al Jazeera, Fox International, the Smithsonian Institution, The Imperial War Museum and others. He specialises in finding alternatives to expensive material.

Jeremy Humphries – Director of Photography.
An award winning cinematographer with over 30 years'
experience filming documentaries for BBC, C4, ITV,
National Geographic and the Discovery Channel. Jeremy's
filming has ranged across new reality shows, arts documentaries, history, science and current affairs films, dramas,
commercials and corporate projects. Alongside his filming,
Jeremy also trains production crews for leading TV production companies.

**Jeremy Skeet – Editor BBC Stories and Digital
Current Affairs.** Jeremy is an experienced BBC editor
who launched BBC Stories to attract a younger, more
female audience through digital story telling. His team
of journalists produces written, audio and video stories
on BBC Online, iPlayer, Facebook, YouTube, Instagram
and Twitter. Jeremy has also been Editor of BBC Radio
Current Affairs and a commissioner at BBC World Service.
Among the awards Jeremy's won are a Peabody and Sony
Radio Gold

**Kathleen Lingo – Executive Producer, New York
Times Op Docs 2013–2018.** During Kathleen's time at
Op Docs, the series published over 250 short films, vir-
tual reality and interactive documentaries, received two
nominations for Oscars, and won three Emmy and two
Peabody awards. In 2018 Kathleen became the Editorial
Director for Film and Television at the New York Times.

Lareine Shea – Head of Production and Production Manager. With over 30 years' experience in Production Management, Lareine has worked at some of the UK's leading production companies overseeing a wide range of award winning factual programming. She's managed projects in current affairs, documentary, drama doc, factual entertainment, observational documentary, reality shows and online. Credits include the BBC's *Who Do You Think You Are?* and the Grierson Award Winner, *George Orwell: A Life in Pictures.*

Leo Eaton – Emmy Award Winning Documentary Filmmaker. Leo has written, produced, directed and executive produced TV factual series and specials for US and overseas broadcasters for more than three decades. Recent films include 'The Story of China', a six-hour PBS/BBC series, and 'After Fire' a 90-minute Obs Doc looking at the problems facing three women after they leave the US armed forces. Leo is President and CEO of Eaton Creative Inc.

Louisa Compton, Head of News, Current Affairs and Sport, Channel 4 TV. Louisa has run the department since the spring of 2020. Before that she edited the channel's award-winning *Dispatches* programme, a strand that investigates issues in the UK and overseas. Louisa was also responsible for launching, devising and editing the Victoria Derbyshire programme on BBC 2 – winning a BAFTA and numerous RTS awards for the show. She has been the Executive Editor of BBC Newsbeat on Radio 1/1Xtra and Daytime Editor at BBC 5live.

Matt Danzico — Head of NBC Left Field, 2017–2018. Matt founded NBC News's experimental video unit with the aim of giving the company a stylistic edge with lovely cinematography, slick editing and 3D augmented reality graphics. Left Field collaborates with filmmakers around the world and can be found on NBC's website and various streaming and social media sites. Matt now runs his own consultancy and production company.

Mike Cleaver – US-based attorney. Mike provides pre-publication legal advice for TV programmes and feature documentaries broadcast by Discovery Channel, Netflix, Amazon, HBO, CNN, National Geographic and Smithsonian. He's worked on Sacha Baron Cohen's *Borat* and *Bruno* and the BAFTA award-winning *The Imposter*. He's a founding partner of the law firm SmithDehn LLP.

Mike Williams – Sound Recordist. Mike has been recording location sound on factual films for major UK broadcasters and online platforms for the past 20 years. He's worked across a wide range of factual genres – covering science, history, lifestyle, investigative, new reality and consumer affairs projects. Mike's experience also includes commercials and corporate work.

Peter Zacaroli – Managing Director of West Digital Post-Production. Peter established West Digital in 2002 and combines running this London based post-production house with his work as a colourist across a range of genres. Most recently he's specialised in factual, factual entertainment and features. Recent credits include, *Railways of the Holocaust* (Channel 5), *The Last Testament of Lillian Bilocca* (BBC4) and *Chris Tarrant: Extreme Railway Journeys* (Channel 5).

Prash Naik – Media Lawyer. Prash is the former General Counsel for Britain's Channel 4 Television in the UK where he worked for 23 years, offering advice and defending filmmakers across a wide range of high profile programmes – among them *Da Ali G Show*, *Beneath the Veil*, *Death of a President*, *My Son the Jihadi* and *The State*. He now lives in Sydney, Australia, where he continues his work as a media lawyer through his international practice Prash Naik Consulting and the London based law practice Reviewed & Cleared.

Raney Aronson-Rath – Executive Producer, PBS Frontline. Frontline is the flagship investigative journalism strand run by the American Public Broadcasting Service. Aronson-Rath oversees Frontline's reporting on air and online and directs the series' evolution and editorial vision. Under her leadership, Frontline has won every major award in broadcast journalism, including most recently, a duPont-Columbia Gold Baton. She earned her bachelor's degree from the University of Wisconsin and her master's from Columbia Journalism School.

Tom Giles – Controller, Current Affairs, ITV. Tom oversees ten different current affairs strands as well as documentary series and one-offs at Britain's ITV channel. Programmes that he commissioned won International Emmys for Current Affairs in 2017 and 2018. Before joining ITV he spent more than 20 years at the BBC working for the World Service, TV News, Newsnight, and making science and history programmes. He also edited *Panorama*, the BBC's flagship current affairs investigative strand.

Part 1

Survival Skills

1   The Factual Filmmaker's Skill-Set

A Survival Guide for Newcomers to the Industry

KEY CONCEPTS

- The attitudes and the abilities that a factual filmmaker needs to survive and thrive in the industry.
- Why multi-skilling is the name of the game.
- Why this is a collaborator's – not a 'loner's' – profession.
- Why creative imagination might be a necessary skill for good producers and directors but, on its own, it's not sufficient to guarantee success.

Factual filmmaking is a highly competitive profession on both sides of the Atlantic and anyone with a passion for documentary or current affairs considering a career in making films that reflect our world or reveal wrong-doing, must equip themselves with the right skill-set and the right attitude. A failure to do this will shackle your career prospects. So, in this chapter, I am going to outline the key issues that you need to consider.

Multi-Skilled Filmmakers are in Demand

The transformation of the media industry mentioned in the introduction to this book has given filmmakers who are multi-skilled a distinct advantage. Easy to use digital cameras, editing software that can be installed on home computers, declining factual budgets and a profession dominated by independent production companies and freelancers, have all ensured that producers and directors who can do more than simply produce and direct are highly prized. Combining two or three jobs into one person saves big money on budgets and many lower-budget factual films now expect the producer/director to do *all* the creative tasks involved in the making of a factual film: that is, producing, directing, shooting, recording sound, interviewing and even editing.

In today's competitive market, it is definitely an advantage to have a CV that includes self-shooting and editing skills. You might not become the best shooter – or the best film editor, but being competent at both will give you a distinct advantage – whether you are working in the UK or in America. But multi-tasking is not something to be taken lightly. The pressures on a producer/director who also

> If you're up-and-coming in the industry, if you have at least a couple of skills – you're a producer but you can also shoot – it's much easier to start being a filmmaker that way … The industry is really teeming with makers. If somebody walks in the door and they can shoot and produce we're much more willing and eager to hire them. Especially if their filmmaking is high level.
> Raney Aronson-Rath, Executive Producer, PBS Frontline

has to film a project are very severe. Doing this successfully demands the ability to keep tabs on many things at once – and it is not for the faint-hearted. See page 40 in Chapter 3 for more information on what self-shooting involves.

Collaborative Filmmakers are in Demand

> If you are just starting in this industry, make sure you surround yourself with people who are experienced enough and know what they are doing. A lot of time when people are doing their first gig, they feel almost like they have to do everything themselves, to prove themselves … And actually the best first time directors I've worked with are the ones that let you do your job but have good input at the same time.
> Peter Zacaroli, Managing Director, West Digital Post-Production

My first job in TV was on a now long-forgotten, but then much-watched current affairs programme called 'Nationwide' that went out nightly all over the UK on the BBC. I was a weekly newspaper journalist who had long-harboured an ambition to make documentaries, and the offer of a job on 'Nationwide' was a fantastic opportunity to take the first steps towards realizing this goal. So I moved to Plymouth, in the south west of England, and turned up at the BBC studios to begin my first day's work. I was a regional researcher. The job was finding guests with interesting current stories to tell to feed into the networked programme. On my first morning, I got a call from the London-based daily production desk telling me about a story my predecessor had found just before he left. "Hi Tony," said the producer. "Welcome to the show. There's a great story in Cornwall about a ghost seen by several people on a stretch of road where there's been a string of accidents. Ghoulish appearances distracting the drivers, or something like that. A good last item for tonight's show. So take a crew down there, speak to the locals and make a 3 minute film." There was no training for newcomers to BBC Nationwide. It was sink or swim. Knowing little to nothing about directing a short on-the-day factual film, I set off in search of ghostly apparitions on a haunted stretch of highway on the Cornish coast. My mind was reeling as I drove out to meet my camera operator and the local news reporter. I had no idea what to film, or how to structure a three-minute segment for the show. So disaster, a three-minute hole in the programme and an early end to my fledgling career, loomed! In fact I was saved by the goodwill, experience and supportive nature of my camera operator and the news reporter. They were very sympathetic to this very green researcher, guiding me through the process – deciding on the sequence of shots, the interviews, what the reporter would say on camera, and the way the piece was cut together. I soaked it all in without the need to face on-air embarrassment. It was an early and a salutary lesson to me, a newspaper journalist used to working entirely on my own, that collaboration and listening carefully to the advice of those with whom you are working, is part and parcel of factual filmmaking. This is true at every level of the profession.

Written journalism is an individual pursuit. You get a brief from your editor, you go out and research the issue, conduct interviews, find stills, commission graphics and then write the story. You'll have occasional briefings with your editor, of course, but the story is yours: you write it, you take the credit. Filmmaking is really not like that at all. Yes, the producer, of a film should have a well-defined conception of the story that he or she would like to tell; the director must possess a clear sense of how to visualize it; and a producer/director, of course, needs both. But filmmaking is a complex, layered process. Its success

> The most difficult PDs to work with are the ones who effectively think: 'OK. I've got this programme commissioned now, I'm going to go off and do my own thing and I'm not going to report back until the edit suite'. And actually that just doesn't work because you end up in the edit suite with someone like myself sitting there thinking: 'why on earth have we done X, Y, or Z?'. In order to get the best out of any programme, it has to be a constant conversation. The PD has to keep the commissioning editor or the exec, fully briefed on what they're doing and why they're doing it. And the more you talk about something, the more likely you end up with a better product because always, hopefully, several brains are better than one brain.
>
> Louisa Compton, Head of News, Current Affairs and Sport, Channel 4 TV

rests on a very wide range of abilities, and it is unlikely that they will all be present in one person. To use a motoring analogy: you, the filmmaker, might be in the driving seat as you motor down your narrative highway, but there are others in the car with you who can help discover the most interesting path to your destination: your eyes might be fixed on the horizon in front of you, but those around you can look left and right and might just spot a route that you have missed. Filmmaking requires the abilities of a range of professionals for its successful completion and it is well worth asking for the advice of creative individuals whose training and experience are different to yours: the combination of their skills with yours will enable you to produce a much better film than you can on your own. Conversely, if you try to take all the key decisions about everything yourself, you're likely to produce a dull film. So it is about teamwork and the most talented and successful producers and directors realize and accept this on a deep level.

The Many Creative Decisions that go into the Making of a Factual Film

You have to appreciate the many creative calls needed in the conception and the making of a documentary or current affairs film. Here are some examples:

What makes a good televisual interviewee? Content is king when you're interviewing someone for a newspaper article. But content is only part of the decision-making process when you're making a film. How the person looks, how they speak, the tone of their voice, are all important issues to consider in deciding who is going to appear in your film.

Where and how am I going to film my interviewees? Inside? Outside? Artificially lit? Standing still? In a chair? Walking along a road? In a vehicle? And how do I frame and light my interviewees? All in close-up? Or filmed in a mixture of shot sizes? Heavily side-lit to emphasize mood? On a long lens to blur the background and focus attention on the speaker?

What other kinds of images will I need of my interviewees? I need sufficient visual material to cover commentaries that speak about them and for use as 'overlay' to cover edits in interviews. What will I film them doing? What's the most appropriate image to complement my story? And how much of this imagery will I need in the film?

What other images will I need? I must give viewers a strong sense of location and illustrate the issues under discussion in my film. How and where do I shoot these images to give visual interest? And what is the best time of day to film them?

Do I need dramatic reconstruction? This can help tell a past-tense story for which no stills or archive exist. But is this approach appropriate for my film – or is the subject too sensitive for this technique? If it is justified, what style will it be filmed in? Will there be dialogue? And what are the key parts of your story that need such dramatization?

Do I want to use a presenter or reporter? If so, will they be filmed in vision or just used as an off-camera narrator? And if in vision, which parts of the story will they tell to the camera? And how much other imagery will I need of them? Will they be filmed on their own or with some of my interviewees? And, anyway, is the person I'd like to be the presenter good enough on (and off) camera to do this job?

> I could be working with a producer who has his or her vision, a reporter who has his or her vision. And then I have my vision – and we won't always see eye to eye. And you never always see eye to eye actually, there's always tension and sometimes quite bad clashes, but I firmly believe that creative tensions and collaboration often lead to better filmmaking. You've got to be able to push for what you want but at the same time understand the perspective of others. And if you can collaborate, people will want to work with you as well. I think it is an extraordinarily collaborative job.
>
> Diana Martin, Executive Producer, BBC TV, *Panorama*

> Whether you've come straight from school, college, university or just as a freelance out of the university of life, then however good your idea, it is worth having people around you who can help you deliver it. And there is a certain amount of humility that's required in this game to ensure that you realize that this should really be a collaborative process. And there's nothing wrong with that. It can be really good if people are encouraging you to be the best that you can and to get the best out of what you are doing. If you haven't done it before, I think that's a good thing.
>
> Tom Giles, Controller of Current Affairs, ITV

What's the style of the programme? Do I want to use a lot of hand-held camera to give a sense of drama, or danger? Or do I want a much more stylised approach – with beautiful compositions and the camera on a tripod for most of the shoot? Or perhaps a mixture of the two is best? Do I need any special camera equipment to achieve the images I want: A camera harness? A dolly and track? A car mount? An aerial drone camera?

Will archive or stills enhance my narrative? If so, what's the best place to use them in my story? And can I afford to pay the royalty fees charged for their use in my film?

How do I cut my rushes into a strong story? There are many ways of cutting a film story together. There's no right way, just better and worse ways. Some cuts engage the viewer from start to finish. Others make them yawn and switch off after five minutes. But how do you find the best cut?

How do I transform my edited programme into a finished film? Once you have cut your story together, there's another raft of creative decisions to take. The sound tracks have to be mixed together at a pleasing balance; you might need to adjust the colour, hue or brightness of some of the images – or blur out some faces if you're making an investigation. All of these decisions are taken in collaboration with creative post-production staff.

> None of us make a film on our own. It's all about collaboration. If you think: 'oh, this is my film, I'm going to make it and I'm the auteur' the chances are you're going to fuck up because the best ideas can come from the least expected sources. I grew up in the theatre. My mother was an actress and a stage manager in the West End. And I remember one of the things she absolutely used to say: 'you listen to everybody whether they are the star, the producer or the stage hand. They've all got good things to say'.
>
> Leo Eaton, Documentary Filmmaker and Executive Producer

At some point in your career, you are likely to be working with camera operators, reporters, commissioning editors, executive producers, film editors, researchers, assistant producers, online editors, sound mixers, foreign fixers and production managers. The task of making all these choices is made significantly easier if you open yourself to the insights offered by other creative individuals. And the decisions made as a result of such collaborations usually produce a stronger, more watchable film.

Factual filmmaking is teamwork – it's not a loner's job. Creative collaboration is a vital skill a filmmaker needs to understand and develop. It can take time to open up to the ideas of others, but doing so is a sign of a mature programme maker whose aim is to get the best out of their project.

Organized Filmmakers are in Demand

The ability to collaborate creatively and the acquisition of a broad technical skill-set place a factual filmmaker in the best possible position to succeed in today's industry. But successful film production is also underpinned by a rigorous approach to logistics, organization, finance, health and safety and staffing decisions. Here's a selection of the calls that you might have to take as a producer/director.

Managerial skills. Planning a practical filming schedule means knowing how long to allow for each film sequence or interview you need in the programme, how long to get to your location, how long to unpack and repack your filming gear, and how long to get to your next location. If you're not on top of these logistics, you might lose a key interviewee who gets fed up waiting for you to arrive because an earlier sequence has over-run. Or worse still, you might overrun so badly that you have to put yourself, your camera operator and reporter up in a hotel overnight and complete the shoot the next day. If you are working to a very tight deadline, how can you organize yourself to start editing as soon as you've finished filming, with no time to prepare a paper cut of the film? How do you make sure contributors to your film give informed consent to participate in the project? How can you efficiently find any image or interview clip during the edit? And what's the best way of keeping track of all the archive and stills in your film so that you don't get sued for failing to pay someone their royalty fee? To avoid chaos, you've got to be organized before your shoot begins, on location, during the edit and during post-production.

Risk assessing skills. How can you keep yourself, your film crew and your contributors safe on location? How, for example, can you know whether the local fixer you've found who says he can get safe access to frontline fighters in Syria, really can do this? How can you be sure that the interviewee re-telling her story of imprisonment and physical abuse at the hands of Islamic State won't face reprisals once the programme is shown? There are serious questions that must be considered before you embark on any shoot, whether you are travelling to a danger zone or not. Health and safety is taken very seriously by all reputable broadcasters, independent production companies and factual filmmakers. Each film or research trip has a unique set of risks that you will need to consider and take steps to minimize in a formal risk assessment. If you don't treat these issues seriously, and things go wrong, you can end up in court being prosecuted under health and safety legislation.

Filmmakers with their 'Ears to the Ground' are in Demand

You also have to develop keen ethical, editorial and legal antennae.

Ethical awareness. A factual filmmaker has to be acutely aware of the ethical dimension of their work. Ethical 'bear traps' abound in serious factual filmmaking. For example: you've got permission to secretly film in a care home for children where you've gathered evidence that physical abuse of the residents is taking place. Your reporter has managed to get a job in the home and you're planning to send her in, wired up to a body worn covert camera. But does your reporter know how to care for children? Is it ethical to send her in if she doesn't? And what does your undercover reporter do if she sees abuse taking place? Just film it? Isn't that immoral – shouldn't she intervene to try and stop it even if that blows her cover? What should she do if she's asked to carry out an action she feels is wrong? Ethical issues like these have to be discussed in advance with your commissioner and a protocol put in place to ensure the team acts ethically. This is how you avoid negative publicity being aimed squarely at the production team – rather than at the bad guys you're trying to expose.

> Filmmakers, particularly young filmmakers, are often focused on the editorial ambitions of their projects. They have often spent a lot of time and effort in focusing on the access, the narrative, the editorial structure and I think the issues about legal jeopardy, duty of care, ethics, etc., although they are important, are often of secondary consideration. The more you become familiar with this area, you suddenly realize how important it is to understand the potential that these issues can raise and how to identify them early. This is the essence of good filmmaking.
> Prash Naik, UK Media Lawyer and Channel 4 TV General Counsel 2014–2017

Editorial awareness. You have to keep on top of the established editorial principles that guide factual filmmakers. If you obtain filming access to the police raiding a crack house, what do you do if they want to see the edited programme before it is transmitted? Does the answer always have to be 'no' to preserve editorial independence? Or can there be editorial justifications for agreeing such a request – for example, to reassure the police that you have, indeed, blurred the raiding officers' faces as promised? If so, what ground rules need to be set to guarantee your journalistic independence, to ensure the police can't insist on editorial alterations?

Legal awareness. You also have to be aware of the law as it applies both in the country where the film is being made – and the country in which it is being screened. In that film about the police raiding a crack house, can you show the faces of the drug dealers? Can you show the police raid before the case has been concluded in court? And, more generally, can you film children without their parents' permission? Can a child sign a release form giving their consent to be filmed? The answers to these and many other questions that raise legal and regulatory issues will differ depending on whether you are filming in the UK, the US or another country. And you need to develop an awareness of when to seek informed legal advice.

The Independent Producer's Skill-Set

Once you've got some filmmaking experience under your belt, and a track record with commissioners, you'll need to cultivate two more abilities as well if you want to run films through your own company:

Staffing skills. Who is going to work on the project? Do you need, and can you afford to pay, a professional camera operator or should the film's producer/director or assistant producer do the filming? Perhaps you can do both: self-shoot the images you need and get a good camera person to light and shoot the interviews? You might not want to pay for a sound recordist, but can your self-shooting producer/director really manage to record the sound of ten people, as well as the subject of your film, in that key town council meeting without one? Do you really need to pay a local fixer to set up your filming in war-torn Syria? And do you need an experienced executive producer to guide your undercover investigation of that corrupt politician?

Financial skills. Broadcasters and online platforms are very cost conscious these days. If you're lucky enough to be commissioned by one of them, you have to bring your film in on budget and, to do this, each part of your film production has to be carefully planned. If you're not on top of this process, you'll over-run and if that happens too often, it's going to drain your budget and tip you into an overspend. If you can't manage your budget, you won't get a second chance.

Part 2

Creative Skills

2 The Art of Treatment Writing

Persuading a Commissioner to Read your Proposal from Beginning to End

KEY CONCEPTS

- Key dos and don'ts in the preparation, writing and presentation a strong treatment for a factual film.
- Advice on how to pitch your film in person.

Factual filmmaking is an overcrowded profession. There's an almost limitless supply of people who want to make documentaries and other factually-based films and, of course, no shortage of good ideas being sent to broadcast and online commissioners, many more than there are slots or web pages to fill. In such a competitive world, only the best ideas find a buyer. But how can you distinguish between a strong and a weak idea for a factual film? And how do you present a film proposal in a way that grabs the attention of a reader from the top and keeps them reading to the very end? There's a rigor to first testing an idea to make sure that it's relevant to the platform at which it's aimed – and then drafting it into a strong, easy to read proposal that captures the essence of the idea.

So let's start at the beginning: you've got an idea for a factual film and want to persuade a TV programme or an online platform to offer you a budget to make it. I'm going to suggest ways of approaching this task that will maximize your chance of success. I'm not saying that by following my suggestions, you're guaranteed to get a film commissioned. You have to be realistic: commissioners pick the crop of the bunch and there's always a very high rejection rate. But following the basic principles I am going to outline will help your idea be relevant and get serious consideration.

However strong you think your film is, if it doesn't fit easily into an existing broadcast slot or online content creator's output, it isn't going to get made – unless you fund it yourself and put it on YouTube or Vimeo. That, of course, is likely to limit its reach. So if you want a wider audience, you need to aim your idea at an established outlet for factual films. To do that with any chance of success, the first step is to understand what the commissioner wants, as follows.

Understand what the Commissioner Wants

You have to research the strand at which you are aiming the film, finding out about its overall ethos and the kind of shows it commissions. And you can only do that by watching its output. You also need an awareness of what the strand or platform editor is actually looking for at the time you are pitching your film. The idea might fit their broad brief, but you'd be wasting your time, and the time of the editor, if you pitch it when this is exactly the kind of film that the editor does *not* want at that moment. Or if it's an idea that she has just commissioned. So call up the outlet. Speak to the editor or her assistant. Find out what the current priorities are, what they do and don't want. You're not going to get ideas for films this way, but what you will get is a strong steer about what not to offer – and guidelines about the kinds of issues or approaches that might interest the person in charge.

> If you're going to pitch you absolutely have to watch our film series. You need to know what the house style is. You need to understand what we're after. You need to know we're investigative. That we're not a show that does a lot of social, personal stories. We always have an investigative edge. A lot of time people will pitch us stuff and we just know immediately that they haven't watched us because it's so far from what we do.
>
> Raney Aronson-Rath, Executive Producer, PBS Frontline

I am going to suggest three 'don'ts' when considering potential film stories.

● **Don't suggest film stories about things that might happen in the future**

> Where's the humanity in the film? Where's the richness of humanity? I think across TV generally, we can end up making interesting but very dry subjects and the real deal is thinking where are you going to inject the emotion and the humanity into programmes.
>
> Louisa Compton, Head of News, Current Affairs and Sport, Channel 4 TV

Not every story makes a strong film. Some ideas are much better conceived as written pieces and this often is the case with ideas that are pitched into the future. Take a look at this example[1] of an opening sentence to a film treatment.

> *One of the country's biggest mining companies has been given permission to bury tons of toxic waste chemicals – a decision that environmental groups have condemned as unsafe and as potentially compromising on the health of local residents.*

Strong films need emotion at their core, and issues that point to problems which are likely to happen if a particular course of action is pursued next month or next year, cannot contain personal testimony from people who have been directly affected by the decision. So I'd have been more engaged if this story had been present day – rather than pitched into the future – and if the opening sentence had read something like this:

One of the country's biggest mining companies has been condemned by environmental groups for illegally burying tons of toxic waste chemicals over the past ten years. They say this secret, unsafe practice has severely compromised the health of thousands of local residents.

At the heart of a strong documentary is human emotion and story-telling – rooted in present day or past experience. In an investigative film, painful testimony retold on camera is a direct and powerful illustration of what a filmmaker believes to be injustice, corruption, illegality, violence, etc. In historical filmmaking, personal story-telling is the most engaging way of bringing past events to life – whether it's a pilot's wartime reflections, or a politician's memory of an unexpected election victory. And science films are always more watchable when they're told through the eyes of the men and women who took part, people who can tell first-hand stories of the struggle to bring a scientific development to life. Ideas that lack illustrative stories make much better newspaper articles or perhaps television discussions than they do documentary films. So don't pitch an idea that doesn't have strong emotion at its heart.

- **Don't offer a film about an issue that's already in the public domain – unless your project reveals significant new facts or offers a unique approach to the subject.**

> I think the biggest omission I see is originality. Basically people will pitch us films that have either been done or reported on and they are not truly original. The other thing that I see: we get these pitches that we don't trust and when we start to dig in on the pitch, we very immediately are able to take apart something that's exaggerated in journalism terms. So we ask people to be really straight. We don't need it presented to us in a fancy way. We just need something that's real. And if it's just a real pitch and it's really original then we commission it.
>
> Raney Aronson-Rath, Executive Producer, PBS Frontline

Commissioning editors want new subjects – or new approaches to subjects – and part of the task of a treatment is to convince them that this is what you are pitching. Ask yourself: what coverage is already 'out there' – in the papers, on TV, on the net? If you can find other films/articles on the subject, so can the person at whom you'll be pitching the idea. So why should they do it again? You might think you've got a new angle to last week's story, but with such a huge choice from which to select films, it's going to take a lot to persuade a commissioner to have a second bite at the cherry. A treatment I read about the problems facing disabled people reported that:

A long film investigating the lives of physically disabled people was recently broadcast.

It tells readers that this film looked at the difficulties and prejudice they faced, and at positive stories – people who had overcome disabilities and realized their ambitions. Well, full marks to the author for researching and revealing what's been done before. But, if that is the case, why should a commissioning editor give this producer a budget to make a documentary about the same issue? If another film has just been made about your subject, you might be able to make a case for a second film – if what you are doing is significantly different and distinctive from what's been done before. If, for example, you adopt an undercover approach, and suggest that you fit secret cameras to three disabled people and follow their lives. In this case you'd be showing first-hand the problems they face rather than simply telling your audience about them. So you do have to acknowledge what's gone before, because without a significantly new angle or a new approach you are unlikely to get a sympathetic hearing from a commissioner.

- **Don't offer an impractical film**

The practical challenges of making a factual film, along with the risks to filmmakers and contributors, must be addressed before you pitch an idea. You need to be sure that what you are suggesting can really be achieved – and be achieved safely. Here's the opening paragraph of another treatment for a film based in Jordan:

> *Some radical Islamist movements are spreading Jihadist ideology – recruiting and training fighters to send them to conflict zones like Syria.*

The film, we're told, will show where these Islamist groups are operating in the country, investigate the training of the recruits and show how the Islamists are:

> *… brainwashing young guys to convince them to join up.*

So how does the filmmaker propose to turn this idea into a film? It can't simply be a series of interviews with experts – or former Jihadi recruits. That's not a film, it's a TV discussion. You'd need filming access to the groups – their training, their recruitment, etc. In this treatment none of the practical questions that naturally arise with such a suggestion are raised.

> Lots of people pitch me ideas which on the face of it are really good subjects and they say, for instance: 'We want to make a film about how awful it is for children whose parents are divorcing, and how the family courts make things worse'. And you think: 'Oh, that's great. Yes, we'd love to do that'. But then you think: 'But how? How would you do that if you can't identify anybody, or talk about anybody's cases or film any of the courts or even report the court cases? So what do you mean?' And then they go: 'Oh yes'. More than anything else, you've got to think, is this film really a viable proposition? Am I sure it can be made?
>
> Diana Martin, Executive Producer, BBC, *Panorama*

How is the team going to get such access: overtly, with the knowledge of the group? If they can get in, what safety guarantees have been agreed to ensure that the crew won't end up kidnapped or worse? Perhaps you're instead considering an undercover expose of the Jihadists, asking someone to pose as a newly recruited fighter? In that case, what's the cover story this person will be telling the group? What happens if your undercover 'fighter' is rumbled and the hidden camera is discovered? What's your back up plan to prise them alive and well from the jaws of such a disaster? You need a lot of specialist advice before embarking on such a risky mission. And, ultimately, it might not be possible to make such a film safely. Without a realistic assessment of the practicality and safety issues involved in your proposal, it won't be taken seriously by any commissioner.

Write and Present Your Proposal in an Effective Way

The content of your treatment is, of course, the prime issue. But the way in which you present the proposal is also very important. It says a lot – both about the idea and about you. Treatments are selling documents. Often your proposal is the first contact between you and a commissioning editor or independent production company, so you really do want to impress with your presentation. To achieve this, your treatment must be compellingly written and sufficiently interestingly laid-out to persuade the reader to continue past the first paragraph to the very end. After all, if you can't make an impression with the content and layout of a paper proposal, you are certainly going to find it difficult to impress a strand editor with your ability to actually make the film. So here are some suggestions to guide you on the writing and layout of a treatment. First – four approaches to avoid when writing a proposal.

Avoid the Following when Writing Film Treatments

- **Don't ask questions when setting out the reason for your film.**

Here's a selling sentence from another treatment, about the care of disabled children. It tells the reader the film will:

> … *determine whether government support of rehabilitation centres for disabled children is providing a sufficient number of qualified staff and well-equipped centres.*

It will also ask:

> *What are the reasons leading to early childhood disabilities? Are they caused by medical errors during childbirth, or a failure by the Ministry of Health to provide care to pregnant women before delivery?*

Why should I be interested in an idea that poses a lot of questions but fails to tell me what is really going on? What happens if I give the producer a budget for this project and he/she comes back saying the government is in fact funding plenty of well-equipped centres for disabled children; that most of them are very good at dealing with the problems of disability; and that there have been few complaints about conditions in the centres? What happens to the film then? There isn't one – and I've wasted my precious broadcaster's money. So, avoid unanswered questions when setting out the main point of a treatment. Instead, make strong statements about what you understand is happening or what you wish to do. You will have to do some research to obtain that information. Find the facts first, then you'll begin to interest a strand editor. If your research hasn't answered all the questions, by all means flag this up. It's good to be honest about the state of your knowledge. But your opening has to make a strong, unambiguous case for your film. I might have been persuaded to read on, had the writer told me the film would:

> … *show that the government is underfunding rehabilitation centres to such an extent that they are poorly equipped, have far too few qualified staff, and are completely failing to help disabled children learn how to survive in the outside world.*

And that:

> *The conditions in many of these centres are atrocious – with some children facing repeated physical abuse.*

- **Don't misunderstand the overall aim of your film.**

Another treatment I came across was about the treatment of people suffering from Haemophilia. It was billed as an investigation – and the proposal flagged up the aims of the film like this:

Aims of the investigation – to raise awareness in the community:
- *About Haemophilia and the numbers of hemophiliac people in the country.*
- *About the number of people affected with virus C and the number of disabled suffering from Haemophilia.*
- *About the different ways in which virus C can spread among people.*

The spreading of public information is *not* the aim of a film that is selling itself as investigative. And statistical information about Haemophilia or explanations of how a virus spreads are for textbooks. The Ministry of Health should do the former – and schools the latter. Raising public awareness might be a *by-product* of the programme, but it is not the right selling line for a filmed investigation. These programmes reveal wrongdoing, inefficiency, corruption, negligence, anti-social behaviour and so on – and the sales pitch of this film would have got more attention had its aims been set out along these lines:

> *This film reveals how a widespread failure to diagnose Haemophilia in children – combined with a lack of public awareness about the disease – is leading to serious medical complications, including arthritis, limb deformities and even a shortened life expectancy.*

- **Don't bury the key point of your film.**

Commissioners are busy people, they get hundreds of treatments and you have to capture their attention from the first sentence – or they will simply stop reading. So if the main point of your investigation is not set out in the first few sentences, you have failed. No commissioning editor is going to wade through 20 pages of text in the hope of finding a strong story. You have to sell the essence of the idea to them as strongly as possible at the top of the document. Here's an example of a treatment that fails to summarize the key aims of an investigation in the opening paragraph. This is about disabled people:

> *Physically disabled people offered places at one of the capital's leading colleges often turn up for their first day only to find they can't get into the building because it lacks an entrance accessible to people in wheelchairs.*

This appears to be a narrow story about one college's insensitivity to disabled people. It could make a strong but fairly short news film for the local TV station. If I was a commissioning editor looking for 30 minute films I'd stop reading at this point. So it's lucky that I had the time to read on – because way down on page 3 I discover there's a much wider story about the disabled. I learn that:

> *People with physical disabilities – face widespread discrimination in the workplace.*

And on page 5, I find out that we're going to meet a disabled person whose story will illustrate:

> *... the prejudice against the disabled that has seen two of her friends badly beaten up – and wider problems that wheelchair bound people face on buses and trains, in shops and cafes.*

And further down in this over-long treatment, I read that we will meet several disabled people who have managed to overcome these obstacles to make a success of their lives. I'm getting more interested, but why have I got to read the entire treatment to understand that this is more than just a film about disabled students at one college? The opening paragraph of this treatment could have been written like this – giving the reader a much better idea of the programme you're pitching:

> *Physically disabled people are suffering widespread discrimination – and even violence – at work, in colleges, on public transport and on shopping trips. In this film we'll see the problems first-hand, ask the*

authorities why so little is being done to stop prejudice facing disabled people and we'll learn how some have managed to overcome huge obstacles to rise to the top of their professions.

Your opening paragraph has got to summarize the essence of the story in a compelling way — or you'll lose the attention of your reader and your ideas will be ignored.

- **Don't try to 'pull the wool' over a commissioner's eyes.**

You have to be honest and straight-forward when writing a treatment. Don't pretend that you've got access that you haven't yet negotiated. Don't say, for example, that the FBI is opening its doors for the very first time, allowing you to film on-going investigations, raids and operations, unless you really do have such access. And don't offer exclusive interviews with top people unless they've really agreed to speak to you. Commissioners will have *more* respect for you and your idea — not less — if you flag up the weak spots in your research but say that a period of development is needed to close the gaps. Over-selling a story is the quickest route to rejection.

> ## Being Straight with your Commissioner
>
> I quite like it when people have clearly identified some of the weaker spots in an idea. I don't mind if people say to me: 'it might be difficult finding this particular person but we're going to try and do it this way. If we can't find this person we'll cover it in this way in the film'. The fact that they have thought about the bad points as well as the good points in an idea is a really, really good thing for me.
>
> Charlie Phillips, Head of Documentaries, *The Guardian*
>
> Don't bullshit. Don't lie. They are the key 'don'ts'. I think people are so keen to get a commission, there's a tendency to over promise. So be honest, be realistic. If some of what you are saying you're going to do is on a wing and a prayer and a hope that it will happen, then say that. So honesty is really important.
>
> Louisa Compton, Head of News, Current Affairs and Sport, Channel 4 TV

Follow These Suggestions When Writing Treatments

That's enough negatives. I'm now going to suggest some positives to take on board when writing short film proposals. These are guidelines — not hard and fast rules. Each project is different, and your proposals can't all necessarily be molded into one shape. So these recommendations are meant to be helpful suggestions rather than a set of compulsory rules. But they will help to ensure you write powerful proposals.

- **Sum up your idea with an opening 'hook' containing the essence of the film — 100 to 250 words.**

Your opening paragraph must sum up the story in a way that entices your reader into the story — it must 'hook' him or her from the top, making them want to know more about the subject and keep on reading to the end. This opening paragraph is *really* important. There's a skill to writing it, the skill of assimilating information about a subject, deciding the main points and then summarizing them in a pithy, stylish manner. You need drama here – not detail. There's another, underlying reason for doing this as well…

If you can't sum up the idea in one paragraph – you probably don't have an idea worth telling.

So here's some tips for writing that strong opening paragraph – for different genres of films. Ask yourself: what is the USP – the *unique selling point* – of your film? What will it reveal that is new, different or exclusive. Your opening line is vital and you must 'big' it up. Here are three examples. First – an exposé of the abuse of elderly residents in a series of Government-run care homes.

> *Elderly residents at state-run care homes are being physically and verbally abused by their carers. In this special undercover investigation we show shocking images of vulnerable old people being hit, left alone in distress for long periods, shouted and sworn at by the very people supposed to be looking after them. We hear from angry relatives who demand the closure of these care homes.*

Keep it short and make it absolutely compelling. Don't give somebody a 30, 40 page shooting outline they won't read. What I've discovered with any commissioner, it doesn't matter what the network is, what the distribution platform is, they will probably glance at about a page. So have that really, really, focused page, page and a half. It's the elevator pitch, a Hollywood phrase, which is actually very appropriate. You're trying to pitch a movie to a studio head, and always the door's shut, the gatekeepers won't let you in. And suddenly you find yourself in an elevator with the studio head. And you've got between the ground floor and the fifth floor to pitch them the show … It's exactly that, but on paper … Make it focused, sharp and really sexy.

Leo Eaton, Documentary Filmmaker

Those three sentences are just 65 words long – so this opening is very tightly written but it conveys the essence of the idea. That's enough to get a reader interested, but you must now build on this top line. Investigative films point the finger of blame and raise issues of public policy illustrated by the problem they're exposing. So the next sentence in the care home treatment might read:

> *We reveal how corruption is undermining the inspection system designed to prevent such abuses – and we ask the Ministry of Health what it's going to do to keep residents safe and prevent such abuses in future.*

That's another 36 words – making 101 in all in this opening 'hook'. Not a lot of detail here – but enough information to get your reader engaged with this issue – and wanting to know more.

If you're not chasing bad guys – harm and blame won't be the issue – but the approach will be similar. Here's a fictitious observational example: the first-ever filming access to Britain's crack Special Air Services (SAS). Your treatment might start along these lines:

> *For the first time the SAS, Britain's crack special forces squad, opens its doors and lets cameras film new recruits undergoing the army's toughest training course. We follow three SAS hopefuls as they march*

> I'm always looking for what is the USP – the unique selling point – of a film? What's good about it? What's new about it? Really, what's the point of it? 'In this film, for the first time …' That's always a phrase that I like to hear: 'For the first time we're going to film inside the country's leading Pupil Referral Unit to see how it should be done. But we're also going to film inside one of the failing Pupil Referral Units to see how it shouldn't be done'. I also want to know you've thought about what sort of film this is going to be – is it an access film, is it an investigation, what's the tone? So you might say: 'We're really going to understand it from the pupil's point of view, and we're going to speak mainly to pupils rather than teachers'. That gives the film a certain character.
>
> Diana Martin, Executive Producer, BBC, *Panorama*

40 miles in full kit against the clock, learn to survive and navigate in the jungle, and take part in fake battles. The training is so tough, that only one in five make it to the end.

Then ask why this story matters to your audience – what is so special about the access that makes this a must-watch film in the TV schedules or for an online platform? With that in mind, the next sentence might read like this:

This secretive special forces unit has only been seen in action once since its formation in 1941: during the dramatic televised rescue of hostages held inside the Iranian Embassy in 1980. Its troops are the most highly trained in the British army; they've played key roles in all Britain's conflicts since the Second World War, and this film offers a unique insight into the making of a special forces soldier.

The two sections of this opening paragraph are 141 words long. It is deliberately short on detail – but offers a strong overview of the film, its exclusive access and the reason for watching it.

My own company made a documentary about childhood for the BBC called *Parents Under Pressure*. The opening paragraph, very short, read:

The surveys and the experts have laid it on the line: Life in modern Britain is proving toxic for young people. They are unhappier, unhealthier and more unruly than they've ever been. So what's going wrong?

That's a very tightly written hook – just 36 words that end with a question. It doesn't contain much detail – but it is full of drama and encapsulates the essence of the film in a succinct and pithy short paragraph. The second paragraph added a little flesh onto the selling line of this story – and answered the question:

In the past few years, academics have learnt a great deal about the experiences that can harm children – and how the damage occurs. And the latest research has a clear, consistent and uncomfortable message, one that we ignore at our peril: our children are suffering because parents do not realize how easily what happens in the family, can make or break a child for life. They are also suffering because we've allowed this generation of kids to come under commercial pressure like no other generation before them. This film reveals surprising new evidence that shows how our kids are being harmed.

With another 101 words we now know that this film will use the latest scientific insights into childhood to explain why Britain is rearing an unhappy and unhealthy generation of young people. There is no right or wrong way to draft an opening paragraph for a film proposal. But it is vital that you convey the overall tone and content of your project in a brief and engaging way for your reader.

- **Write a more detailed breakdown of the project – 1,000 words maximum.**

After the opening – you have to unpack the idea with more detail – and explain the approach you plan to take to realize the film. You have to do a certain amount of research to be sure the story will stand-up when you come to make it. That doesn't mean you have to fully research the film before pitching it. But it does mean that you must do enough to convince an editor that there really is a strong story to be made – and that you are aware of, and acknowledge, any existing gaps in your knowledge. The balance between not enough and too much research is often hard to judge. Don't write more than two pages or 800 to 1,000 words in all and do include the following.

The Narrative and the Context

You need to give a strong sense of the argument that the film will pursue – in other words, the major building blocks of how the story will progress from the beginning, though the middle to the end. This must give an overall sense that you know what you wish to say journalistically – or a sense of how the lives of your characters will unfold in an observational film. You are only offering a 'sense' of this: you are not writing a script. This part of your proposal is meant to convince a commissioner that you really do know what the story you wish to tell is all about. So add some context – the economic, political, social, scientific or historical backdrop to your story You can illustrate the text with quotes from key interviewees to add emotion or impact.

Style, Method and Practicality

You must outline the kind of film that you envisage: its visual style – and the method you'll use to realize it. This is a key part of a film proposal, often omitted entirely by producers new to the profession. But you have to convince your reader that the idea really is realizable as a film rather than as a discussion programme or a newspaper article. So this is where you have to think visually to give your reader a strong sense of what the film will be like on screen, along with a sense of its practicality. How, for example, will you film that undercover investigation in the old folks care home? Can you overcome the safety and ethical issues raised by this kind of filming (for more on this see pages 190–194 in Chapter 10). Would dramatic reconstruction help to convey what's already happened – or will that be misplaced in such a sensitive area? And how will you convey those stories of angry relatives? Filming them at their homes to get a strong sense of their family lives? Or in an 'atmospheric' location like a park or by a river? In the SAS training film, exactly what filming access have you negotiated? Has the army insisted, for example, on a preview before screening that might compromise the independence of the project? Do you want to draw a clear distinction between the hand-held observational sequences and images filmed elsewhere (at the soldiers' homes, for example) by making a point of filming these on a tripod, in a more considered way? Perhaps the contrast you want to draw is between the hand-held filming and some beautifully shot imagery of the locations in which the training is taking place plus nicely lit interviews for more reflective thoughts. How many key characters will your film follow – and will you interweave their back stories with the actuality of the training course to keep an audience's interest? The practical and visual aspects of your film must be outlined in some detail.

Reporters and Presenters

Whether you have a reporter or presenter hosting a factual film, use an out-of-vision commentary or let the actuality and interviews convey the narrative is a major 'method' decision on a factual film. Before making a decision about this, look at the previous output of the strand at which you'd like to pitch the idea, and understand whether an on-screen personality is part of its approach. If you do think a presenter or reporter is an advantage, and the choice is not obvious, attach two or three names to the treatment for your film and explain why you've made these suggestions. If a very well-known TV personality/reporter/expert is the obvious pick, approach them with the treatment and get in-principle agreement before offering it. If you don't, your credibility will take a dive if your choice turns you down once you've caught the eye of a production company or a commissioner. Ultimately, whether a film has an on-screen talent and, if so, who this is going to be, is a decision taken after a discussion with the film's commissioner. But it helps to demonstrate that you have thought about possible hosts, and securing the agreement of a well-known individual can increase the attractiveness of your idea. If you are suggesting an on-camera host who is not well-known – an expert perhaps who has not fronted a factual film before – then consider including a 'taster tape' with the treatment. You might be convinced of their on-camera abilities and the quality of their narration, but your commissioner will want some evidence that they really are strong enough to carry an entire project. So film your choice doing a number of camera pieces to show off their abilities.

The Team

You need to convince your reader that the production team you've picked is capable of producing this film. Commissioning editors, like anyone else, have careers to think about. They want successful films that pull in big audiences and they are more likely to commission from someone who's already made successful factual films than someone who hasn't. If you offer the idea directly to a TV or online platform and don't have a track record in the genre of filmmaking, or if you're an inexperienced filmmaker, you're unlikely to get any editor to commission you to make the film by yourself. It's not impossible, of course. Some online platforms welcome ideas from newcomers especially if they've got a cracking good idea or exclusive access that no-one else has got. But one way round a lack of experience is to include someone, an executive producer or a producer/director, on your team who does have credibility in the arena in which you wish to work. A better route for new filmmakers is to approach an independent production company that's already been commissioned to make films of the kind you are pitching. Their track record is the guarantee that a commissioner will get a strong film at the end of production. As the originator of the idea, you should be able to negotiate a role on the film plus a share of any profits. That's the upside. The downside is that you lose overall control of the project. It becomes the property of the company with whom you've been paired. That might seem harsh but, for an inexperienced filmmaker, a small share of something is better than a big share of nothing. And you also get your foot in the filmmaking door: a difficult task at the best of times. So if you're in this position, research the most relevant companies, and offer the idea to the one you feel is the best of the bunch. They are in a better position to get it commissioned than someone with little credibility in the industry.

> If it's a strong pitch and it's a story we're going to want to do, then the producer's experience or otherwise doesn't make any difference. Then it would be trying to work out: can we place him with a production company that's got some more experience so that they can lean on that production company? So strong pitches from inexperienced producers are very much welcome. It would just be trying to pair them then with another company that they could work with.
> Louisa Compton, Head of News, Current Affairs and Sport, Channel 4 TV

- **Find a strong, attention grabbing title.**

You also need to think up a good title for your film. I've put this last on the list because it's often easier to think up a good title once you have crystallized the essence of your story in a treatment. You want something stylish, something that will grab attention whether you're pitching a film for broadcast or at an online outlet. Before the rise of the internet when, in the UK at least, there were only four TV channels, programme titles could afford to be oblique and clever – because broadcasters didn't have to fight so hard for an audience as they do today with hundreds of available channels plus the competition that the online world now poses for viewers' attention. Now factual film titles tend to be direct and explicit WYSIWYG titles: this '*What You See Is What You Get*' approach has migrated from the written labels on the lids and sides of processed food to the world of factual filmmaking. Here's a range of factual film titles taken from TV and online listings. They come from current affairs, history, new reality and science films.

How The Wild West Was Won with Ray Mears (BBC)
The challenge facing the early pioneers of the North American continent.

All Star Driving School (Channel 4)
A series about minor celebs learning to drive.

To Catch a Cat Killer (Vice)
Investigation of a serial animal murderer.

UN Sex Abuse Scandal (Frontline, PBS)
An investigation into sex abuse by United Nations peacekeepers in the
world's conflict zones.

World War 2 – The Price of Empire (History Channel)
History of the conflict, showing how different countries were drawn into the war.

Why Mum Died: Britain's Sepsis Crisis (BBC)
Investigating the deficiencies in the way sepsis is diagnosed.

World's Scariest Drug (Vice)
A film made in Colombia about a drug called Scopolamine, also known as
'The Devil's Breath'.

Koko: The Gorilla Who Talks To People (BBC)
The story of the only 'talking' gorilla in the world and her relationship
with Penny Patterson.

You barely need to read the second line that I've penned for each of these titles to know the essence of the film. They are not very imaginative – but they are immediate and if you're at all interested in these subjects, you're more likely to stop and read on than for a more obliquely written top line. If you can combine immediacy with imagination – so much the better.

So when you are thinking up a title for your treatment, consider what it will look like in the TV listings page or attached to a clickable still frame on an online platform. If it does what the examples above do – then it's going to be good enough for the strand editor reading your proposal.

Good titles sometimes come in a flash – and sometimes they take a lot of thought and discussion. They will be phrases or short sentences that symbolize the film and the best ones use grammatical plays of words to convey interest and catch the eye. So, for those of you who might have forgotten all you were taught at school about grammar, here's some more titles that combine immediacy with basic language techniques like alliteration and double entendre. The examples below are from British and American films.

Hitler's Henchmen
From Channel 5 in the UK. A simple title that elegantly conveys the essence of the programme.

Making a Murderer
The widely acclaimed in-depth Netflix series about an alleged wrongful conviction. The title doesn't tell us exactly what it's about – but it does say enough to get anyone interested in factual films about detectives and violence to read on.

Born into Brothels
Academy Award winning independently made British documentary about the children of prostitutes working in Calcutta's red light district. The title tells you pretty much all of that – apart from the location.

The Climate and the Cross
Evangelical Christians tussle over climate change.

Parents Under Pressure
The BBC film, discussed above, investigated why British parents are bringing up such an unhappy, unhealthy and unruly generation of children.

Arafat's Authority
This title was one that I used for an investigative BBC documentary looking at the Palestinian Authority – when there were claims that, under Yassir Arafat's guidance, there were extensive human rights abuses and corruption.

Life and Death Row
The title of a BBC series about capital punishment as seen through the eyes of young people whose lives have been shaped by it. Elegantly combining two phrases to give an immediate sense of what the film is about.

- **Present the proposal with care – using pictures, highlighted quotes and subheadings.**

By now you've got the contents of your proposal written, you've thought up a title. And all that's left is to think about the way you present it on paper. Remember: you are pitching a film proposal, if your commissioning editor sees two pages of closely typed text and nothing else, he or she might wonder if you have any visual sense at all. So layout your treatment in an easy-to-read, engaging way. Illustrate it with photos, perhaps pick out one or two dramatic quotes from individuals and place them in larger type at the top and bottom of the page. Break the text up with subheadings. These are all basic journalistic skills – and you must use them to good effect in your treatments

Finally – be aware that that treatment writing is an iterative process. Good treatments can take time to write – and the first draft is usually not the last. So show versions to team members and colleagues whose judgments you respect, and listen to the critique. Dialogue and discussion is often essential in the preparation of a good treatment.

Pitching in Person

If you are lucky enough to be invited to pitch your project in person you've got to convince the individual in whose hands the future of your film rests, with your knowledge of the subject, your passion for the idea, and your understanding of how to turn it into a practical film. This meeting can tip the commissioning scales in your favour – or result in a 'thank you – but no thanks' letter. So take it seriously and that means doing some preparatory thinking and planning. Consider the following.

- **Decide who needs to attend this meeting.**

It's usually better to have two people to represent your idea. While you certainly don't want a big delegation at this meeting, it helps to have more than one person, so that if you forget a key point, your colleague can fill in. Established production companies will often send an executive producer (who will have a clear overview of the project) with the producer or producer/director (who will have more command of the detail). You might be accompanied by the person who has the most first-hand know-

> Knowledge and passion are key. There's nothing worse in a meeting where you ask a few questions and very quickly it becomes clear that the person in that meeting room knows nothing more than is written on that piece of paper. And that bit of paper in a pitch should be the starting point for a conversation, where I will normally end up reading it and writing notes to ask lots of follow up questions. And if I'm not getting answers then that can make you question the story itself – [and] how much the person sitting in that room knows about it.
> Louisa Compton, Head of News, Current Affairs and Sport, Channel 4 TV

ledge about the story – for example, a whistleblower or specialist researcher on an investigative story, or an academic on an historical or scientific film. These individuals will underpin the detail of the story. They'll be able to respond to probing questions and add to the credibility of the proposal. Some films might rely on a named director – that is, someone with a long track record of making distinctive films in this arena. In which case, take them along, they can speak about their directorial vision for the film. Sometimes your presenter or reporter is also worth bringing to the meeting – especially if they have a personal connection to the story.

> I don't mind if people are nervous, I don't mind if people stutter and are tongue-tied and I don't mind if people wear jeans, flip flops. For me, it's not really about you, it's about your idea and your relationship to the idea. I don't mind too much how you present yourself, but I do want to know that you know what you are talking about and that you really have researched this idea and that you can have a sensible conversation with me about what would the next steps be in the journalism. Passion really, really, helps to sell an idea – but it's not enough. I want that passion underpinned with a proper understanding of the subject.
> Diana Martin, Executive Producer, BBC TV, *Panorama*

- **Decide the key points you wish to make. Write a list – divide them up amongst the team in an intelligent way.**

One person, the executive producer for example, can deal with the narrative structure – the overall thrust of the story, what it's going to say and why it's important to do the story now. Another person, the producer and/or director, can deal with the practicality of making the film, the characters and the directorial vision. And if you've decided to take a specialist with you – they can handle the detailed content queries.

- **Think about your body language.**

This speaks as much about you as what you say: you're in effect a sales-person in this meeting and you need to infect a commissioning editor with your conviction and passion for the idea – so don't slump in your chair, yawn or talk in a monotone with your eyes looking at the floor.

- **Take key visual material with you – but only if it's vital to convincing your commissioner of the idea's viability.**

You might have some video evidence on which your story rests – perhaps some revealing footage shot by citizen journalists of the conflict in Syria, or footage shot on a phone by prisoners showing physical abuse inside a jail. If it is key to your film – take it along to the meeting.

> I think the passion has to be there. But then so does the back-up. If it's a journalistic story, show that you've got the access. Don't go in with bullshit. Don't say: 'Oh, it's a wonderful idea!' Show that you've done your homework. You have to know what you're talking about – make sure also that you know the answers to those few questions that the commissioning editor's going to want anyway. But also don't come across as arrogant. Come across as grateful for the chance to pitch – in other words, a little humility.
>
> Leo Eaton, Documentary Filmmaker

Chapter Summary

Key Points to Remember When Writing a Treatment and Pitching a Proposal

1 **Understand what the commissioner wants**

   - Don't suggest film stories about things that might happen in the future.
   - Don't offer a film about an issue that's already in the public domain – unless your project reveals significant new facts or offers a unique approach to the subject.
   - Don't offer an impractical film.

2 **Write and present your proposal in an effective way**

   Approaches to avoid:
   - Don't ask questions when setting out the reason for your film.
   - Don't misunderstand the overall aim of your film.
   - Don't bury the key point of your film.
   - Don't try to 'pull the wool' over a commissioner's eye.

   Approaches to follow:
   - Sum up your idea with an opening 'hook' containing the essence of the film – 100 to 250 words.
   - Then write a more detailed breakdown of the project – 800 to 1,000 words maximum. Include:
     - The narrative and the context.
     - Style, method and practicality.

- Reporters/presenters.
- The strengths of the production team.
- Find a strong, attention grabbing title – use techniques like alliteration and double-entendre.
- Layout the treatment using pictures, highlighted quotes, sub-headings.

3   Pitching in person

- Decide who needs to attend this meeting.
- Decide the key points you wish to make. Write a list – divide them up amongst the team in an intelligent way.
- Think about your body language.
- Take key visual material with you – but only if it's vital to convincing your commissioner of the idea's viability.

Note

1 The examples used in this chapter come from treatments that I read while commissioning documentaries for BBC Arabic and while training filmmakers from the Middle East. Some appear with the kind permission of the authors. Others have been altered to make them untraceable while retaining the essence of the approach taken in the original.

3 On Location

Filming Images, Directing Sequences and Working with Reporters

KEY CONCEPTS

- The pros and cons of shooting-it-yourself or using a professional camera operator.
- How to direct well-composed images that will edit together and complement your narrative.
- How to give reporters an on-screen presence to guide viewers through a film.
- This chapter is illustrated with 24 filmed examples on *The Insiders' Guide* website.

Whether you are directing a professional camera operator or self-shooting, you need three key skills to visualize your film effectively: an ability to choose images that are appropriate to the part of the narrative that they will illustrate; a clear view of how you wish to film each image; and an understanding of the basic rules of filmic grammar. These rules are often deliberately broken to create stylistic impact – but you can't break a rule unless you know what it is in the first place. And if you lack this knowledge, you'll get back to the edit suite to find your film editor complaining that they can't cut a sequence together because you've missed a crucial shot or 'crossed the line' or simply shot a load of uninteresting, wobbly-scope 'wallpaper'.

To help you avoid such embarrassment, I am going to list the core information you'll need to direct or shoot well-composed, editable sequences of images to illustrate your narrative. I will also offer some suggestions for making the best use of on-camera reporters – and to resolve the 'Catch-22' dilemma facing factual filmmakers (see Chapter 5, pages 100–102): if you don't write a script until your film is edited together, how can you decide what words your reporter should say to camera on location?

Some of the examples in this chapter are illustrated with still images within the text. Others by an icon: [▶] and an ID number which point to specially filmed examples that can be viewed on the book's accompanying website.

Shoot it Yourself – or Pay a Professional to get the Images?

If you're struggling with a low budget, and can't afford to pay for a professional camera operator, the first question you're going to have to answer when planning your shoot is: 'Can I film it myself?' By that I mean, do I have the skills to do the job? Conversely, if you are able to afford a camera operator, what should you be thinking about before including this creative individual on your team? I'm going to look at the pros and cons of both self-shooting and using a paid for camera person.

Self-shooting. Filming it yourself is cheap. You're only paying for the kit and the best semi-pro digital cameras won't be as expensive to hire as a full professional kit. Working on your own, you have the ability to move fast, to change your plans rapidly where needed without major additional expense, and you can spend more time on location without worrying about crew overtime payments or hotel bills pushing you into the red. So self-shooting definitely has it's upside. But there's a downside as well: bringing a well-shot selection of rushes back to your edit is not easy. Learning to handle a camera is like learning to play the piano: it's time-consuming and requires a lot of thought, concentration and practice to get it right. You will have to master the physical movement of the camera on a tripod and on the shoulder, the different uses of the lens and how focal length and aperture affect your image. You have to understand the grammar of filming, the importance of lighting, of composition and have an ability to select imagery that's relevant to your narrative. Add to that the need to pay close attention to the sound that's being recorded, to the content of your interviews, while also keeping in the back of your mind all the logistical, financial and editorial issues of your film schedule – and you can see that self-shooting is *very* physically and psychologically demanding. Its success rests on a rare combination of editorial, technical, directorial, managerial and visual skills. You have to be an adept multi-tasker. So it shouldn't be undertaken lightly.

> Someone who's starting off shooting must come into the edit to see what shots they are missing. It can be simple things that they have to pick up on: they might not be holding their shots long enough. It might be not holding the camera level on the shoulder. It might be they have a technical issue, not quite getting it in focus sometimes. And editors are known for telling you things straight. I haven't gone through all my career without at some point going in and seeing an editor. And you learn the hard way. Sometimes it can be tough, but it is the best way of learning. So, to start off with, please get involved with the person that's actually editing your material.
>
> Jeremy Humphries,
> Director of Photography

Using a professional camera operator. The downside, of course, is the high cost of hiring a professional. Along with the kit, you're also paying their fee, any overtime if your schedule gets knocked off course, and all their travel, hotel and subsistence costs. So your time on location will be precious: you'll feel under a lot of financial pressure. And you have less intimacy with your interviewees – more people means more disruption. On the upside, all the technical and some of the creative pressures of filming and recording sound will be taken off your shoulders, and you'll be freer to pay attention to interview content and directorial thoughts.

When I joined the BBC it was all men that operated the cameras. But that's changed. The gear isn't quite as big now, not so heavy, so far more accessible and, certainly from my experience, three quarters of the people on my camera training, are young women. What I'm looking for is someone who's got the flair to just use that camera to tell a story. So I'm coming at it from a more creative aesthetic way, which women can be as suited at as we are, to be honest. Forget about the past. I mean the time now is for taking and a young woman should be no different from a young man. There's opportunity for all.

Jeremy Humphries,
Director of Photography

Your money will buy you distinctively filmed images, so long as you select your operator carefully. Their strengths have to match your project. A strong observational camera operator used to following action on the shoulder is not necessarily a strong compositional camera person. A camera person used to working in a war zone might not be the best choice for an historical documentary with dramatized reconstructions involving significant lighting and actors. Some camera operators do straddle the divides between these different skills but you must check out their abilities by asking for their CV and speaking to those they've worked with. You also want to work with a team player – not a prima donna. However talented a camera operator might be, you don't want your creative juices to be sapped by personality conflicts. Due diligence in the choice of a camera operator is essential.

It is always worth setting a little time aside to discuss your aims and objectives with a camera operator so that he or she can feed ideas into the process. Two creative heads are usually better than one – and this early dialogue is a good basis for a harmonious working relationship.

Making the Most of Your Images and Your Reporters

Whether shooting it yourself or directing a camera operator, getting good images for your story requires an understanding of four different directing issues:

1 *The camera:* how movement, lens adjustments and composition affect your images.
2 *The narrative:* making the emotional tone and geography of your images appropriate to the story being told – and thinking symbolically when there's no relevant imagery.
3 *The edit:* bringing an editable selection of images back to the cutting room by understanding the basic rules of filmic grammar.
4 *The reporter/presenter:* making your programme host look and sound good on-screen.

Directing with the Camera in Mind

Whatever camera you or your camera operator decide to use, you must understand the key terminology used to describe the way you want your image to be filmed. Here are descriptions of the different kinds of camera movement and their impact on the image.

Pans[1]

These describe a horizontal camera movement, from left to right or vice versa, from a fixed position. A slow pan might be used when filming a beautiful landscape to allow a viewer time to fully appreciate the image. A fast pan is used when the most important images are at the start and end of the move – for example, when panning from a busy road to a train speeding along its track. A whip pan is a specific effect and describes a rapid move from one field of view to another, fast enough to blur the intervening image. Whip pans can be used to cut unnoticeably from one scene to an entirely different scene so long as the direction of the 'whip' remains the same. So if the camera leaves image 1 by whipping left to right, it must arrive on image 2 moving in the same direction. So long as the whips are fast enough to blur the image, the cut from one image to the other will not be noticed. However – there's a catch. It's easy to begin on a static frame and pan the camera away fast. But it's very difficult to stop a fast camera pan smoothly on a static frame. Take a look at Film 3.1 on the website – the blur disguises the edit but the camera pans a little too far at the end of the shot and has to re-frame. The solution is to film the second of the shots in this example in reverse – starting on the subject and whipping away from right to left. The shot is then reversed in the edit before cutting the two together. The effect in Film 3.2 has been achieved by doing this.

Film 3.1 Watch a poor whip pan from static subject to static subject with unsteady camera at end of edited sequence

Film 3.2 Watch a whip pan with steady ending achieved by filming the 2nd camera move in the opposite direction to the first and then reversing shot in the edit

Tilts

A vertical up/down motion of the camera from a fixed position – tilting up from the image of a doorway to reveal the full height of a building, for example. Or tilting down from the sky to reveal a landscape.

Cranes

A vertical movement of the camera in space. So craning up involves the camera rising up above the ground. Craning shots can provide very interesting images because physically moving the camera provides a perspective that, with the right framing, emphasizes the difference between objects that are near the camera and those that are further away. Small craning shots can be achieved simply by rising up from a crouching position holding the camera. And, in the right location, larger craning shots can be filmed with no extra cost or equipment: a glass-sided lift going up the exterior of a tall building can do the job, as can a forklift truck on a building site (although you'd need to check out the insurance issues for this last suggestion – or you risk invalidating your production cover). Professional craning equipment which allows the camera to rise smoothly up down on a long arm is too costly for all but the biggest of factual budgets. A camera mounted on a gyro-stabilized aerial drone can offer similar imagery without punching such a large hole in your budget. They're also quicker to set-up and much more manoeuvrable. The downside of using a drone is the need to comply with safety and licensing legislation in both the UK and US, which limits the kind of images you can film[2].

Figure 3.1 A camera mounted on an aerial drone offers directors a relatively cheap way of filming craning shots and aerials

Tracking Shots

These describe images taken from a camera that is physically moving horizontally in space. At their simplest, tracking shots are achieved by a camera operator walking and shooting simultaneously or filming from a moving vehicle. Inevitably there will be some shakiness in such images and there is equipment to allow perfectly smooth tracking shots. One such is a 'dolly and track', consisting of a set of rails on which sits the dolly – at its simplest, a flat board on wheels that runs on the track (see Figure 3.2). The camera operator plus tripod sit on the dolly and can be pushed along, providing smooth tracking images. A stabilizing harness is another way of minimizing camera shake – some systems use springs and a counterbalance weight to iron out camera shake, some use a gyroscope. Stabilizers allow very smooth tracking shots even when the operator is running or climbing stairs. The disadvantage of using either a dolly and track or a harness is the cost and set-up time of both. Once again, producers on tight budgets can be inventive to achieve smooth tracking images. A camera mounted on a hospital trolley running along a smooth floor, for example, can achieve the same effect.

How Changes to the Camera Lens Impact on the Image

Pulling Focus

This is used to guide a viewer's attention from one part of an image to another. It is achieved by the camera operator moving the focus ring during filming so that what was in sharp focus becomes blurred, and what was blurred becomes sharp. You might use this when filming a child playing in a garden to emphasize the laughter of parents sitting behind their loved one.

Zooms

The camera zoom offers a variable focal length – from wide angle to a narrow focus telephoto, giving the operator a choice of perspectives on the world from one camera position. But because the camera doesn't physically move, the relationship between the various elements making up the image doesn't change, as it does when the camera closes in on a subject by physically moving

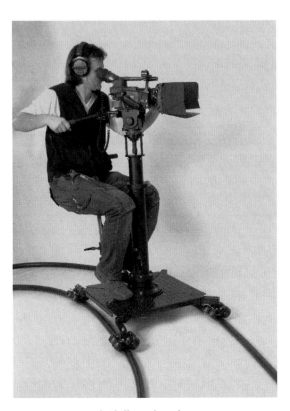

Figure 3.2 A simple dolly and track

towards it. So zooming in and out can feel artificial and some documentary camera operators and directors dislike this effect. But stylized uses of the zoom can be useful. Crash zooms, where the image transforms very rapidly from wide to close, blurring the intervening images, is a useful dramatic emphasis in a fast paced music sequence, for example. Staggered zooms, where a wide shot of a person or object is progressively shot at closer perspectives, can be edited to look like a crash zoom but without the blurring. As the time that each shot is on-screen is shortened, the apparent speed of the staggered zoom increases. A staggered zoom will only work if the camera is locked off on the closest shot before the series of zooms is shot. Film 3.3 on the website shows a series of unedited shots and the staggered zoom that results when they are cut together. Notice in these shots that the subject's eyes are in the same position in the frame in each shot. If there is any camera movement at all between each image, the subject of your staggered zoom will appear to move around in the frame as the camera zooms in – as you will see in Film 3.4 on the website.

Film 3.3 See an effective staggered zoom: camera locked off in one position

Film 3.4 See an ineffective staggered zoom: camera moves position between shots

Focal Length and Depth of Field

The kind of lens used to film your images has a big impact on what ends up on the screen. Although most professional video cameras can use a range of different prime lenses, with fixed focal lengths[3] varying from very wide angle to extreme telephoto, documentaries and current affairs films are mostly shot using the camera's own zoom lens – which offers a variable focal length and hence a changeable visual perspective (see Figure 3.3). The photos in Figures 3.4, 3.5 and 3.6 show a scene filmed from the same camera position but using three different focal lengths on a zoom lens. In Figure 3.4 the lens is set at its widest angle. Notice that the background in this image is in sharp focus all the way back to the horizon. As its name implies, this lens setting offers a very wide perspective and a large depth of field, so near and distant objects remain in focus. Figure 3.5 is the same scene filmed using the zoom lens at what can loosely be called its 'standard' setting – that is, a focal length approximating the view seen by the human eye. The background is not quite as sharp now. The lens is set at its longest telephoto setting in Figure 3.6. Telephoto lenses narrow the field of vision, and are able to focus in on and enlarge distant objects. In doing so, they offer a very narrow depth of field, throwing everything around the distant object out of focus. So the background in Figure 3.6 is completely blurred.[4] When focused on distant objects, like a landscape, telephoto lenses also decrease the apparent separation between the different elements in the visual field – so powerful telephoto lenses can be used effectively to make distinctive 'crushed perspective' images.

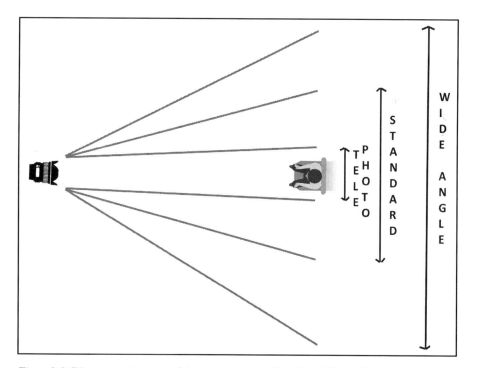

Figure 3.3 Diagrammatic view of the perspectives offered by different focal lengths

Figure 3.4 Wide angle lens

Figure 3.5 'Standard' perspective lens

Figure 3.6 Telephoto lens

Exposure

The aperture of the lens on a camera works much like the adjustable iris in the eye: narrowing the size of the pupil (the opening that allows light into the eye) in strong light, and widening it in low light conditions. Most high-end consumer digital cameras have an automatic aperture setting that can be used when light values across the scene you're filming are evenly lit. But where the light varies widely, you will get rapid changes in exposure as your camera image moves to differently exposed parts of the scene. In this situation, if you're self-shooting, adjusting the aperture manually offers more control and gives better results. For example, on automatic exposure panning the camera to the backlit subject in Figure 3.7 will produce an underlit foreground, as the camera narrows the aperture to cope with the bright background. By manually adjusting the aperture, you can find a better balance between the background and foreground, as in Figure 3.8. Filming a sunset is another obvious image that requires manual adjustment. Take a look at Film 3.5 on the website which shows two camera moves to a sunset. The first was filmed on auto exposure, and you can see the iris is slow to compensate for the bright sun. On the second shot, the camera operator manually adjusted the iris during the move – for a more pleasing result.

Figure 3.7 Backlit subject. Auto exposure

Figure 3.8 Backlit subject. Manual exposure

Film 3.5 See the difference between auto and manual exposures when filming a sunset shot

Composition

A director must also consider the arrangement of the visual elements in each image she wishes to film – and the positioning of the camera in relation to those elements. In a fast-moving situation like a riot, there is often no time to do anything other than point, shoot and hope to get something 'in the can'. But when there is no urgency, giving some thought to the ingredients that make up the visual field can give the images you shoot a more distinctive look – for example, by using foreground to frame a subject or by looking for unusual perspectives. Figure 3.9 is a not particularly inspiring approach to filming two people talking on a garden terrace. The camera has been plonked down and pointed at the subjects. Figures 3.10 and 3.11 offer more interesting perspectives on the same scene – using foreground and height. Figure 3.12 is another straight-forward way of filming two people walking through a garden. Figures 3.13 to 3.15 show a more thoughtful approach to the same walk: using height, framing the subjects with leaves or positioning the camera on the grass for a low angle shot that fills the foreground with leaves and grass. Film 3.6 on the website shows two compositional approaches towards filming a person walking down a road – one straight-forward and uninteresting, the other imaginative and so more likely to persuade a viewer to want to watch it.

Figure 3.9 Table scene, filmed with little compositional thought

Figure 3.10 The same scene, framed in a doorway with an interesting reflection in the glass

Figure 3.11 A little height also adds interest. This shot was filmed from a flat roof

Figure 3.12 Walking through a garden. Camera pointed straight at the subjects. An 'obvious' perspective

Figure 3.13 A top shot frames the subjects with foliage – giving a more pleasing result

Figure 3.14 Partially hiding with subjects with foliage also adds interest and intimacy

Figure 3.15 A low angle, camera–on–the–grass, unusual view

Films 3.6a and 3.6b Watch two approaches to filming someone walking: a point-and-shoot 'newsy' version. And a more thoughtful, compositional approach

Directing with the Narrative in Mind

Whether you are filming an analytical factual film, in which characters appear to explain different parts of the narrative, or an observational film in which a chronological unfolding of the lives of your characters is the story, you won't be going on location to illustrate a pre-written script (see Chapter 5, pages 100–102). But what you must have is a clear sense of your objectives for each of the sections that will become the building blocks of your film, and how each contributor will further those objectives. Once that's clear, you can tailor what you film to fit the overall purpose of the sequence in which the images will be used. If you don't do this, the images you film will not gel with the story you're telling. You can avoid this by planning what you're going to film for each part of your narrative, ensuring that the locations you choose, and the way you film the images, reflect the emotional tone of each sequence.

Getting the Emotional Tone Right

Choosing a Relevant Location

If one interviewee is going to tell you about the tragic death of their husband in a plane crash, then you'll be looking to film images with this person that reflect the sombre mood of the story, that will feel relevant when used either for the commentary introducing her story or as overlay to cover edits in the interview. You might, for example, want to film the deceased's wife at her loved-one's graveside, or alone in a park sitting meditatively on a bench, or looking through a family album of photos of her husband. You wouldn't want to see her shopping, eating lunch or playing tennis. Those images would jar with the tone of the sad tale. Similarly, in an observational film in which your story follows a woman's recovery from a double amputation after an accident at work, you'll want to find a relevant context for her to tell the story of the tragic event. You might take her back to the location of the accident, to hear this part of her story, so she can show and tell what happened at the same time. You wouldn't ask her about it at her 5-year-old son's birthday party. You might, of course, use the party as a means of illustrating her feelings about the impact of her new disability and how she now struggles to care for her son.

Choosing a Relevant Perspective

How you (or your camera operator) use the camera also has a big impact on the feel of the images you use to tell your story. Before reading on, take a look at Films 3.7, 3.8 and 3.9 on the website showing three different ways of filming a person walking down a street.

Film 3.7 Camera on tripod

Film 3.8 Handheld camera

Film 3.9 Point-of-view

All the shots that make up sequence in Film 3.7 were filmed with the camera mounted on a tripod. The effect of shooting this way is emotionally neutral. Images filmed like this might be appropriate for a character whose role in your film is to convey information rather than emotion – an academic, a politician, an author, etc.

The three shots in Film 3.8 were filmed with the camera on the shoulder. The shots are always in motion, the camera moving with the subject as he walks. There's more urgency, more drama in these images. They'd be more relevant when filming a character in a state of emotional tension – on his way, for example, to a vital job interview, or about to meet his mother for the first time after losing touch with her as a child.

Film 3.9 is a composite. The first and last shots are the subject's point-of-view filmed with a body-worn camera. The middle three shots are filmed on a tripod but shot in a more stylized way. Using a first person perspective plus foreground and reflections adds intrigue and an element of jeopardy to these images. This might be appropriate for someone on a risky mission – so could be used in the run-up to an undercover sequence, for example.[5]

Getting the Geography Right

In documentaries and current affairs films, conveying an impression of the geography in which a narrative unfolds takes significant time and fulfils two different roles, as discussed below.

IMAGES THAT CONVEY A SENSE OF PLACE, COMMUNITY AND SPECIFIC LOCATION

To give viewers a strong sense of the location in which your story is set you have to paint a vivid picture of an area. This can involve three or more different filming locations: one offering a panoramic view of the area – perhaps London filmed from a distance with the camera on top of a hill or at the top of a tall building. A second, offering a narrower perspective, providing images that give a sense of community. This might be a district in London showing images of its people, shops, homes, etc. And finally images that convey a specific location that help to introduce a character or storyline: this could be the exterior of someone's home, or a school or community centre, for example. Add up the time it takes to film at the three locations, with the time spent, moving from one location to another, and conveying a strong sense of geography can take several hours to achieve. But these kinds of images are important parts of your visual story-telling kit, helping to introduce characters or issues.

GEOGRAPHICAL IMAGES AS A PAUSING DEVICE

Images that convey place and community are also useful for providing breathing spaces in an unfolding narrative. So they can also be used at the end of a train of thought as a pacing device to allow a moment's reflection before your narration picks up the thread and moves the story forwards again. This prevents an audience from feeling rushed from one thought to another and, combined with a moody music track, can draw out the emotion in a film.

Thinking Figuratively

Sometimes there is no easy way to visually convey the thoughts that need to be expressed in a story. For example, when dealing with the recollection of past-tense events for which there is no archive or stills, or for conveying abstract notions or where your duty of care to a contributor rules out a direct approach. To get round this problem you need to look for images that point to, represent or symbolize – the subject under discussion. There are three approaches you can consider.

DRAMATIC REPRESENTATION

If the events are sufficiently dramatic, re-creating them is a powerful way of visualizing a past-tense story. But once you involve actors and specialist filming kit, the costs escalate beyond the reach of all but best budgeted films. There are, of course, cheap ways of dramatizing events – if you abandon costly kit and actors and are persuasive enough to get friends or colleagues to help you out for free.

Film 3.10 Watch a short dramatized reconstruction made on a low budget

This is what I did in a lower budgeted film for the BBC investigating Yasser Arafat's links to the Al Aqsa Martyrs brigade, a group that admitted carrying out 13 suicide bombings in Israel. We included a story about the violent abduction of the Governor of Jenin by men from the Al Aqsa brigade – and dramatized the event in a reconstruction achieved with very little money thanks to friends of our Palestinian fixer, who played the roles of abductors and abductee. You can watch the reconstruction on the website – it's Film 3.10. The only payments were for fake guns from a toy-shop and small gratuities for the people who played the parts. One precaution worth noting: this sequence was filmed in East Jerusalem, where the sighting of guns (fake or otherwise) could easily trigger an incident with either the Palestinian or Israeli authorities. So warning both sides that a reconstruction was taking place involving fake weapons was a necessary safeguard. This is a precaution you should take when filming any sequence involving fake weapons – or simulated violence.

Dramatic reconstruction is sometimes the only way to visualize the story to protect vulnerable contributors. In 2013 a film called *Leave To Remain,* looking at teenagers trying to get political asylum in Britain, began life as a documentary. But when the director[6] realized that seeing these young people on camera could jeopardize their asylum applications, their stories were dramatized to protect the contributors.

SYMBOLIC REPRESENTATION

There are stories in which the use of a dramatized reconstruction would feel inappropriate. Consider a documentary investigating the sexual abuse of young children. You could consider reconstructing the grooming that led to the sexual abuse – but, however tastefully done, this might feel inappropriate in such a sensitive subject. So what do you film to illustrate these past tense stories? Just filming street scenes or countryside shots won't do the trick: this is generic 'wallpaper' imagery with no real connection to the disturbing thoughts expressed in your narration. The solution is to think symbolically, to find visual metaphors that will complement thoughts about lost innocence and stolen childhoods. You might take your camera down to film in a playground. You wouldn't, of course, want to film children playing – in part because that's a happy scene and will jar with the tone of your story, but also because identifying any child in a commentary about the sexual abuse of children is likely to lead to mistaken impressions that the children in the images are the ones who have been abused. That kind of inadvertent association will lead to angry letters from parents, and potential legal actions. But filming a swing gently swaying, an empty slide, a climbing frame, or a roundabout slowly turning resonates with childhood. Stylizing the way you film and edit these images can also add to the emotion – perhaps letting the camera drift slowly across the images, and emphasizing the impressionistic feel by using mixes between the moving shots in the edited sequence. Or you could shoot a series of static images of the equipment – framed through trees and bushes – to create a silent, sombre mood. Both these approaches provide relevant symbols of youthfulness that will complement your story. Another approach in such a film would be to take your camera into the bedroom of a child of the right age and film a series of gentle pans across the toys, clothes and other symbols of childhood.

GRAPHIC REPRESENTATION

The medium of film is much better suited to conveying passion and excitement than it is at delivering factual content – because it is much easier to engage a viewer's attention with a visually arresting sequence or a moving personal story than it is to capture their minds with abstract facts. But most films have to convey some facts to their viewers – and sometimes a graphic device is the best way of doing this.

Most audiences can take in one fact, one statistic, without needing much visual help. So:

> *'There's been a dramatic 84% fall in the number of children killed or injured in road accidents since the late 1970s'*

This requires very little effort to comprehend. But the series of facts in this statement is more difficult to digest in one hearing:

> '*In 1979 almost 12,500 children were killed or injured in road traffic accidents. By 2013 this had fallen to just under 2000. That's an 84% drop in the past 35 years*'.

In a newspaper or magazine you can linger over the words, re-reading them if necessary. In a film you get one chance to convey this information to a viewer – and you have to do it in a simple and visually compelling manner, where the pictures complement the words in your commentary, or you risk losing your audience's attention. And keeping them engaged with the story is, of course, a key task. Graphic representation of abstract facts is sometimes the best way of helping viewers digest complicated statistical information. There are many different visual approaches towards the use of graphics in a factual film. My own view is that graphic representation of facts should not feel like a 'bolt-on' caption but should grow organically out of the film itself: for example, filming a camera pan off a busy road to a close framing on a car door – and using this as the backdrop for those road traffic accident statistics. With careful timing, you can add interest by including a second move away from the door to, say, the road surface to give a new backdrop for the conclusion to the statistic.

One last tip about graphical content on-screen: always marry the words contained on a graphic closely to the spoken narration. If you place visual facts on-screen in an attempt to enhance a related but separate commentary, you will confuse your viewers because it is difficult to attend to separate visual and verbal streams of thought at one time.

> When you go off filming, you've got to know how much you need to film to make the sequence work. So for instance if you're sent out to film a patient who's going to meet their consultant to find out whether they've got diabetes, you need to think 'how many cutaways do I need?', 'how many close-ups?', 'how many wides?'. Do you need to get people to repeat things? You need to have enough experience in the edit to know what to film. You need to understand how the shots cut together. You need the basic film grammar. What I've noticed a lot recently is that people break the rules of basic film grammar – and that can look quite stylish. But at risk of sounding old fashioned I would advise you to learn the rules first before you break them, because different programmes want different things and some still want the conventional look.
>
> Diana Martin, Executive Producer, BBC, *Panorama*

Directing with the Edit in Mind

When I first started directing short factual films for the BBC, I picked up the skills I needed on-the-job. There was no formal training, so I stumbled through my early days as a director. Not really understanding the core principles of what works and what doesn't when it comes to the edit, I'd over-shoot some scenes – and under-shoot others. I remember being asked by my film editor why I'd filmed 15 different shots of people's feet in a film about a traditional British Town Crier, but had failed to shoot a close up of the bell he rings to announce his presence. A good editor can usually find ways of getting round poor directing, but with a little fore-thought and planning you can avoid such embarrassing feedback. When you lack experience as a director, it helps to think through the kind of images and the different perspectives you are going to need on location and make a list. Over time, you can dispense with this security blanket. As your experience grows, you can quickly assess what you need once you see the layout of the location and understand what you want your characters to do. You'll need to consider the following.

Establishing the Key Elements of a Scene

There are no hard and fast rules about the number of shots needed to cover any action in a film, but as a rule short news stories will use a minimum of images to convey a sequence. With more time to play with, documentaries can offer viewers a greater visual texture, with close-ups and different perspectives offering variety and interest. It's usually worth over-estimating what you'll need, as cutting some images out is much easier than finding you don't have enough.

Take a look at Film 3.11 – one 12-second take of a man getting out of a car, walking down a front garden path into his house. It's much too long for one shot – lacking variety and not especially engaging for a viewer. And our subject is really too far away from the camera to be properly identified. Now watch Film 3.12: the same action but edited together using seven shots filmed from different camera perspectives. The result is a much more interesting watch. By using a close-up of the subject in the car we identify him at the start. And by using close ups of his feet, his hand opening the gate, the subject walking towards the camera as he opens the gate and putting the key in the door, the viewer obtains a more detailed impression of the scene.

Film 3.11 One shot covers the action

Film 3.12 The same action edited together from different shots

Versatility in the Edit

Filming one action from different perspectives also gives your film editor maximum versatility. Film 3.13 on the website is one unedited shot showing two people coming out of a front door, moving a wheelie bin onto the pavement, collecting a bag from a car and walking off down the road. It lasts 27 seconds in all. If you only have one take of an action, you have two choices: either write a commentary to fit the length of the shot. Or cut the beginning or end off the shot, to shorten it. Cutting a section out of the middle will, of course, result in a jump cut that's obvious to your viewer.

Film 3.13 Filming an action in one shot restricts editing. Only the front or end of the shot can be removed to change its length

Film 3.14 Several different edits of varying length possible when the action is filmed from different perspectives

Figure 3.16 to 3.26 Screen grabs showing the 11 different perspectives filmed for the five different edits of this sequence – shown in Film 3.14 on the website

Instead, if as in Film 3.14, you film the action as a sequence of different sized images your editor can cut the same action to different lengths by focusing on the significant parts of the action (hand on bin; bin out of gate; hand opening door, etc.) and ignoring the less interesting bits: the full walk down the garden path, the full walk to the car, etc. Even shorter cuts are possible now by only showing parts of the action. This condensing of time is an artifice that's acceptable to a viewer so long as you stick to the rules of filmic grammar when filming your images (see the next section). The different perspectives also, of course, have the bonus of adding variety and interest to the sequence. The four different edits shown in Film 3.14 required a total of 11 different shots of the same action. They've been used to produce edits of 27", 23", 15", 11" and 8".

Directing an Editable Sequence

Filming or directing a sequence of images that will edit together (as above) requires an understanding of the key rules of filmic grammar. If you don't pay attention to these principles, your film editor will struggle to make visual sense of the images. There are six key points to keep in mind.

Avoid 'Crossing the Line'

A sequence of images covering one action will only cut together if the direction of travel of each image through the camera frame remains consistent, unless the change in direction is made obvious to the viewer.

All the images used to make up the edited sequence in Film 3.15 on the website, were shot with the camera on the right hand side of the subject. I've illustrated what I mean in Figure 3.27. So the direction of travel of each image is from left to right as seen through the camera viewfinder. The 'line' that mustn't be crossed is the imaginary line (the arrow in the diagram) that marks out the path along which our subject is walking. Any images filmed on the side where the camera is located will be travelling from left to right and will cut together. Cross the line to the other side of the subject, and the images you film will be moving from right to left and won't cut together. Take a look at Film 3.16 on the website. Two of the images in this sequence 'crossed the line'. One is obvious. The other is more subtle. See if you can

> You've got to have some knowledge of film grammar to actually put a sequence together. The rules are great, and we adhere to them most of the time, but I have absolutely no problem with people breaking the rules so long as they know why they are doing it. And by breaking them, they are doing it for a reason which hopefully will benefit the story. If you want to break the rules, do so. Just know why you are doing it.
>
> Jeremy Humphries, Director of Photography

spot them, and then look in note 7 at the end of the chapter.[7] If you want to shoot from two sides of a moving subject you have make the move to the other side transparent so that it is not such a shock. The cut sequence in Film 3.17 does this by using a physical camera move from one side of the line to the other.

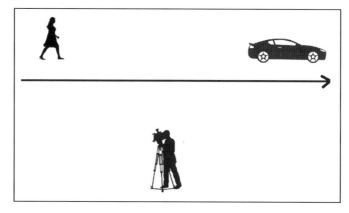

Figure 3.27 Keeping to one side of 'the line' to keep the direction of travel through the viewfinder consistent

Film 3.15 Crossing the line. Watch a correctly filmed sequence – camera keeps to one side of subjects, so direction of travel is always left to right

Film 3.16 Crossing the line. Spot the mistakes when the camera crosses to the wrong side of the line and direction of travel is not consistent

Film 3.17 See how crossing the line in a transparent way keeps the viewer at ease with a change of direction of travel

Keeping Continuity of Action

Actions that are repeated to obtain different camera perspectives must be identical.

This might sound obvious – but is an all-too-easily forgotten rule. Take a look at Film 3.18 on the website and see if you can spot the four continuity errors in the sequence. The answers are in note 8 at the end of the chapter.[8] Mistakes like these happen under the pressure of filming, and no-one spots the error until it's too late back in the edit suite. Your subject might not be in quite the same position when you repeat a shot. Or you run out of time to complete a sequence of images on one day, have to finish the next morning and forget to tell your subject to wear the same clothes – even if they are a bit dirty after a day's wear. If you're in any doubt about continuity, check the previous takes on the camera viewfinder before filming.

Film 3.18 Spot the four continuity errors in this short film sequence

Overlapping Action

An action filmed from more than one perspective must be repeated in full to give maximum flexibility in the edit.

If the repeated action is only partially performed, you restrict your editor's ability to cut the two shots together at the most natural moment. You can see the problem that results from only partially overlapping actions by viewing the edited sequences in Film 3.19 – where the action has been fully overlapped – and Film 3.20 where it hasn't. Each edited sequence is preceded by the four unedited shots used in the two examples.

Film 3.19 See an edited sequence with action overlapped

Film 3.20 See an edited sequence with actions only partially overlapped

To make this clearer, take a look at the series of screen grabs of the significant shots in these two films.

Figure 3.28 In the wide shot the subject walks down the path, opens the gate, shuts it and walks away

Figure 3.29 The close-up of the gate opening. In Film 3.19 this begins with the subject out of shot and ends when she's left the frame as the gate closes. This is a complete repeat of the wider take of this action

Figure 3.30 The same close-up. But in Film 3.20 the action is not fully overlapped. It starts as you see in this still frame, with the gate open and her arm ready to close it. So the first half of the action is missing

Figure 3.31 The wide shot of the subject walking to the car, opening door and getting in

Figure 3.32 The close-up of the car door being opened and the subject getting in. In Film 3.19 she comes into frame, puts her hand on the door opens it and gets in. This fully overlaps he wide take of this action

Figure 3.33 In Film 3.20 the close-up shot starts with the subject's hand on the door. This is not fully overlapped – and the edit can only take place at that precise point

Figure 3.34 Interior view of subject getting into the car. In Film 3.19 the entire action is repeated – from the door opening to the sit-down, giving the editor maximum flexibility on when to cut

Figure 3.35 The interior shot starts in Film 3.20 with the subject already seated in the vehicle, forcing the editor to hold the exterior image for longer than feels natural before cutting to the interior shot

Figure 3.36 The key going into the ignition. In Film 3.19, the shot starts with an empty frame, the key goes in and the hand rises to start the engine. A complete overlap of the wider version of this action, again giving the editor flexibility on when to cut to the close up

Figure 3.37 We only see the key hanging forlornly on its own in Film 3.20. No movement. No hand. So the editor is forced to stay on the wider shot until the subject's hand has risen away from the key. And the lack of movement also feels unnatural – keys jiggle about a little after they've been put in place

Fully overlapping any action that you repeat in close-up gives your film editor maximum room to craft a fluid, engaging sequence out of the images that you film.

Entrances and Exits

When filming a character on-the move, make sure your shot contains an entrance or an exit or, for continuously moving subjects, both.

Entrances and exits offer useful edit points. They are another way of allowing you to condense time while also giving your editor maximum flexibility. So if you are filming someone walking, allow them to come into the shot, follow them for a while, then let them leave the frame. Once they have left the frame, you can cut to the same subject in a different context, opening a door perhaps or sitting down in a chair, without the audience being disturbed by the speed at which these actions take place in the cut sequence compared to the time they'd have taken to do the action in reality. If you don't allow your subject to enter or exit the frame you can only edit successfully to a wider or closer take of the same action. Take a look at the four sequences in Film 3.21 on the website.

1   Clip A is an unedited one-shot take of our subject coming out of a front door, walking down a garden path onto the pavement and then getting into a car.
2   Clip B is an edit that attempts to shorten the 23" it took to do this walk down to 12" by editing out the walk down the path. But because she never leaves the first frame before we cut to the second our subject appears to 'jump' from one position (walking down the garden path) to another (opening the car door). That's what is meant by a 'jump' cut. It jars on the viewer. It looks like (and is!) a mistake.
3   Clip C rectifies the problem simply by lengthening the first shot sufficiently to allow the subject to leave the frame. Although this is an artifice and the audience implicitly knows that the actual walk to the vehicle must have taken longer than is shown, letting her exit from the first shot allows this edit to work. You only need one exit or one entrance to achieve this – not two.
4   Clip D only when you are repeating a live action shot – that is, doing a wider or closer take on the same action – will an edit work without an entrance or exit, as this example shows.

Film 3.21 Watch edits that use and don't use an exit. Decide which works and which doesn't

Slowing Down Action for Close-Ups

The closer you film a repeated action, the more likely you are to have to physically slow down the action (i.e. the speed at which you perform the action – rather than the speed at which you film it).

Take a look at the two shots of a cup being picked up in Film 3.22. The first, where the subject picked up at his own pace, feels rushed – as if he's sat in the sun for too long and is desperate for a drink! Only when he was asked to slow down and pick the cup up at less than the natural pace does it feel right – as in the second shot. Comparing the two shots, the difference in time that it takes the hand to come into the frame and the cup to be lifted out is only half a second. So a subtle timing change can make a significant difference in impact on a viewer.

Film 3.22 See the difference half a second can make when filming a close-up action

Significantly Different Shot Sizes Cut Together – Similar Sizes Don't

When you film one action from different perspectives, make sure the difference between the shot sizes is sufficiently distinct to enable the images to cut well together.

Look at Film 3.23 on the website which contains two edited sequences. First, you'll see a recut of the long 27" edit of the wheelie bin sequence from Film 3.14. This time the perspective on the action varies only marginally from shot to shot. The edit is unsatisfactory in part because the eye naturally wants to focus in on some of the detail – but also because there's a visual monotony to the sequence of shots. They are all wide-ish shots, very 'samey' in feel. So the result is visually uninteresting. Now look at the second version in Film 3.23 which shows the original edit of Film 3.14. When you look at it this time, notice the variety in shot sizes that make up the edit: it uses images whose perspective varies from wide to close-up. Each edit takes you to a shot that is distinctly different in size from its predecessor.

Film 3.23 Watch what happens when similar shot sizes are cut together

Directing Actuality Sequences

If you are filming – or directing a camera – at an unfolding event like a political demonstration, or following a character in an observational film, then interrupting actions to obtain different visual perspectives is either impractical or undesirable because it interrupts the very actions you're trying to capture on camera. Filming actuality sequences is a highly skilled job, requiring a camera operator who is confident shooting 'on-the-shoulder'; who can apply the basic rules of filmic grammar instinctively in a fast-moving situation; who can keep one eye on what's being filmed and the other on the surrounding context, allowing camera movements to respond intelligently to the action; and who can shoot a wide enough selection of images of the event plus relevant cut-away shots to allow your editor to cut a strong sequence together. So a director's role is limited to setting the tone of the shoot, laying down editorial and visual priorities. Stating, for example, that the key focus of a demonstration is a character whose story you wish to tell – and that just one of three political speeches at the demo needs to be filmed, giving the camera operator the freedom to pick up audience shots during the other two speeches. Once the demo starts, the camera person bears the major burden of responsibility for coming back with the shots. Directors then act as the operator's wider 'eyes and ears' by looking out for and alerting them to significant scenes that might develop off camera. They also help keep the camera operator safe, watching out for potential trouble or simply guiding the operator as he or she walks backwards to get a shot of your interviewee on the move.

Directing with Reporters or Presenters in Mind

An on-screen reporter or presenter who is passionate about a subject, who can convey complicated issues in an accessible way, can bring an otherwise dry subject to life and entice an audience to watch with a combination of expert knowledge and personality. The director's job is to decide exactly how to use their reporter or presenter on screen. How much imagery of your host will be needed; what parts of the narrative, if any, they will speak to camera – in other words, how and when is the best time to film their 'stand-ups'? Here's some suggestions that will help in making those decisions.

Working with an On-Screen Reporter or Presenter

Reporters and presenters who appear in vision in effect become *characters* in your film whose on-screen presence has to be carefully thought through. For example: is the narrative of your film going to be constructed around a 'journey of discovery' for the reporter, in which the issues you wish to explore become clear as he or she travels around meeting and speaking to people? The reporters in these kinds of films inevitably have a big on-screen presence – because they are the guides, leading the viewer through the story. As they learn about the issues and the interviewees, so does the audience. But not all factual films lend themselves to this treatment. In many, the journalism drives the story, and a reporter's presence is used more strategically, to draw threads of thought together, to sum up a key issue, to take the viewer out of one sequence and into the next, or to draw the film to a conclusion. The less visual your story, the more useful a reporter's visual presence becomes to help convey the content. Conversely, the more dramatic and visually engaging your film sequences, the more strategic you can be in the placing of your presenter/reporter's image in the structure.

Whatever kind of factual film you are making, it's vital that you engage creatively with your reporter or presenter, setting aside time to discuss your visual approach to their role in the film – and to hear and respond to their input into the editorial content and the creative process.

Speaking to Camera: The 'Pieces-to-Camera' or 'Stand-Ups'

Recording what are called 'Pieces-to-Camera' (PTC) or 'Stand-ups' – where a reporter or presenter looks straight down the lens and speaks to the audience – raises an obvious question for a filmmaker: what parts of the narration are going to be spoken to camera, and what parts will be recorded as a voice-over to the images once the film is edited together? At first sight, this decision appears to place the producer in a dilemma: if the final script for a factual film is not written until the structure has been edited together (see Chapter 5, pages 100–102), how can a reporter say anything on camera during the filming, way before the edit even begins? This predicament is only apparent and is resolved by looking in more detail at the different function of PTCs in documentaries and current affairs films – and when they are best filmed.

Ad Hoc, Impressionistic, Descriptive PTCs

These camera pieces convey immediate reactions to unfolding events. They are not pre-scripted, but are emotional responses to what a reporter or presenter sees happening in-front of them. Here are two examples:

> *The demonstration has now become very violent. Rocks are being flung at the police to my left. And we're now having to run for cover or we're going to get hurt.*

> *The night sky here, high up in the Andes is quite fantastic. There's little dust and no streetlights to obscure the view – and there are millions and millions of stars visible above me. This observatory is 4,000 metres above sea level. And at this height, the Milky Way is a truly spectacular sight.*

These kinds of stand-ups don't rely on a pre-conceived script. They are instead eye-witness statements describing what a reporter is seeing or hearing at that moment. This kind of PTC can be very engaging and help draw viewers into a story by capturing the emotional tone of a situation. When such immediacy is appropriate, it's always worth recording a good selection of such stand-ups so that you have choice back in the edit suite. Which ones you eventually end up using in the film will ultimately be driven by the structure put together.

Formal, Pre-Planned Stand-Ups

The other kind of stand-up are 'set-piece' PTCs designed either to convey abstract information; to introduce or conclude significant chapters in your programme; or to covey context, interpretation or opinion. It's difficult to write such PTCs without knowing precisely where they fit in the film structure – and they are best written and filmed towards the end of your edit. Sometimes, of course, this just isn't practical: if part of your film is in Israel, but the edit is in New York you won't have the cash to send a reporter back to Israel to pick up a PTC late in the edit. But you would like to see your reporter on-screen at some point during the Middle East sequence saying something more than a descriptive, eye-witness camera piece. By understanding the purpose of the Israeli sequence, and how it will fit into the overall narrative that you are constructing, you could use your reporter on-screen to introduce the reason for coming to Israel and perhaps also convey the conclusion of the sequence. These more formal statements help glue the story together and establish your reporter or presenter on-screen. It's likely that they won't fit perfectly into your final film structure, because they've been written with no knowledge of the precise words that will precede and follow the stand-up in the cut film. But a little strategic editing – losing the opening line in a PTC, for example, and replacing it with an out of vision sentence – can often make such a camera piece work.

Writing and Filming Pieces-to-Camera

Writing a PTC

The writing of a PTC is usually a collaborative process because, although reporters are the voice and face of a film, it is the producer/director who's in charge of the film's structure and the way in which the content is realized on-screen. To put it more simply: because the PD's job is to decide how the story is going to unfold visually and editorially, decisions about which parts of the narration will be spoken to camera, and which will simply be out-of-vision voice-over are usually taken by the PD. The reporter's role is to conduct interviews and write the exact words that will be used to convey the content at any point in the film. So it usually works like this: PDs suggest the kind of stand-up that they'd like a reporter to say, and the reporter devises the words to express the thoughts. The division of responsibilities between a PD and a reporter varies somewhat from film to film. Reporters who are involved from the very start of a production, or who bring specialist knowledge to a film, will have a big role in the kind of story that's being told, and therefore more involvement in the kind of camera pieces that would benefit the film. Conversely, presenters who are taken on board later on in the process, when the content of the story is in place, just to record interviews, PTCs, and read the script, will be more of a mouthpiece for the PDs vision. But the process should always be a collaborative one. If it isn't, it's usually because a reporter misunderstands the role of the director – easy to do if the reporter is from a newspaper background and used to calling all the shots. Then you can end up with extenuated two or three minute camera pieces that show little awareness of an audience's attention span or the overall film structure. So best to explain the process in some detail up front to hosts who are new to the medium.

The Written Style of a Camera Piece

A camera piece should always be written in an immediate, straightforward way and lack sub clauses. It is English as it is spoken – not written – and a producer/director's job is to act as the eyes and ears of the audience, judging whether the stand-up is clearly intelligible on one hearing; whether the reporter's delivery is engaging and ensuring there are no visual or audible distractions that will interrupt the flow-of-thought. It's always worth recording more than one take of a PTC.

Filming Stand-Ups

One Shot – Two Sizes   How long you can sustain a PTC on one shot really depends on the quality of the performer. The stronger their televisual presence, the more at ease they are in front of the camera, the more passionate and knowledgeable about their subject, the longer they will be able to engage the audience without the need to change the image to add variety. For lesser mortals, I'd suggest that a camera piece of up to 15" to 20" long can be filmed in one shot – without worrying about losing audience attention. But it is always worth filming the PTC in either a wider or a tighter framing, to give you editing options and to help you cut around any editorial issues that might arise between recording the PTC and completing the film. For example, you record this camera piece on location.

> *The night sky here in the Andes is quite fantastic. There's little dust and no streetlights to obscure the view – and there are millions and millions of stars visible above me. This observatory is 4,000 metres above sea level. The Milky Way is a truly spectacular sight.*

But back in the edit suite you discover an error: the observatory is in fact 5,000 metres above sea level. You could, of course, cutaway from the PTC early, and rescript the penultimate sentence, using images of the observatory and the sky to get round the factual error. But you like the delivery of the presenter's last sentence, it's spoken with passion and you'd like to keep it in vision to the end. If you've filmed a wider version of the entire PTC, you can simply cut out of the camera piece after the words '*visible above me*', and edit straight to the wider take for the last sentence. The correct height of the observatory can then be added somewhere else in the commentary.

Two or more Shots – Varying the Perspective   Varying the camera perspective on your reporter can also help to keep an audience engaged with a longer PTC. Take a look at the raw unedited footage in Film 3.24. These are two shots of a stand-up in which the director has asked the reporter to turn their head to face a new camera angle halfway through the camera piece. Notice that, in the first shot, the reporter continues to speak even after turning away from the camera. And similarly, he begins speaking in the second shot before turning towards the camera. This is to ensure the flow from one shot to the next feels natural, as if the reporter has turned from one camera to a second without pause, even though there is only one camera filming. You can see the result in the edited PTC that follows the unedited shots.

Film 3.24 Watch a two shot stand-up – using a head turn and a shot size change to give the impression of a two-camera shoot

Demonstrative PTCs Stand-ups where a reporter demonstrates an activity – showing the safety kit required for a potholing expedition, for example, should be filmed as a mini sequence with the action repeated a number of times to obtain a variety of shots. Their length will of course be driven by the time it takes to illustrate the activity.

Chapter Summary

Key Issues to Consider when Directing or Filming Images or Reporters

DIY or Pay a Camera Operator?

Self-Shooting

- *Pros:* cheap – small budgets stretch much further; can spend more time on location.
- *Cons:* not easy to bring back well-shot selection of rushes; physically and psychologically demanding; success requires rare combination of editorial, technical, directorial and visual skills. Shouldn't be undertaken lightly.

Camera Operator

- *Pros:* with no technical camera and sound operating pressure, you'll have more energy for creative directing; carefully chosen, a pro will give you distinctively filmed images.
- *Cons:* the high cost – much more financial pressure, less time on location.

Directing with the Camera in Mind

- *The different kinds of camera movement:* Pans. Tilts. Cranes. Tracking shots.
- *Changes to the camera lens:* Pulling focus. Zooms. Focal Lengths. Depth of field. Exposure.
- *Composing your images:* Finding interesting or unusual perspectives to engage an audience.

Directing with the Narrative in Mind

Getting the Emotional Tone Right

- Choosing relevant locations.
- Choosing a relevant perspective.
- Getting the geography right.

Thinking Figuratively

- Dramatic representation.
- Symbolic representation.
- Graphic representation.

Directing with the Edit in Mind

Establishing the Key Elements of a Scene

Different approaches are taken by short and long films towards conveying a visual sense of a scene.

Versatility in the Edit

Filming one action from different perspectives, varying the shot sizes.

Directing an Editable Sequence

- Avoid 'crossing the line'.
- Keeping continuity of action.
- Overlapping action.
- Entrances and exits.
- Slowing down action for close-ups.
- Significantly different shot sizes cut together – similar sizes don't.

Directing Actuality Sequences

Director's role limited to setting the tone of the shoot, laying down editorial and visual priorities. Major responsibility rests on camera operator's shoulders.

Directing with Reporters in Mind

- *Working with an on-screen reporter or presenter:* deciding the nature of their on-screen presence – from full-on 'journeys-of-discovery' to more strategically placed in-vision reportage.
- *Speaking to Camera. The PTC.*
  Ad hoc, impressionistic PTCs.
  Formal, pre-planned stand-ups.
- *Writing and Filming Pieces-to-Camera.*
  A. Writing pieces-to-camera is a collaborative process.
  B. The style of a Stand-up: English as-she-is-spoken, immediate and straight-forward.
  C. Filming pieces-to-camera.
     One shot, two sizes.
     Two or more shots – varying the perspective.
     Demonstrative PTCs.

Notes

1 When the camera is used on a tripod, the quality of pans and tilts described here depends critically on the quality and construction of the tripod. See page 220 in Chapter 11 for more information on the choice of a tripod.

2 In the UK, to operate a drone commercially (i.e. if you are being paid to fly it) you need to be trained and obtain permission from the Civil Aviation Authority (CAA). If you try and dry hire one you'll be asked to show evidence you have such permission. So most hired out drones come with an approved operator. Recently introduced legislation restricts all drones from flying above 400 feet without CAA permission, with much stricter flying limits near airports, and insists that users of drones weighing more than 250g pass an online theory test. Commercial drone operators must also comply with the CAA by conducting a flight risk assessment to ensure that the drone is being flown safely within regulations which stipulate how near to airfields, schools, built-up centres, etc. it's allowed to fly. Getting good results also requires many hours of practice.

   Similarly, to use a drone commercially in the US, you also have to be trained and have permission from the Federal Aviation Administration (FAA) to fly in airspace managed by air traffic controllers. Most hired out drones in America come with an approved operator. Operators also have to comply with the FAA by conducting a flight risk assessment similar to the one required by the CAA in the UK. More information can be found here:

   UK: www.caa.co.uk/Commercial-industry/Aircraft/Unmanned-aircraft/Small-drones/Regulations-relating-to-the-commercial-use-of-small-drones/

   https://dronesafe.uk

   US: https://uavcoach.com/drone-laws-in-united-states-of-america/

   www.faa.gov/uas/getting_started/

3 The focal length of a lens is the distance from the point in the lens where light rays enter to the point where they come together or converge on the light sensor in the camera. This distance is small in wide angle lenses and much longer in telephoto lenses.

4 The aperture of the camera can also affect the depth of field. So if there is sufficient light, closing the aperture will sharpen up the background around a subject that's been filmed on a telephoto lens.

5 The quality of the tripod images, filmed on a professional camera is, of course, much better than those filmed on the body worn, pinhole camera.

6 Bruce Goodison – as he explained to an audience at Sheffield Documentary Festival in 2017.

7 The close-up of the feet 'crosses the line'. But so does the last shot in the sequence because the subjects entered the shot on the right hand side of the frame – the same side as they had exited in the previous shot, changing the direction of travel through the frame.

8 A grey hoodie jacket changes into a yellow T-shirt; an empty plate suddenly contains a half eaten banana; arms that are folded on the table in one shot are raised in the air in the next; and a watch mysteriously disappears between shots.

4 Talking Heads

Choosing Contributors, Conducting Interviews and Making your Characters Look and Sound Good on Camera

KEY CONCEPTS

- What to look for when selecting a contributor for your film.
- Teasing the best performance out of an interviewee.
- Using camera framing, eye-lines, shot sizes, lighting, lenses and background design to make your interviews look great.
- The importance of capturing good quality sound.

Whether you are planning to shoot it yourself or direct a professional camera operator, crafting a factual film requires careful thought about how you're going to film, question and record the sound of your interviews. You don't want to be the butt-end of an editor's jests because an interviewee is so poorly lit they look like they have asked to appear in silhouette; or because they appear to have a lamp-post growing out of their head or an eye-line that makes the interviewer appear to be seven feet tall. Even fantastic lighting and framing won't make up for an interviewee who's so nervous they can't string two coherent words together, or a reporter in such a hurry to place follow-ups that the questions repeatedly overlap the last words of an interviewee's answers, making them un-editable. So in this chapter I am going to offer some broad visual, editorial and interview management principles to guide directors and self-shooters on how to bring back nicely composed, well lit, interesting, cuttable interviews. This will be enough information to keep your editors happy, but not so much that you become overwhelmed with techniques that you are not likely to need on many factual film shoots, and certainly not in the early part of a filmmaker's career.

Unless you are making a narration-only film – like a wildlife film – some of your screen time will consist of 'talking heads', as interviewees tend to be called. That casual term belies the many detailed questions that must be answered before you embark on filming an interview. Choosing an interviewee simply because they've got the right qualification to speak on a subject, and then plonking the camera down with little fore-thought risks a poor-looking image, badly recorded sound and a range of potential problems with the content. To avoid this, before you press record, you have to address questions about the kind of person you want to include in your film; the context in which you're planning to film them; how they are lit; where you locate the camera and position the person in the frame; how you arrange the background; what shot sizes you're going film; the focal length of the lens; how you record the sound of the interview, and, of course, how you go about preparing for and conducting the interview itself. All of these decisions impact on what your audience will see and hear – and therefore how engaged they are likely to be in what's being said. If you are working with a camera operator, they will take some of these decisions, in consultation with you. But a good director should always be aware of the possibilities so that they can make stylistic suggestions. I'm going to break the task down into its component parts.

Choosing an Interviewee

At the heart of all factual films are personal stories told on camera by individuals whose experience, knowledge and recollections illustrate your narrative. More often than not you'll be looking for the raw emotion that brings the story to life: strong feelings engage an audience much more than detailing factual content. Think of the following when considering someone as a potential contributor to your film

How Will They Perform?

Your first decision is one of character: will your potential contributor tell a great story on camera or will they become self-conscious and dry up once you switch on and start asking the questions? On film, how a message is conveyed is just as important as the content of that message. I once went to film a neurologist for an 'on-the-day' film made for a nightly BBC current affairs show. There was no time to meet the academic before filming and, once the camera was switched on, he either dried up or added so many qualifications that what he wanted to say lost all meaning. I had to collaboratively prepare a written version of what he wanted to say which he learnt by heart and then spoke to camera. As you can imagine, it wasn't the best of interviews! So it pays to meet a potential interviewee before turning up with a camera to film them. It's much easier to judge *in person* whether someone is going to flail on camera or be the engaging character that you hoped to find.

Idiosyncrasies that can Distract an Audience

By meeting your contributors before asking them to be interviewed, you'll also be better able to judge whether other idiosyncratic character traits are going to be an asset or a liability. Remember: your aim is to capture an audience's attention and keep it firmly fixed on the unfolding narrative. If you choose a middle-aged interviewee with day-glow pink hair, unless your film is about hair styles, viewers are likely to be distracted when they first see them. That means they will miss what's actually being said while they take on-board the unusual hair colour. You've lost their attention – and they've lost the message. You might decide to choose someone else to do the job in your film. But if this person's story is significant, you might instead get round the problem by introducing your interviewee before he speaks, filming him at work or at home and adding an out-of-vision narration. By the time your audience hears his first words they will have got over the shock of their coiffured pink hair. That lessens the likelihood that the audience will miss any of the precious content.

Getting the Best Performance out of your Interviewee

Producer/Directors working without a reporter or presenter will, of course, be sitting in the hot seat asking the questions during an interview. If you are self-shooting my advice is: get someone else to operate the camera for the interviews. Thinking about content, responding sympathetically and intelligently to an interviewee's comments, while also paying attention to the quality of the sound and the image being recorded, is too much for one person to achieve effectively. So find a camera-savvy friend and focus only on content when interviewing. Here are some basic techniques that you should follow to maximize your chance of coaxing a strong interview out of your subjects.

Before you Arrive at the Interview Location

1   Prepare a list of questions based on your story structure. In an analytical film, that entails anticipating the sections in which your character will appear, and tailoring a list of questions accordingly. In an observational film, you'll have to decide which part of your character's unfolding story you wish them to reflect on during the interview.

2   Avoid questions that elicit yes/no answers like: 'Did you feel upset when you first heard the news about the exam results?' Much better to ask a question that requires an explanatory response like: 'Describe how you felt when you heard about the exam results'.

3   Design each question to contain only one thought – or you risk an interviewee only responding to one part of your question. So avoid questions like: 'Tell me how you managed to escape from the boat before it sank and describe your feelings at the time'. Instead, split such a question into two.

4   Design questions to which an interviewee will respond with a full statement rather than a sentence that begins with a pronoun. For example, asking: 'What happened when the child fell into the lake?' will most likely be answered with: 'We ran as fast as we could to the bank and just jumped in'. Because the interviewee has picked up the story after the child fell in, you might be forced to include your question in the film to make sense of the answer. If you want to exclude the interviewer from the final cut, a better question to ask is: 'Tell me what happened while you were sitting on the park bench having lunch?' Your interviewee is then forced to tell you the entire story, giving you more scope when you come to edit this sequence together.

5   Design questions that will elicit story telling or emotion. Facts are much better relayed with a considered commentary illustrated by relevant visuals.

6   The order in which you prepare your question list is important: leave hard questioning – or emotionally demanding questions – until your interviewee has relaxed and, as tends to happen mid-way through an interview, the presence of the camera becomes subliminal. You'll get better answers that way.

7   You must be able to adopt an opposing viewpoint in an interview, to ask the questions that a sceptical viewer might be thinking as they watch – particularly when making investigative films. You can phrase such challenging questioning politely, but by playing 'Devil's Advocate', you often provoke strong, emotional responses as your interviewee defends their position.

When you Arrive at the Filming Location

1   Put subjects at ease. Never rush into an interview. Remember that most people are not used to being filmed and the presence of a camera is usually a source of considerable anxiety. Even on a pressured schedule, take some time to chat, away from the interview set. Explain the purpose of the film, even if a researcher has already done that at an earlier meeting. Give them an overview of the question areas you'll be addressing (but not the actual questions – or you risk them over-rehearsing their answers). Tell them that your only concern is to help them express themselves in the best possible way, that there are no 'trick' questions, and that if they are not happy with something they've said, then you can simply ask the question again.

2   If you are producing a reporter or presenter who is asking the questions, keep out of the interviewee's eye-line. If you sit near to the interviewer, or even on the other side of the camera, there will be a temptation for the interviewee to glance at you during answers. To the audience, a shifting eye-line can appear to make the subject look anxious or even untrustworthy. So position yourself at right-angles to the interviewee or, better still, a little way behind the person to avoid being a distraction.

During the Interview

1   Maintain eye contact and use body language to demonstrate your interest. A good interview is achieved by listening acutely to the answers. Your attention is vital feedback for an interviewee, especially someone not used to being filmed. If you are not listening, their ability to express themselves declines. They will most likely be worried about how they are coming across, and eye contact puts them at ease by letting them know that you are actively following their words. You can further ease a subject's anxieties by using silent assent – nodding affirmatively at times or shaking your head in sympathy. Do not use your voice to convey understanding. 'Hmmm' sounds or repeating 'I see' can be very irritating for viewers and can complicate the job of cutting an interview to length if they happen to coincide with an edit point.

2   Regard your prepared question list only as a security blanket – a list that you can look at *once the interview is over*, or during a break in filming, to check that you have indeed asked all the questions you prepared. You can't both be attentive to what an interviewer is saying and also continually checking the list. Your next question will be a natural follow-up to the answer you have just heard, it will be obvious, it won't need thinking about. It might be a request for clarification, or it might be a question designed to plug an obvious gap in what you've just heard. But the question will appear in your mind without effort. Often the best answers in an interview come in response to spontaneous follow-up questions.

3   Be wary of acronyms (abbreviations). If your interviewee uses an acronym that you feel your audience won't understand don't be frightened to act as their interpreter: as soon as you hear some jargon, or an acronym, interrupt the flow and say, for example: 'By USMCA you mean the new United States Mexico Canada free trade agreement'. That will make the answer usable. Of course that means the interviewer has to be well versed on the subject being discussed – and able to respond confidently and quickly in this way.

4   Be patient – don't hurry onto another question until you are sure the interviewee has completed their thought. Sometimes waiting that extra second or two at the end of an answer can evoke the best part of the reply. Be especially careful not to overlap the end of an answer with an incoming question – or you will find your interview very difficult to edit. The only exception to this is during a confrontational part of an interview, where you feel

the need to press hard for an answer. But breaking into an interviewee's train of thought should be used very judiciously.

5   At the end of an interview, if a little voice inside you is saying that you haven't quite got that key answer you need for the narrative – listen to your instinct: apologize to your interviewee, and say something like: 'now that you've warmed up, I think you'll be able to give a much stronger answer to question X and Y etc. So do you mind if I ask them again?' Most people want to be seen at their best and usually won't mind doing this. Explain that you'll most likely only use one of the answers and warn them against using phrases like 'as I told you before'. In fact it's always worth asking important questions more than once. A significant answer given early on in an interview, before your interviewee has relaxed, will be more stilted, less emotional, than an answer to the same question given near the end.

The Look of Your Interview

In all but the most uncontrollable situations, directors of factual films should be thinking about the stylistic, camera, lighting and design issues that affect how their interviewees are going to appear to an audience These decisions have a big impact on the way in which a contributor is presented to a viewer – so let's look at these decisions one by one.

Interview Style

You have three options.

Static Interviews

The questioner and interviewee are stationary in one location as they chat with the camera on a tripod or handheld. There are advantages and disadvantages to both approaches.

On a tripod. With the framing of your interviewee limited to different shot sizes on one perspective, you can use lighting and set design to fine tune the look of your interviewee and the surrounding background. In the hands of a skilled lighting camera operator, you can achieve very distinctive looking sit down interviews in this way. The downside is the time you need to allow on your schedule to set up lights and design the distinctive 'look' you want.

On the shoulder. The more physical camera movement you allow, the less you can control the 'look' of your interview with careful composition and lighting. The upside is an ability to convey immediacy, a sense of being present at an unfolding event, and variety because a mobile camera can offer a changing perspective on an interviewee. I once used a camera operator who, unusually, much preferred to shoot sit down interviews hand-held. He worked out the best camera positions beforehand and, during questions, he'd physically move and reframe a very different perspective on our subject. This gave an interesting selection of static images to work with in the edit suite.

Walking Interviews

Interviewer and interviewee are on the move, walking and talking together, while the camera operator walks backwards ahead of them – or alongside the speakers. The audience will be aware of two kinds of movement: the changing perspective of the landscape as they move through it, and changes in the framing of the speakers as the camera moves around them.

Action Interviews

Working and talking at the same time can sometimes help to put a nervous interviewee more at ease when talking on camera. With the focus on a manual task – it can be anything from making a model airplane to cooking an omelette or driving a car – there's less room for the contributor to worry about the presence of the camera, making for a more relaxed performance. The task being filmed must, of course, have some relevance to what's being said: filming a solider digging a flower bed in his garden while talking about a violent incident while on duty in Iraq, doesn't add up. Watching him clean his Heckler and Koch sub-machine gun might make more sense. Working in his garden could be appropriate if the focus of what he's saying is about the stress of the incident that's forced him to leave the army and left him unable to work.

Framing your Interviewee

Whether the camera is on a tripod or hand-held, and whether your interview is static or on the move, you need to think about the position in which your interviewee appears in the frame. There are two aspects to this.

Horizontal Framing

Take a look at Figure 4.1 which shows a diagrammatic aerial view of a typical interview set-up, with the interviewer in this case sitting on the left of the camera. Then look at Figures 4.2, 4.3 and 4.4[1] showing three possible horizontal framings of the interviewee. Which position looks most appropriate for this set up? To my eye, Figure 4.2 showing the interviewee sitting in the right hand segment looks correct. Notice that the interviewee's eyes in Figure 4.2 are looking towards the left of the frame. If you pull the camera straight back a little as in Figure 4.5, so that your framing includes a rear view of the interviewer, he appears to block out the gap on the left hand side of the frame – in the very position towards which the interviewee was looking. That's why this interview position looks 'right'. It fulfils natural expectations of where the elements of the interview should be in the TV or computer frame. The further to the left you seat the interviewee, as in Figures 4.3 and 4.4, the more unbalanced and unnatural the framing appears. In Figure 4.4 the interviewee is sitting fully in the left segment, she is looking out of the frame entirely, giving the impression of looking to the left of her questioner rather than straight at him. When you pull the camera back to see the interviewer, as in Figures 4.6 and

4.7, to keep the interviewee in the same position in the wide shot as in the close up, the interviewer and interviewee are progressively pushed onto the left side of frame, making for a very unbalanced looking picture. If you try to get round this by re-positioning the wide shot of interviewer and interviewee to appear as in Figure 4.5, then cutting from close-up to wide shot will make the interviewee appear to suddenly jump from the centre of the frame (as in Figure 4.3) or the left side of frame (as in Figure 4.4) across to the right hand side of the screen, and the cut will look very odd. You can break this rule of course – plenty of filmmakers do – but they do so in full knowledge of the general rule, to achieve a specific 'look' or effect for their film.

Figure 4.1 Diagrammatic aerial view of interview set-up

HORIZONTAL FRAMING EXAMPLES

Figure 4.2

Figure 4.3

Figure 4.4

Figure 4.5

Figure 4.6

Figure 4.7

Vertical Framing

The vertical position in which you locate an interviewee is just as important as the horizontal plane. And the key issue here is the headroom you give your subject – the gap between the top of their head and the top of the screen. Figures 4.8 and 4.9 show two alternative vertical framings for an interviewee. This time I've divided the frame into quadrants. Both look rather odd: in Figure 4.8 the interviewee's eyes are just beneath the top and bottom half of the screen – and there's too much headroom. She now looks too small to fit in the frame or possibly has had one too many drinks and is slumping in her chair! In Figure 4.9, with her eyes well above the centre line leaving no headroom, she appears to have grown rather too tall. The most pleasing or natural looking framing, shown in Figure 4.10, has the eyes placed just a little above the centre of the upper right hand quadrant and a small amount of headroom. Finally look also at Figure 4.11.

VERTICAL FRAMING EXAMPLES

Figure 4.8

Figure 4.9

Figure 4.10

Figure 4.11

Cutting back from Figures 4.10 to 4.11 will work because the headroom remains proportionate to the size of the shot and the change 'in height' of the eyes within the quadrant is still acceptable. This would not be the case if you tried to cut from either Figures 4.8 or 4.9 to 4.11.

Eye-Lines

When we talk about an interviewee's eye-line, we are referring to the direction in which they appear to be looking. The eye-line contains clues as to where the interviewer is positioned in space relative to the interviewee. Take a look at Figures 4.12 to 4.15, which show different eye-lines – and compare with the eye-line in Figure 4.16.

Figure 4.12 either gives the impression that the interviewee is falling asleep or is looking down at her questioner, who is sitting on the floor.

Figure 4.13 makes the interviewer appear to be much larger than the interviewee. If your interviewer really is much taller than your interviewee, then sit him or her on a lower chair – or put a couple of cushions underneath your interviewee.

Figure 4.14 has an eye-line that makes the interviewer appear to be seated much too far to the left of the camera.

Figure 4.15 shows the interviewee looking directly towards camera, and therefore at the viewer, rather than answering questions from an off-camera interviewer. This eye-line is mainly used in films by reporters or presenters doing pieces-to-camera, although asking a contributor to talk to camera is sometimes used by filmmakers[2] to give added intimacy to an interview.

Figure 4.16 has the interviewer on the same level as the interviewee while also sitting close to the camera. This eye-line is the most frequently used approach in documentaries and current affairs films.

There are no hard and fast rules about eye-lines. Directors have their own preferences and may well use extreme eye-lines to create an effect. It's always worth looking at your list of interviewees and deciding how many will be looking to camera left (i.e. with the reporter sitting to the left of the camera) – and how many looking to camera right. If everyone in the film is looking in one direction, your interviews will be rather predictable. Where you know you might cut one interviewee against a second (for example, two people with opposed viewpoints) shoot them with opposite eye-lines because they will appear to be looking towards each other when you cut one against the other.

EYELINE EXAMPLES

Figure 4.12 Too low

Figure 4.13 Too high

Figure 4.14 Too far left

Figure 4.15 Straight to camera

Figure 4.16 Eyeline frequently used in documentaries

Shot Sizes

The interviewee. Most people don't speak in succinct, self-contained clips – they might use sub-clauses, or wander off the point before coming back to it, or fluff an answer and have to start again. So the interview clips in a film are often the best sentences of an answer strung together from different parts of the interview. You'll then have visual 'jumps' between the sections. One way of making these edits invisible is to vary the size of the filmed image of your subject during the interview, allowing you to cover an edit by cutting from one shot size to another. Figures 4.17 to 4.20 show examples of shot sizes on my illustrative interview set. A director will usually agree these sizes with his or her camera operator prior to beginning an interview. A good camera operator will listen to what's being said during the interview and vary the shot size appropriately – for example, zooming in to a big close up (Figure 4.17) or a close up (Figure 4.18) to emphasize emotion. Only *distinctly different* shot sizes cut well together. If you edit the image in Figure 4.17 straight after Figure 4.18 it will look like an error – the interviewee will appear to 'jump' from one frame to the next. By contrast, Figure 4.17 will cut with either Figure 4.19 or 4.20. Although this is also a 'jump' cut – because you are editing two significantly different images of the interviewee together – the cut will feel acceptable.

SHOT SIZES: INTERVIEWEE EXAMPLES

Figure 4.17

Figure 4.18

Figure 4.19

Figure 4.20

The interviewer – 'noddies'. Of course, you can't *guarantee* that two clips of interview you wish to cut together will have been filmed at different shot sizes. Or you might have taken a stylistic decision to film all interviewees in just one size. Or you might have too many edits in an answer to use the technique more than once. Or, like me, you might just dislike the idea of cutting two different shot sizes together. To cover edits in these situations you have two options. Directors who want to include their interviewer's image and questions in the finished programme, sometimes film listening shots of the interviewer once the interview has finished. The camera is moved behind the interviewee and the reporter is filmed silently listening while the interviewee talks on any subject they wish. These are commonly called 'noddies' because they are images of your reporter 'nodding' their head and looking sympathetic in assent to the interviewee's words. Although 'noddies' can be used to cover edits, it's difficult to make this artifice look realistic. I would only use 'noddies' if they are shot at the same time as the interview, using a second camera focused on the reporter. That way you obtain real emotional responses to an answer. Of course, you need the budget for a two-camera shoot to do that – and not all factual films are sufficiently well resourced to permit this. I prefer to cover sound edits in an interview with separately filmed images that have a relevance to the subject matter under discussion. So listen carefully to your interviews and note down suitable cut-away images to be filmed later on to cover edits.

Interviewer/Interviewee editing shots. If you are using an in vision reporter or presenter you might wish to give a sense of your host asking the questions without actually seeing their lips moving. If so, you'll need to film wider perspectives on the interview set, once the interview itself has been filmed, showing the interviewee listening and the interviewer speaking. This allows you to cut to a wider image of the setting, showing both participants (Figures 4.21 to 4.23 show different examples) to cover the question. Because you don't see the interviewer's face, these images can be used on any question. Profiles, as shown in Figure 4.24 have to be sufficiently wide so that an audience won't see that the words being spoken during the filming of the profile, are not the words of the question recorded during the interview. Figure 4.24 would not be wide enough. You need a big room or the space provided by an outside location to achieve this. Two camera shoots are normally needed to provide the actual 'lip sync' questions at the time of asking. Filming them 'wild' at the end of an interview has the same problems attached to it as does filming 'noddies': it is very difficult to make them convincing.

SHOT SIZES: INTERVIEWER EXAMPLES

Figure 4.21

Figure 4.22

Figure 4.23

Figure 4.24

You can, of course, capture the real questions along with the answers with one camera by positioning it between the two speakers (see Figures 4.25 and 4.26) and panning onto the reporter as a question is asked. The camera must hold on the interviewee until *after* the start of any question before panning to get the question – or you will find it difficult to edit out of any answer. The eye-line of your interviewee will inevitably be angled further away from the camera (because the interviewer has to be some distance from the camera to obtain an image once it pans onto her). And your interviewer will be profiled. You can avoid angled eye-lines and profiles, by going hand-held and letting the operator physically move position to frame good shot sizes on both participants.

Figure 4.25 and 4.26 Capturing both questions and answers in a tripod interview setting

Lighting

How an interviewee is lit makes a huge difference to the way in which your subject appears to a viewer. You create atmosphere with lighting – but are you going to use natural light? Or do you want to use artificial light to set a specific style, using shadows to model their faces and a backlight to help pick them out from the interview setting? If you are shooting with a camera operator, you won't need to know how to achieve a particular effect, but you should have a vision of how you'd like your interviewees to appear. If you are working alone, self-shooting, you will need some basic lighting skills, if for no other reason than to get you out of a fix. How do you film an interview when there's too little light to produce a good image, for example? Or if there's too much light? I am not a lighting camera operator, so can't offer an in-depth primer on lighting techniques. But I have self-shot and used a basic lighting kit to film interviews for broadcast on TV – so am going to offer some basic techniques to ensure you get back to the edit suite with a decent image.

If there is sufficient natural light where you wish to film, aim to use it – unless you wish to create a very specific and consistent interview style. On documentaries and current affairs films using natural light is always quicker and easier than spending time setting-up and fine tuning a lighting kit – which only adds pressure to your daily schedule.

Exterior filming. If you're outside on a partially cloudy day when the sun is sometimes visible and sometimes obscured, changes in the light level can play havoc with your image. If you've set the exposure while the sun is out, when it goes behind a cloud, the light drops and your image becomes under-lit, forcing you to open the camera aperture to compensate. If you've done the opposite, and set your exposure when the sun is behind a cloud, your image will become too bright when the it comes out again and you'll have to close the camera aperture to lower the amount of light going into the lens. Unless you are an experienced camera operator, this is a complication best avoided. But, as I indicated on pages 47–48 in Chapter 3, relying on the auto-exposure function of a digital camera can result in sudden changes in the light level on your interviewee and this is also best avoided. If you have to film outside on a day like this, find a shady area where foreground and background remain in shade during your filming. If you can't, learn how to change the exposure manually – once mastered, altering the camera aperture can be achieved much more smoothly.

> My preference when I'm lighting – and not everybody would necessarily agree with me – is to always use daylight. In fact it's the lights I turn off – in terms of the artificial lights – not the lights I turn on, that creates my shot. I will use daylight time and time and time again wherever I can. I think we're programmed to respond to daylight, engage with daylight, much more than anything else. That having been said, if I'm in a big office where there's a mixture of light and you can't really turn them off, one inevitably has to use that. But even then I might be steered to doing an interview near a window, where I can use that main daylight coming through as a source and model my character accordingly. But, yes, I very much prefer natural or available light.
>
> Jeremy Humphries,
> Director of Photography

Interior filming – using light coming through a window. Look for a spot next to a window – see Figure 4.27. Place your interviewee so that light from the window falls on one side of their face. Side-lit subjects look better than subjects lit from the front as the contrast between the light and dark sides of a face give a more 'moody' image. A face that's lit from the front, without shadows, looks flat and uninteresting. Consider the following issues when filming an interior interviewee by natural light.

1   *The distance of your interviewee from the window*. The nearer they are to the window, the bigger the difference between the light from outside and the light inside the room – and therefore the more the contrast between the light and dark sides of the face.

2   *The position of the camera with respect to the window*. The closer you place the camera (and, of course, the interviewer) to position B in Figure 4.27, the more your interviewee's face presents a profile to the window and so the greater is the contrast between the sunlit side of the face and the side in shadow. Conversely, the nearer to position A, the more the interviewee is turned towards the window and so the contrast will be less. Exactly how much side lighting you desire is a matter of choice. Figure 4.28 shows a side lit subject resulting from positioning of camera and interviewer as in Figure 4.29 (close to position B in the diagram). Figures 4.30 and 4.31 show the same for a subject who is angled towards the window and so lit more from the front (close to position A in the diagram).

Figure 4.27 Side and front lit interviews

Figure 4.28 Side lit subject

Figure 4.29 Position of camera/interviewer for side lit interview

Figure 4.30 Subject lit from front with little shadowing

Figure 4.31 Camera position for front lit interview

3   *The difference in the colour-temperature of interior and exterior light.* Filming an interview by a large window on a bright day should let you turn all the artificial lights off and still obtain a good camera image, even on the shadow side of the face. But on a dull day or if the window is small, you might be forced to raise the level of light inside the room to prevent a complete loss of detail on the unlit side of your interviewee. There are two ways of doing this:

Using a reflector. Ask for a reflector to be included with your lighting kit. This is a sheet of material that unfolds into a circular shape and is used to reflect sunlight. It has a white and a silver side. Place this out of shot, of course, on the 'dark' side of your interviewee with the white side angled so that the soft, diffuse light that it reflects from the window lights the interviewee's face. By moving the reflector nearer or further away from your subject you can raise the light level sufficiently for you to obtain good contrast. The silver side reflects a more dazzling light that can be used to raise the overall level of light in a room by, for example, reflecting daylight coming in through a window and bouncing it off a wall or ceiling.

Using the room lights. Switching the room lights on means you'll be filming in mixed lighting conditions. Digital cameras need to be adjusted to the prevailing lighting conditions to ensure that the colour of a person's skin looks normal.

> If somebody is self-shooting, then just think: where is the natural source of light coming from? If you have a window, in daytime you have a source of light coming through. You could use that. You may well be in a situation where there is light there, but it's just not enough, so that's when we supplement with a light panel, maybe bounced off a wall, maybe direct but dimmed down, just to lift the ambient light there. Not to ruin it all, not to destroy the effect of the light coming through the window, but where it is just not quite bright enough, I might just lift it up a little bit as well.
>
> Jeremy Humphries, Director of Photography

This is called white balancing.[3] But filming under mixed lighting presents a problem: if your room is lit by tungsten – in which the colour orange dominates – and you 'while balance' for this light, then the side of the face lit by daylight – in which blue dominates – will appear bluer than the shadow side. Conversely, if you white balance for the daylight, the shadow side of the face will appear orangey. Fluorescent lights, in which green light dominates, present a similar problem. One solution is simply to ignore this difference: audiences are used to it. But there are also several fixes to this dilemma: you can use a camera that offers a compromise white balance setting that is halfway between tungsten and daylight. Alternatively, you can white balance the camera – making sure your white card is angled in such a way that it picks up both kinds of light. Or you can light your subject with what are known as 'bi-colour' LED lighting panels whose colour temperature can be adjusted between tungsten and daylight.

Interior filming – using artificial light. There are filming situations where lighting is unavoidable. It might be pouring with rain outside, or the window in a room might be too high up to throw sufficient light on an interviewee. Or you might want to film an interview using the view through a window as a backdrop, where the large contrast in lighting levels between the room and the daylight outside will make it impossible to obtain an acceptable exposure: opening the aperture on the camera to expose for the face bleaches out the background. Closing it, to expose for the window, turns your interviewee into a silhouette. In these situations you'll need a basic lighting kit.

Here's a simple way of getting a decent result if you're self-shooting, by taking two Bi-Colour 1x1 LED panel lights with you. Place one light facing your interviewee, on the same side as the camera and positioned a little to one side of her. (Figure 4.32 shows the rear of this light. Figure 4.33, the front). This will light the left side of the subject's face, leaving the other side more in shadow. Place the second light diagonally opposite the first, behind and a little to one side of the interviewee (as in Figure 4.32). This will help throw some light the other side of her face and also separate

What we're trying to do with anybody we're interviewing is just give form and modeling. The face is an oval shape, and reacts very well to modeling. So we need one light coming in from behind the person over the shoulder. The light will catch the person's shoulder and the side of the face. And one light diagonally opposite from the front, just off to one side. If you're clever with that key light, it can be so angled that it will also catch on the other side of the face as well so that it actually covers both eyes: you want to be able to see a bit of light in both eyes. And that's the skill you can pick up very easily.

Jeremy Humphries,
Director of Photography

the subject from the background. You can adjust the position and the brightness of the two LED panels until you get the result you want. You can also change the colour tone of the Bi-Colour LEDs to match the lighting in the room or to match daylight coming in through a window. Figure 4.34 shows the interviewee lit with these two lights. Notice the highlight on her hair provided by the second LED light positioned on her right side. Figure 4.35 shows what she looked like lit only with the tungsten lights in the room. The distinction between the lit and unlit versions of these images is lost in black and white – but colour versions of Figures 4.34 and 4.35 are available both on the website that accompanies this book and in the ebook version of the *Insiders' Guide*.

Figure 4.32 Interview set, using two LED light panels

Figure 4.33 One light behind camera to lift light level on front of interviewee's face

Figure 4.34 The subject lit with the two LED lights

Figure 4.35 The subject lit only by the tungsten lights in the room

Designing the Frame

One other visual issue that a filmmaker has to take on board to help keep an audience's attention focused on what's being said is the design of the frame in which your interviewee appears. This can be looked at in both a negative and a positive way.

Visual distractions. If you don't think carefully about where you place your interviewee, you can end up with an eccentric composition that drags a viewer's attention away from the content of the interview. A TV left on in the background, or a lamp stand placed behind an interviewee's back so that it appears to grow out of her head, can have a distracting effect on a viewer.

Visual enhancements. Designing a harmonious and attractive backdrop for an interview is part of the process of keeping an audience engaged. So think about the balance of visual elements around your interviewee. Does that empty cup of coffee really enhance your setting? Would it be better to move your interview away from that pure white wall to a more subdued and interesting background? Even the most pressured of current affairs schedules permit simple 'set design'. But if you have more time – and particularly if you're working with a skilled lighting camera operator – then create a distinctive style for your interviews. Doing so is as significant a part of engaging an audience as is the content and structure of your film.

What you don't want is something going on in the background that's going to distract. Now ways round that are just focusing on your character and putting the background out of focus, or just framing it out altogether. At the same time, background activity can be important because, if it's a farmer working out in his fields, then obviously linking the interview to the job they are doing is rather important. But not if the background is too intrusive, if the farmer's employee is coming up behind with a plough, tuning round and going off again completely drowning out the crucial point! So you've got to learn how to mitigate it when it's excessive. It's just striking that balance where it is not distracting. This is crucial.

Jeremy Humphries, Director of Photography

Lens enhancements. I've already discussed (on pages 45–46 in Chapter 3) the visual impact of using different lens focal lengths. They can, of course, also be used to adjust (and occasionally spoil) the look of an interviewee setting. Look at the interview images in Figures 4.36 to 4.39, all filmed from the same camera position. The camera zoom is set at its widest angle in Figure 4.36, offering a very sharply focused, wide view of the interviewee and their background.

THE IMPACT OF DIFFERENT FOCAL LENGTHS ON YOUR INTERVIEWEE

Figure 4.36 Lens set at widest angle

Figure 4.37 Standard focal length

Figure 4.38 Telephoto lens

Figure 4.39 Distortion caused by using very wide angle lens too close to the subject

Figure 4.37 is the same setting filmed using a 'standard' focal length setting (similar to the view offered by your eye). And a telephoto lens was used in Figure 4.38. The narrow depth of field of this setting has blurred the background, focusing attention squarely on the interviewee. One word of warning: wide angle lenses exaggerate the distance between the foreground and background in the image they shoot – so placing the camera too close to an interviewee when using a wide angle lens results in a distorted facial image, as in Figure 4.39

The Sound of your Interview

Capturing good quality sound is a critically important part of the filmmaking process. That fact is, unfortunately, sometimes overlooked by self-shooting assistant producers or producer/directors. There are moments in factual programmes when capturing decent sound is much more important than the image recorded by your camera. Take a look at what happened to the

BBC reporter John Simpson when he and his crew were caught up in a 'friendly fire' incident during the Allied invasion Iraq in 2003. You'll find a version of this here: www.youtube.com/watch?v=ulHpAjUPco0.

There are moments in this documentary account of the incident (5'05 to 5'17" and 6'01" to 6'31") when the image is static, showing nothing but a mound of earth or grass and shrubs, but the actuality sound recorded by a camera that was kept switched on is compelling.

Recording good quality sound in more controlled situations, particularly during an interview, is also not something you can leave to chance. Whatever camera you are using, you have to have an external microphone to be certain of hearing every word that your interviewee says with clarity. The quality of the sound recorded by a microphone that's attached to a camera can pick up the sound of the motor, the zoom lens or the camera operator shifting position. If you're filming hand-held any movement of the camera away from the interviewee, will move the microphone away from your subject and produce a sudden dip in the sound. And on a tripod, what proves to be a good camera position for the image of your interviewee will more than likely give the sound a very 'wide' feel, with ambient noise from the surroundings leaking annoyingly onto the track. The solution, of course, is to separate the microphone from the camera and place it in a fixed position close to your interviewee.

> If you haven't got pictures you can always cut to something else. But if the dialogue isn't there you can't cut to other dialogue if it's essential to the narrative. So the story continues if the dialogue is there. That's my priority as a sound guy: I know that it's carrying the narrative and without it, you're going to lose a chunk of your film, aren't you?
>
> Mike Williams, Sound Recordist

What kind of microphone you need is driven by the conditions in which you are filming your interview. There are three main options.

Hand-Held 'Shotgun' Microphones

You'll see these being used by reporters in noisy situations – conducting an interview by a busy road or at a demonstration, for example. Shotgun mics are highly directional: they capture good audio in a narrow arc to the left and right of the front end of the microphone. Sounds outside this angle are not picked up as well as those inside the axis. So when the microphone is pointed directly at your interviewee, it relays clear audio of the interview while also minimizing background noise. There are three types of shotgun mic: cardioid, super cardioid and hyper cardioid: the first of these has the widest 'on mic' sound arc, the last the narrowest. You might use a cardioid or super cardioid microphone in a meeting because when you are pointing the mic at one person and a second starts speaking, it will still pick up their 'off-mic' voice while you swing the microphone in their direction, so that you don't lose their first words. A hyper cardioid microphone might be used by a reporter speaking in a very noisy location – in a storm perhaps or standing beside a busy road – because so long as it is pointed directly at the reporter's mouth, it will minimize irritating off-mic sounds. The super cardioid mic – with a narrower sound arc than a cardioid but not as narrow as a hyper cardioid – is considered a good 'all round' shotgun microphone by some sound recordists.

When you see a shotgun mic in use they look rather like a small furry animal being held near the speaker's face. Here's why: the microphone has three different shields to guard against operator and wind noise. The first is a shockproof mount to minimize handling noise from leaking onto the sound track (as shown in Figure 4.40); the entire assembly is then covered by a rigid wind guard (Figure 4.41) and finally by a second layer of protection against air currents, a furry windsock (Figure 4.42).

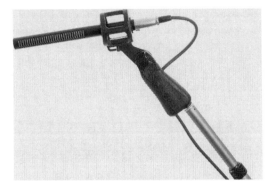

Figure 4.40 Shotgun microphone held in shock proof mount

Figure 4.41 Shotgun microphone in shock proof mount and covered in rigid wind guard

Figure 4.42 Shotgun microphone in shock proof mount then covered with both wind guard and a windsock

The directional shotgun microphone is often attached to a long pole to capture the sound of groups of speakers – in a public meeting for example – allowing it to be quickly moved across the heads of the group to capture good quality audio from different speakers while also minimizing off-camera sounds. Self-shooters obviously cannot film and record the sound of a big meeting on their own. And although operating a boom mic, as it's called, is technically a sound recordist's job, with a little practice in keeping the microphone out of shot, it's quite possible for those of you working on low budgets to persuade a colleague to handle the boom pole.

Wired Lapel Microphones

This is the microphone of choice for one or two person documentary and current affairs interviews. It is also called a lavalier or clip mic. It is very small, picks up sound in all directions, but by being placed very close to the speaker, clipped onto clothing a few centimetres under-neath the chin, it achieves clear and consistent audio of your interviewee. Some precautions are required to avoid extraneous noise from spoiling your sound track (see Figure 4.43): only the clip and not the microphone should touch the item of clothing to which it is attached or your inter-view will be accompanied by irritating rustling (this would happen if attached as in Figure 4.44); use the clip to leave some slack on the wire connecting the microphone to the camera, to protect the microphone from being accidentally yanked out of place; and cover the microphone with a small wind shield. If you hear an irritating sibilance ('ssss') sound or a popping sound (sometimes caused by air coming out of the speaker's nose and hitting the microphone head-on), you can minimize this by placing the microphone upside-down as shown in Figure 4.43.

Figure 4.43 Correct way of attaching a lapel mic to clothing. Only the clip touches the clothing. Here it is attached upside down to minimize sibilance and popping sounds

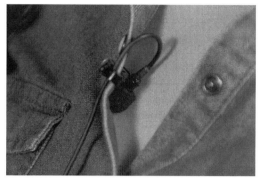

Figure 4.44 The incorrect way. This microphone will pick up rustling from touching the skin and clothing

Wireless Lapel Microphones

A lapel mic attached by wire to the camera is fine for a static interview – but walking and talking simultaneously requires a radio transmitter/receiver pair to send the audio wirelessly back to the camera. The microphone plugs into a transmitter, which you clip onto your interviewee's belt, running the connecting wire underneath their clothing. Your reporter's mic can be attached to a second transmitter. The radio receivers plug directly into the audio inputs on the camera. Be aware of the following: the transmitter/receiver pair runs on batteries, which can fail, and there can be dead spots where radio mics won't work. So you or your camera operator must be monitoring the output on headphones as you record. And a legal wireless frequency for a radio mic in one country – can be illegal in another.[4] If you're caught transmitting on a restricted fre-

If you are self-shooting, make sure you have systems in place. Know your kit, test it, go through scenarios and be as prepped as possible. What happens if there's a radio mic frequency problem? Learn how to go through menus and quickly solve it because people get pretty impatient pretty quickly on location when there are problems. So be as organized as possible so that you're an efficient machine rather than tripping over when the problem happens – and things go wrong all the time. I'm a bit of a stickler for that really.

Mike Williams, Sound Recordist

quency (for example one limited to military use), you can be fined, or have the kit confiscated. Some countries are reluctant to let you in with radio mic equipment. You can of course consider hiring radio mics in the country in which you intend working, because they will comply with local laws – but the quality of such kit can vary. The other solution is to hire what are known as wideband radio mics that allow the user to discover the local prohibited frequencies and select a safe transmission range. If you are working abroad, get your local fixer to check out the local regulations governing radio mic use.

Buzz Tracks – Room Tone

Whenever you are filming an interview you have to keep a weather eye on the problems caused by extraneous sounds recorded on the sound track along with those you actually want. You might not be aware of such noises when focusing on the content of your interview, but your camera doesn't discriminate between the sounds you want and those you don't. It all gets recorded. So picture the following: back in the edit suite you are listening to your interviewee re-telling that key story about their abusive father and you find the perfect edit point on which to cut two compelling parts of the tale together. The only problem is that there happened to be a noisy truck going past the window at the edit point in the first clip. But the road was empty and silent at the start of the second clip. So although the edited content makes sense, the noise of that truck builds in the background and then, instead of tailing off naturally, is cut dead at the edit point. That will sound very odd to your audience and whatever visual overlay you use, it will prevent you from disguising your edit. To get round this problem when recording an interview in anything other than complete silence, you record what's variously called a 'buzz track', or 'room tone', to provide you with a second layer of sound that can smooth out such issues. A 'buzz track' is simply the sound of the room in which you conducted your interview and should be recorded as soon as you've completed the questions. Ask for complete silence from those in the room, switch the camera on and record one or two minutes of the sound of the room which, of course, includes the sound of the road outside with cars, buses and trucks going by. Back in the edit suite your editor can then find a matching sound moment on this 'buzz track' – another truck going past the window – and fade this in to remove the sudden ending of the truck that was cut off in its prime by your editing decision. Recording a buzz track for every interview will be really appreciated by your film editor.

Chapter Summary

Key Issues to Consider when Filming an Interview

Choosing an Interviewee

How will they perform? Meeting your characters to decide if they really can convey their message in a compelling way – and to satisfy yourself that there are no character or appearance idiosyncrasies that will distract an audience.

Getting the Best Out of Your Interview

Before Arriving on Location

Prepare question list; avoid questions that elicit yes/no answers; one thought per question; design questions to obtain full statements rather than partial answers; aim for story-telling and emotion rather than facts; leave difficult questions to later on in the interview; be prepared to be 'Devil's Advocate'.

When you Arrive at the Location

Take time to put subjects at ease before interview begins; explain question areas; keep out of interviewee's eye line if working with a reporter/presenter.

During the Interview

Maintain eye contact and use silent assent; don't slavishly follow your list of questions – listen and ask intelligent follow-ups; be prepared to interrupt to make the meaning of an acronym transparent; be patient – don't hurry onto the next question until you're sure the answer to the current one has ended; if you haven't got that key answer – ask the question again.

The Look of your Interview

Interview Styles

Decide whether you want to film static – handheld or on a tripod; walking and talking, or an 'action' interview.

Framing your Interviewee

Consider the horizontal and vertical position of your interviewee in the viewfinder.

Eye-Lines

Make sure the horizontal and vertical position of your interviewer results in an interviewee who is looking in a direction that feels 'natural' to your audience.

Shot Sizes

Decide the number and size of the shots to be filmed of both your interviewee and interviewer.

Lighting

Using daylight.

- Exterior filming: find a location that avoids extreme changes in light levels.
- Interior filming: use light coming through a window; the problems of mixing daylight and artificial light.

Interior filming – using artificial light.

- Simple interview lighting: using two Bi-Colour LED lights

Designing the Frame

Avoid visual distractions – design a harmonious visual background for an interview, and use different lenses to give sharply focused or blurred out backdrops.

The Sound of Your Interview

Different microphones for different jobs: hand-held 'shotgun' microphones in noisy locations; wired and wireless lapel microphones for quieter interview settings. Make sure you record a buzz track for each interview.

Notes

1 The vertical red line indicates the centre of the frame.

2 Answering questions straight to camera without eye contact with your questioner is unsettling for most people. Eye contact can be maintained using a one-way mirror placed at 45 degrees in front of the camera lens. The camera still sees the interviewee, but the interviewee sees the interviewer reflected in front of the lens. This technique is similar to the way newsreaders see their script as they look straight into the camera. You can see a video of this kit here: https://youtu.be/C4R4_gfWU-Q.

3 You white balance a camera by focusing the lens on a white piece of paper or card, on which the light in which you wish to film is falling, and pressing the white balance button.

4 Sennheiser has a useful page on its website detailing wireless frequencies that do and don't require licences in many countries: https://en-uk.sennheiser.com/sifa.

5 Visual Story-Telling

Constructing and Illustrating a Linear Narrative

KEY CONCEPTS

- Five key rules for constructing the narrative structure of a factual film.
- An explanation of the different visual elements in a documentary.
- An examination of the structure of a film to demonstrate the concept of a linear narrative.

Story telling in a factual film is very different to story telling in the world of writing. A narrative unfolds on paper in two dimensions: content delivered by text with images or graphics as illustrations. The illustrations on a page draw a reader's attention to the story with images or key facts displayed in an eye catching way. But how engaged the reader is from moment to moment is entirely down to the writing skills of the author who conveys the content. Engaging an audience with a film narrative is a multi-dimensional task. It is the way you balance all the sound and visual ingredients one against the other to convey a narrative that can give a film the power to capture an audience's attention. This is what I will be explaining in this chapter – along with some suggestions for the kind of visual mix of ingredients needed to make any kind of film plus an explanation of what's called the linear narrative, kind of story telling that works in factual films.

Constructing a Factual Film: Five Rules

Film Narratives are Direct and Linear

The narrative is the argument that you wish to make, the editorial content that engages your audience and pulls them through the story you're telling. It's the heart of your project. If you are preparing a feature for publication in a newspaper, magazine or online you have considerable room to expand on issues that might not be directly linked to your main theme, but nevertheless add context and deepen understanding of the subject. It might be a chronology of events or some biographical information on a character or a reminder of a previous incident, etc. You can hive-off such information, if you wish, and place it inside a box away from the main content of your story, or hide it in an online story on a clickable link. If it's a book you're writing, you can add footnotes containing information that you consider significant but which isn't directly linked to your narrative. You don't have any of these luxuries in a film.[1] Any information you wish to convey has to be woven into the main theme that you are developing in your story.

So our first construction rule is this: film stories are *direct and linear.* You are on a storytelling highway: you can't meander to your destination in a factual film, stopping off to look at interesting side issues along the way and then returning to the main thrust of your argument. You are motoring to your destination in an unremittingly straight line, without deviating from the path set by the overall objective of the story. No detours allowed. Step A of your argument leads directly to step B; B leads to C and so on. It's very logical, very straightforward. No jumping around from one thought to something completely different. Each building block of the content of your film takes you seamlessly into the next. Film is very unforgiving of producers who don't appreciate that it is more limited than the written medium in the way it conveys factual content – precisely because one of the key tasks a film structure has to do is keep a viewer's attention rooted to the screen. You don't have to consider this in quite the same way when writing a newspaper article. Of course you want to write in a compelling and stylish manner because that will make your reader more likely to continue to the end. But becoming distracted isn't such a great problem in newspapers: the reader can simply go back a paragraph and re-read the section they've missed. In a film, if you lose your viewer's attention, you've lost the battle because there's no re-viewing while the film is playing – it moves on in time and your viewer simply misses that bit and possibly loses interest altogether.

That's what will happen if you fail to follow a linear train of thought, if you lead your viewer down a side alley, raising an issue that is not intimately

> At any point in a film, you have to understand where the film is going. If you are a viewer and suddenly something slightly random and unrelated pops up and doesn't really go anywhere, you just feel the film is drifting and you don't want to watch it any more. You stop concentrating and you start thinking: 'I wonder what's for supper' or 'I wonder what's on the other side'. There may be a reason for the change of direction but you've got to help the viewer understand the journey a bit. And so each little sequence has to have a suspense and a tension of its own, and has to be gripping in its own right. But they also have to link together very coherently in a way that makes you feel this film has a sense of direction.
>
> Diana Martin, Executive Producer, BBC TV, *Panorama*

> Words can be augmented and have their power multiplied by the images that are around them. Absolutely. The fusion of both where needed, is one of the most powerful things known to mankind. Hence the incredible popularity and durability of television. One of my slight frustrations in recent years has been a slight tendency towards: 'oh well, it's just television, you know, someone straight out of newspapers can just as easily do this'. I do think you have to have learnt a certain amount of the craft to understand the difference between a visual medium and a written medium and there is a powerful difference.
>
> Tom Giles, Controller of Current Affairs, ITV

tied into the major narrative you are telling. By the time you've finished, the audience will have forgotten the main thrust of the story and you won't know how to guide them back again. You might wish to argue that this doesn't matter because viewers now have the luxury of recording films or watching the bit they missed on a catch-up service. But the same principles apply the second time around: why should anyone persevere with your film if the way in which you have structured it proves to be un-engaging and you can't keep their attention focused on the screen? So you must appreciate the importance of the linear narrative in making a film. Filmmaking might be more limited in its ability to convey information than other media, but that limitation is also the source of film's great power to engage an audience.

> I think the art of filmmaking takes years and years to learn well. The relationship between script and commentary and pictures and actuality – it's a very, very delicate art and I don't think anyone understands it when they first start out. Even people who go on to become the greatest filmmakers are learning all their lives to do it better. So it's completely different from writing a text article. And the mistake many people make is to think just writing the script first without having given enough thought to the pictures, is alright. And it clearly isn't.
> Diana Martin, Executive Producer, BBC TV, *Panorama*

The filmmaker's task, then, is to find a way of conveying the information of a story in a way that keeps a viewer engaged from moment to moment. And the way to do that is, essentially, to hold the viewer's hand, guiding them from one thought to the next – so that you don't lose their attention.

The Mix of Ingredients that Illustrate Your Narrative Must be in Harmony

> My late wife was once asked what the difference was between a really good PBS documentary and the sort of Discovery, A&E docs they were doing at the time which were basically illustrated lectures. And she used an analogy which I thought was really rather nice. She said: 'imagine you are on a tour bus and you're driving through beautiful countryside in Spain or Italy, and you're looking out the window at these beautiful villages. You're passing through these beautiful mountains, and at the front of the tour bus is your guide saying: "To your left, you'll see such and such, and to your right . . .". OK. You experience a little bit of it. You get a sense of the country. You get a sense of the scenery. [In] the good documentary you have been invited into a world. You have not just been told about a world: the bus stops. The steps are put down. You get out. You sit down at a local café and talk to the locals. You smell the air. You listen to the noise on the streets. And for me the difference between a great documentary and just the cheap stuff is: the good ones, they open a door and allow the audience to walk through, to experience whatever that world is. I'm not just standing back, looking at things on a screen'.
> Leo Eaton, Documentary Filmmaker

Capturing an audience's attention relies on a delicate balance between the visual and audio ingredients that you use to illustrate and explain your argument. The filmmaker's skill is finding the right mix to create dramatic tension and an engaging film. If one or other of the ingredients over-dominates, the film is likely to become difficult to watch. Use too many interviews at too great a length, for example, and you risk a monotonous approach that might bore your viewer. Music is useful to convey emotion and tension – but use too much or the wrong score at the wrong time, and that can also turn viewers off. Silence is golden sometimes! Hurrying from one sequence to the next can confuse a viewer who needs to be given time to digest the thoughts from the first section before moving to the second.

The way commentary is used can also enhance or detract from your audience's attention – as can the televisual qualities of a reporter or presenter, should you be using one, and how you use them on-screen to tell parts of the story. One mix of the available sound and picture ingredients can capture an audience's attention – another can quickly lose their interest. And that fact is independent of the strength of the story you are telling. You can't expect an audience to watch your film simply because you think it is important. You have to entice a viewer into the subject.

Mixing the ingredients together in a film is a bit like baking a cake. You need eggs, flour, sugar, water, flavouring and butter to bake a sponge. So what makes the difference between a mouth-wateringly delicious cake – and a dry, tasteless version? The quality of the chef, of course: a talented cook knows how much of each ingredient to mix together to make the perfect product.

So let's apply this to factual filmmaking. You have the following kinds of 'ingredients' available to make your film:

- Specially shot images.
- Interviews.
- Dramatic reconstructions.
- Archive footage.
- Still images.
- Graphics.
- Actuality sound recorded on location.
- Music.
- Commentary.
- Sound effects.

Not every film has all of these ingredients, of course, but those that you do have must be balanced against one another to engage your audience. At the risk of repeating myself, I'm going to under-score this point because it is sometimes lost on new filmmakers: with the right mix you can create a stylish, compelling programme that powerfully draws together the emotion and the content of your idea into a coherent whole. But if you allow any one of these ingredients to become too dominant, then you risk losing your audience.

Newcomers to filmmaking that uses narration will have a tendency to let the commentaries over-dominate and drive the film. But you won't achieve a powerful programme by writing a script and then setting out to illustrate it with pictures – because films work on an emotional level as well as an intellectual one. A major part of a film editor's job is to cut together the sequences and interviews you've filmed to maximize their dramatic impact. She will do this by the way she paces the picture sequences, by using music and by the way she intercuts interviews with images. Forcing an editor to add pictures to illustrate a pre-written script effectively ties her creative hands. She can no longer construct the film in a way that will engage an

> The people that are writing a film first and then just visualizing it, basically are ending up with a fancy PowerPoint presentation. The pictures that you shoot are going to just be the pictures you need to fill in the script that you wrote ahead of time. It's painting-by-numbers and you end up with a very one-dimensional film, a very flat film. It's very hard to give a nuance to a film like that because you're kind of locked in. For me, the best films are when the pictures are shot first, so the scenes are shot, and then, you figure out what your story is and you tell your story as much as you possibly can with visuals and with the actualities. Then you sort of drive it home with narration if needed and as needed.
>
> Barbara Ballow, Film Editor

audience with the emotion of the subject. She's restricted to adding images to your pre-written words. The result of such an approach is an intellectual construction that will almost certainly bore an audience and lose their attention.

In short: the words you write are determined by and are devoted to your film structure – not the other way round. This is a key issue that you should take on board from the start – and it leads to rule three of visual story-telling.

Your Script is a Slave – It Serves Your Film Structure

> Often, the films that cause difficulties in the edit for me are where producers or reporters write far too much and try and get too many facts out when they haven't really got the characters, the actuality and the pictures to illustrate it and bring it to life, and make it feel like a good watch. But just as many films, I would say, suffer from people who think they don't have to write a script at all. They hope the story will somehow tell itself and they don't really link different sequences in a way that's coherent.
>
> Diana Martin, Executive Producer, BBC TV, *Panorama*

This is a key issue for films that use a written narration: the commentary you write is really the 'glue' that links each section in the film together. In other words: the flow of thought in your narrative is created by the logic of your picture sequences – and by what your interviewees say. So you don't go out filming to illustrate a script. You go out filming to get the sequences and interviews that you can craft into a story in the edit suite. Only then, when you're happy with the edit, do you finalize your commentaries.

So you have to abandon a text-based way of thinking – and embrace a different approach to story-telling. This can be quite a difficult transition as most of us grow up with the primacy of words firmly fixed in our minds. But it's a vital one. The words you write in a factual film are no longer 'top dog'. They have a subservient status, devoted to the film sequences you've cut together, linking them in a manner that keeps the audience engaged. This is why some films can dispense with written narration entirely: allowing actuality sequences and interviews to convey the story instead.

The Content of Each Commentary is Determined by its Place in the Film

Because a film script is written to 'glue' your film sequences together, the content of any particular commentary is rigidly determined by what's gone before and what comes next. If you try and make a commentary do something different, you confuse the viewer. A successful script guides an audience carefully from sequence to sequence, and it can't do that if a commentary ignores its position in the film, and heads off at a tangent to convey information that is extraneous to the particular sequence in which it is placed. The function of any specific commentary is to pick up on the preceding thought in your narrative and ensure that it takes the viewer to the next actuality sequence or interview in the structure, while paying attention to the images that are being used in that section of the film. That's called writing to picture.

Don't Overwrite the Commentaries – Make Each One Fit the Pictures That Have Been Cut

What I've said above also explains why film as a medium is limited in how much content it can convey successfully. Films have to engage viewers emotionally, conveying dramatic tension to help keep an audience watching. But the more information you try to impart, the less you can create a film with atmosphere that keeps the viewers' attention. Adding too much factual content can wipe out atmosphere by overwhelming your viewer with information that is not easy to follow. Then you've failed in that key filmmaker's task: you've lost their attention. So you have to determine what information is absolutely essential to comprehend any particular section of the film – and dispense with everything else. When your editor has left room for a 15 second commentary – and you come back with two minutes worth of words, you'll know you're heading off in the wrong direction. There is some wriggle-room over commentary lengths, but not much. So listen to what your editor says. Brevity in a script is always best.

From the above I hope you'll see that you should only go filming after you're really clear about the following.

> When people come to me wanting to work on *Panorama*, I really do expect them to have watched a lot of *Panorama* and I will check whether they have or not. Not just because I've got a big ego and I want people to tell me how good our programmes are, but because it shows interest in the journalism. Also because you can only really learn the art of filmmaking by watching other people's films. You really need to watch as much as possible. You need to watch current affairs films, but you need to watch other genres too. You need to see what ITV and Channel 4 are doing, you need to watch big, 90-minute docs, you need to see what Netflix is doing. You really need to be watching as widely and as broadly as possible to understand what other people are doing, how they are advancing creativity in their area, and what we can all learn from it.
>
> Diana Martin, Executive Producer, BBC TV, *Panorama*

The Building Blocks of Your Argument

The step-by-step approach you will take to unfold the story for your viewers. One step naturally leads to the next and you must be clear what each section is going to cover. In an observational film the steps of your narrative will be the key events you've decided to cover in the time that you've allocated to your film schedule.

Who is Going to Contribute to Each Step in the Narrative and What You'd Like Them to Say

You must have a good notion of which interviewees are going to be heard in each part of your film – so that, once you know the content of each step of the narrative, you will also be able to devise relevant questions to ask your contributors to ensure you get the right answers for each section. In an observational film you have to choose the key characters around which you will focus the narrative of your film and understand in which actuality sequences each will be filmed and the likely questions that you'll want to ask them – either during the sequence itself or later on in a reflective interview.

In short – you must have a film structure in mind. This is different to a script. It's a plan of action, if you like, a detailed breakdown of each section of the narrative – whether this is an analytical or observational film – an outline of what you want to say in each chapter of the film, and what each interviewee needs to contribute to these different chapters. If you don't have this clearly thought out, you will find yourself filming images and asking questions with no real idea of how they might contribute to your story – and end up back in the edit suite with far too much visual material and little idea of how to use it. The result is unlikely to please anyone. If you have thought all this through carefully, with the help of a good film editor, you'll be able to cut your rushes into a strong film – and, if you are using narration, at the end of that creative process write a commentary to fit that structure.

Using Images in a Factual Film

You also need to be clear about the kind of visuals you plan to use to tell each part of the story. You might, of course, need stills, archive footage, graphics, documents, newspaper clippings for example. These vary from film to film and their use will be obvious depending on the context and story you are following. But most films need specially shot images and you should appreciate some key principles when taking your decisions about what to shoot. Specially shot images fulfill various functions in a documentary.

Actuality Images

These are 'show not tell' images. Not every factual film contains actuality. In some stories there just isn't anything like this to shoot. But where there is actuality to be filmed, it's likely to form the heart of your film and will breathe life into your story. Actuality images convey an event unfolding in the present. It could be a political demonstration, the fighting in Syria, 'action' sequences that you obtain permission to film, like a police drug raid or ones that you film under-cover, without permission, in some investigative films.

Images that Convey a Sense of Place

You need to give your viewers a strong sense of the geographical locations relevant to the films you are making. A story filmed in London, for example, must convey a visual impression of the city, and you do that by finding a good vantage point from which you can see the city skyline spread out before you. That might mean travelling outside the city to a nearby hill with a view of the cityscape – or finding a tall building in the city itself and getting permission to film from the top. Images that convey a sense of place will be wide panoramic views of a location.

Images that Convey a Sense of Community

By itself cityscape imagery is not enough to give a visual impression of a location. You also need a sense of the community that's relevant to your story. This means finding a second, narrower vantage point overlooking the particular community that interests you, and filming within the location to show people, houses, shops etc.

Images that Establish the Precise Location of an Interviewee or Sequence

A third kind of location images are those that give viewers a sense of where specific individuals who appear in the film live, work or play. These can be buildings in which you interview people or that have a relevance to your subject. Or exterior locations like parks, boats, etc – locations that might add emotional tone when introducing a character. Sometimes these images are used not to convey specific information at all, but are used instead as a pausing device between two sections of commentary.

Reporter or Presenter Images

If you work with an on-camera reporter or presenter, they become a character in the film. How much screen time you give them is driven, in part, by the presenter/reporter you pick: you'll want to make the most of a 'big name' or a strong televisual presenter. But it is also driven by the story you're telling and how visual it is. The more you can rely on your film sequences, the more strategic you can be in the placing of your presenter/reporter's image in the story. Conversely, some stories are best told as a 'voyage of discovery' in which a presenter or reporter moves from place to place. The narrative unfolds for viewers as he/she travels around meeting and talking to key characters. You still need to film images that convey a sense of place, community and location but visualizing a strong sense of the physical journey on which the reporter/presenter has embarked is a vital ingredient in this approach to a documentary. You can achieve this by:

- *Filming tracking shots:* images that have been filmed, for example, in and from a moving car showing your presenter/reporter or a key character, plus the environment through which they are travelling.
- *Filming your host on the move:* walking through a location or into a relevant building, using static or mobile camera positions, depending on the emotional tone you wish to convey (see pages 51–55 in Chapter 3). Combined with relevant commentary or interview, these images also give viewers a sense that the programme is not confined to one location.

Reporter Stand-Ups or Camera Pieces

If you decide to film your reporter/presenter on location, conveying a part of your narrative directly to camera, you have to be aware of the different functions that camera pieces provide in a film, decide which parts of your narrative are best conveyed in this way and then write the words for these stand ups well in advance of having a film structure in which they will sit. I discuss these issues in more detail on pages 66–67 in Chapter 3.

Images that Establish Your Characters

The key characters in your programme also need to be visualized for your audience. How much footage you need to cover any particular character will be driven by how much screen time you plan them to give them. A very significant character whose interview clips are going to be used several times in different parts of the film, and about whom you have a number of things to say, might need to be filmed in several locations. This will give you sufficient image sequences to cover your commentary and for use as 'overlay' – in other words, images to cover edits in the interviews. It's always worth erring on the side of caution: better to have too much than too little.

Symbolic Images

Sometimes you need to find ways of representing an issue in a film that cannot easily be visualized: a past-tense story, for example, for which you have no stills or archive to cover a written commentary or to complement an interviewee's re-telling of a dramatic event. You might then reach for graphic devices, dramatic reconstructions or specially shot images that allude to the subject being discusssed. Your approach will be driven by the context of the story and the sensitivity of the subject. You might consider reconstructing the chase and arrest of a drug smuggler, for example, but you might not do the same for a sexual assault on a child, because this would be too insensitive a way of conveying this kind of incident, given the very raw emotions such incidents provoke. There's more information on using images in a symbolic way on pages 53–55 in Chapter 3.

Interview Images

In Chapter 4 I looked at the many decisions that a director has to take in deciding how to film their interviewees — decisions about the location, the lighting, the use of the camera and the design of the interview set, all of which can add to (or detract from) the overall tone and style of a film.

If you want to capture a TV audience's attention with your work you have to start thinking visually. And that means realizing that the ingredients you use to construct your film, and the way you combine them all together, is a critical part of the success or failure of your project. You also have to remember the key importance of the narrative structure: strong narratives are very forgiving of weak directors. But however strong you are at directing, a weak narrative will consign your film to obscurity.

Chapter Summary

Five Rules for Constructing a Factual Film

1   Film narratives are direct and linear.
2   The mix of ingredients that illustrate your narrative must be in harmony.
3   Your script is a slave — determined by your film structure.
4   The content of each commentary is fixed by its place in the film.
5   Don't over-write the commentaries. They must be written to fit the pictures that have been cut, not the other way round.

The Different Kinds of Specially Shot Images in a Factual Film

1   Actuality images.
2   Images that convey a sense of place.
3   Images that convey a sense of community.
4   Images that establish the precise location of an interviewee or sequence.
5   Reporter or presenter images.
6   Reporter stand-ups or camera pieces.
7   Images that establish your characters.
8   Symbolic images.
9   Interview images.

Note

1   There are now some experimental interactive online films that do allow viewers to pause the film and click to discover contextual information that is not directly relevant to the main thrust of the story. But my comments about linear narratives are aimed at the majority of factual films being made today.

6   From Paper Cut to Fine Cut

Editing a Factual Film

KEY CONCEPTS

- The key issues to consider before embarking on an edit.
- Vital pre-edit prep to ensure an edit runs smoothly.
- Deciding whether to work with a film editor – or to do it yourself.
- The stages of an edit and the tasks attached to each one.
- The importance of having a 'fresh eye' looking over your film.
- How to survive a rough cut viewing.

Discovering a film narrative hidden in an unruly mass of specially shot images, interviews, actuality sequences, stills and archive is a *slow* process of discovery. Unlike a jigsaw puzzle where a hundred or a thousand pieces are painstakingly assembled to form a pre-conceived picture, the raw ingredients of a film contain almost as many different cuts as there are filmmakers to conceive them and editors to craft the visuals together. There's no one correct finished version, no one right way to transform your rushes into a finished film. There are better ways to do this – ways that prove to be more engaging for an audience. And there are worse ways that will leave your viewers at best yawning, at worst struggling for comprehension. So I can't tell you how to edit your film. What I can do in this chapter is suggest a method, a way of approaching the edit that, I hope, will help you assemble the spine of your story, then craft it into an engaging narrative and finally polish your cut into a strong, watchable film.

Editing a Factual Film: An Introduction

There are certain basic principles to appreciate about the edit of a longer documentary or current affairs film:

- *Your paper version of the film is never the final version, and the first cut that you watch is never the last.* Editing is an iterative process and a film will always go through many revisions during an edit. You can't go into an edit with a rigid idea about the way the interviews and sequences will work in the film. You go in with an offering, a starting point from which the edit progresses. Flexibility is key – as is an ability to judge the unfolding story from the standpoint of the material you've filmed rather than trying to force your sound and pictures into a shape that was pre-conceived before you'd actually watched anything. That's what I mean by 'discovering' the story hidden in your rushes.

- *Your first cut is always over-length.* It is sometimes double the length you eventually need. It has to be cut long to allow you to judge the strength of the material you've shot. As the edit proceeds, successive viewings allow you to sift out the unnecessary, the boring and the fascinating but not strictly relevant. This sifting process is methodical. It has stages, and your attention has to be in the right place at the right time, as I'll be explaining.

- *The order of your sequences is never fixed in stone until the edit ends.* Until then, you can always move things around if you feel that, by doing so, you'll end up with a better film. Don't be frightened to be drastic! It's always worth experimenting.

- *Your core narrative is constructed from the interviews and actuality sequences you've filmed.* The drive and direction of the story you're telling is not constructed from a pre-conceived and pre-written script. It's built from the specially shot picture and actuality sequences, the interviews, and if you're using it, archive footage. The narrative of your story unfolds through these ingredients.

- *Your commentaries (assuming your film contains narration) are written at the very end of the edit.* Only when your pictures and interviews have been cut together and your film structure is agreed, can you write the precise words that pull the sequences together. You may well have drafted out a rough, guide script before then to make it easier to view the developing film, but the final commentary needs a final structure before it can be written. See pages 100–102 in Chapter 5 for more on the function of narration in documentaries.

- *The decision-making process during an edit has to be approached in stages.* The process of cutting a film together is multi-layered, so refining and improving your film involves much more than simply judging the narrative content of the story. Many of the decisions you take are not based on intellect – they are driven by your 'gut' feelings as you watch a film. And because there are many such issues to address, a developing film has to be watched many times during its evolution so that, one by one, the problems can be resolved. They can't all be taken in at once.

So that's why an edit proceeds slowly and in stages. But as time passes, the film you conceived all those months ago, gradually comes into sharper and sharper focus. All the decisions you've taken over weeks or perhaps months, all that stress and worry, the highs and lows of your shoot, the sifting, editing and re-editing, give birth to what I can only describe as a living and breathing organism: a unique, emotional/intellectual take on a subject. And if you've done your job well, when you press play, the attention of your audience will be focused on your story – and on nothing else – until the credits roll.

Working with a Film Editor or Do-It-Yourself?

Many producer/directors edit their own films these days. Declining budgets and easy-to-use software have forced this change. So if you can 'do-it-yourself' why bother to pay for a film editor? The reason is that a creative collaboration between a filmmaker and a talented editor, will almost always result in a better film than she can produce on her own. A director knows the cost – both financial and the sweat, tears and time it's taken to get all the sequences in the can. An editor comes into the creative process knowing nothing but the value of any sequence to the overall narrative. That outsider's view is invaluable in cutting through to the core of a film. It's much easier for an editor to abandon that hard-fought for sequence that took two weeks to negotiate and an all-night shoot to gain, but doesn't add much to the story, than it is for the director who shot it. Good editors also have creative ideas to throw into the mix that will improve a film. They'll see links between images and interviews that you might have missed; suggest structural changes that will improve the unfolding of narrative; and be able to pace the story in ways you might not have considered. Working alone might make financial sense during the edit – but it doesn't always make creative sense.

> When you go out and shoot and you come back and go: 'God! That was a fabulous scene! That's going to be so powerful in my film', the editor looks at it with a fresh eye. Their response might be: 'well maybe it is and maybe it's really not'. So if you're doing everything yourself, either everything ends up looking the same, every single thing you do has the same style to it, or you're missing opportunities to expand what you've got, to bring another dimension to it that you hadn't thought of. So yeah, if you have the luxury of being able to bring in an outside person, it's definitely better than doing everything yourself.
>
> Barbara Ballow, Film Editor

That said, there are many low budget broadcast and online films where working alone in the edit is the only viable option. The key to success then is to arrange frequent viewings with outsiders whose instant feedback is invaluable to a filmmaker whose aim is to ensure their story really does engage an audience. The benefits of having a 'fresh-eye' looking over your film cannot be over-estimated – and I return to this issue later on in this chapter.

The Stages of an Edit

The stages of an edit are common to most factual films, as are the pressure points during an edit where you are racing to get a cut ready to show to an executive producer or commissioner. In very broad outline they are shown in Figure 6.1.

The precise number of viewings with executive producers and commissioners depends on the kind of film you are making, your experience level, the commissioning hierarchy and the number of co-producers. If your commissioner is the exec, for example, you might have less viewings than if you are making the film for an independent production company that itself has been commissioned by a broadcaster or online platform and has its own executive producer overseeing the project. Some investigative or undercover films might require more viewings with a commissioner and a lawyer to resolve thorny legal or ethical issues. And the rough and fine cut viewing/adapting stages of films co-produced by two or three broadcasters can become quite extenuated.

Let's now look at the key stages of an edit in more detail.

Edit Prep

There are four key editorial tasks before starting an edit.

PREPARE PAPER CUT		
	E D I T	**PREPARE SYNC ASSEMBLY**
		VIEW: PRODUCER/DIRECTOR (PD)/EDITOR
		PREPARE ROUGH CUT
		VIEW: PD/EDITOR
		REFINE ROUGH CUT
		VIEW: EXECUTIVE PRODUCER
		REFINE ROUGH CUT
		VIEW: COMMISSIONER
		PREPARE FINE CUT
		VIEW: PD/EDITOR
		REFINE FINE CUT
		VIEW: EXECUTIVE PRODUCER
		REFINE FINE CUT
		VIEW: COMMISSIONER/LAWYER IF NEEDED
		LAST CHANGES
		VIEW: COMMISSIONER
		PICTURE LOCK
		FINALISE NARRATION
		SOUND LOCK
		POST-PRODUCTION

Figure 6.1 An outline of the stages of an offline edit

Viewing Rushes

If you have the time (some deadlines prevent this) – and the money (some low budgets also prevent this) it's always worth taking a considered look at the rushes, to remind you of the images you've shot – and to make sure what you thought had worked during the shoot has in fact worked in the camera. The two don't always match up. On location, you might think that the fifth and final take of a camera piece by your reporter is the definitive version, but on review you discover that you'd missed an extraneous off-mic sound, a slight camera wobble, a change in the sunlight, or a misspoken word – and take three is in fact the one to use. Looking at the images and actuality sequences is also a good way of reminding yourself of the ingredients available to construct your story sequences. You don't need to listen to all your interviews – that's too time consuming on a long film. Instead, see the next section.

Reading and Marking up Interview Transcripts

It's very difficult to decide which clips of interview you want for your film until you can see them on paper. Interviewees often speak about the same issue more than once, and you might want to edit the first part of one answer to the last part of another. In long interviews, it's easier to make this decision when you can see the words on paper. So you (or a paid typist) transcribe each interview verbatim, with time codes indicating where each new question starts. You need to read these transcriptions, then highlight each interview clip you're thinking of including in your cut and annotate the document by giving each selected section a title. If there are several versions of an answer, or part of an answer, add numbers to the labels to distinguish between the versions.

Researching Archive, Stills and Music

It is possible that some of this research will have been done during pre-production – because, when looking for potential contributors, you often come across useful visual and audio material. But, unless you are working on an historical film that's driven by archive, you're unlikely to know precisely what still images, archive or music you'll need until you begin to cut the story together, so the majority of this research is conducted either in preparation for the edit or during the edit itself. Clearing copyrighted material for use in a film can be complicated – and I have outlined the issues you need to consider on pages 227–230 in Chapter 11.

Preparing a Paper Cut

A paper cut (or cutting order) is your initial conception of the film and it follows a specific format. Figure 6.2 is an illustration of the first couple of pages of a paper cut for a film that I made about a lawyer called Bill Pepper who'd spent many years trying to prove that the American civil rights leader, Martin Luther King, was not assassinated by a lone gunman – instead his murder was the result of a huge conspiracy involving the US government, the army and the Mafia. There is enough in these few lines of cutting order to give you an overview of the basic layout and what needs to be included. My comments below Figure 6.2 relate to the line numbers in the left hand column. You can find an interactive version of this cutting order with my explanations on the website.

	BILL PEPPER CUTTING ORDER	
1	**PICTURES**	**SOUND**
2	**SEQUENCE 1: MLK OPENING**	
3	**Impressionistic – mixing together period archive with specially shot reconstruction of a gun being fired and reconstruction of King being shot on the balcony of the motel. Music throughout.**	
4	**IMAGES** **ARCHIVE** **King 'I have a dream' speech** Ex ITN archive file 1. Speech starts at 10-14-42 **King images** Movietone file 2027A from 10-32-23 Pathe file 65/24 from 10-06-00 **Riots/White on black violence** ABC file 263 from 10-06-20 **Civil Rights March** Ex NBC file from 01-04-52	**AUDIO** **MUSIC** Try Mitch Dalton ex Guitar Gallery (MHS-35). More music suggestions to follow. **ACTUALITY SOUND EX ARCHIVE** King SPEECH – part of the section from 10-24-17 Riot fx ex archive Violence fx ex archive

Figure 6.2 Illustration of a paper cut or cutting order – for a film about the assassination of US civil rights leader Martin Luther King

	MIXED WITH SPECIALLY SHOT IMAGES **Reconstruction – shots of gunman getting ready to shoot)** MLK – 050 **Reconstruction – representation of gun firing** MLK – 044 **Reconstruction – King's hand whipped off balcony and body falling to ground** MLK – 047 **King falling to ground – POV shot and whip pan shot** MLK – 049 **MLK's tomb with flame** MLK – 009 from 09-06-50	**ACTUALITY SOUND EX LIBRARY FX** Gun fire
5	**SEQUENCE 2: BILL PEPPER INTRODUCTION**	
6	**IMAGES** **Dusk over Manhattan** MLK – 02 **New York taxis through glass** MLK – 01 **Bill Pepper past shop window** MLK – 04 **Bill walking thro revolving doors** MLK – 05 **Bill Pepper elevator and walking to office sequences** MLK 10	**AUDIO** MUSIC TBA AND COMMENTARY 1 WE INTRODUCE BILL PEPPER – A MAN WITH A MISSION TO SOLVE ONE OF THE CENTURY'S MOST OUTRAGEOUS ASSASSINATIONS. A MAN WHO HAS SPENT 20 YEARS OF HIS LIFE UNCOVERING EVIDENCE THAT HE BELIEVES SHOWS THAT AMERICA'S GREATEST CIVIL RIGHTS LEADER WAS NOT KILLED BY A LONE RACIST ASSASSIN, THAT HE WAS, INSTEAD THE VICTIM OF A CONSPIRACY THAT JOINED TOGETHER THE MAFIA, THE MILITARY AND THE GOVERNMENT IN AN UNHOLY ALLIANCE

Figure 6.2 Continued

7	ONE OF THE FOLLOWING PEPPER QUOTES – WHICHEVER SOUNDS PUNCHIEST OR POSSIBLY THE FIRST HALF OF THE PAGE 24 QUOTE FOLLOWED BY THE SECOND HALF OF THE ONE ON PAGE 16	
8	**IMAGES**	**AUDIO**
	Pepper interview MLK – 041 at 11-23-05 PAGE 16	**The death of Martin Luther king was a seminal event in my life and in the life of this Republic** and that cannot go un-addressed. That must be responded to. **The people must know what their government did and how it was done and how it has been long covered up and if they learn that lesson perhaps it will not happen, not as likely happen again.**
	Or **Bill Pepper interview** MLK – 041 at 11-27-12 PAGE 24 **POTENTIAL OVERLAY IMAGES** **Archive** Martin Luther King images ex Movietone/Pathe as above **and (IF NEEDED)** Bill walking down corridor and office – MLK 10 and 11 Bill's bag placed on table – MLK 13 Bill at desk – MLK 15	**The assassination of Martin King was a symptom of a sickness in democracy in America that prevails and permeates the whole of the society, even as we sit here. And the only hope of Americans reclaiming their liberty in my view is that they become aware of these actions of government and say at one point in time – no more.**

Figure 6.2 Continued

Line 1 Split your cutting order into two halves – the left side for the images that you wish to use and the right side for the sound. It's much easier for your film editor to comprehend what you are planning by doing this.

Line 2 Break your cutting order down into the building blocks, or sequences, that you've devised to bring the narrative to life – and give each sequence a name.

Line 3 This is an overview of the filmmaker's intention, a statement that gives your editor the essence of what you'd like to achieve. Sequences where you are, for example, simply introducing an interviewee or pulling together a picture sequence for a line of narration won't need such signposting, but as this is the opening of the film, your intention is not necessarily obvious. So best to spell it out here.

Line 4 The left hand column contains a list of the images that the filmmaker wants to use to construct this part of the film. The opening is a mixture of archive footage (Martin Luther King's famous 'I Have a Dream' speech plus other images of King, civil rights marches and white on black violence) plus a selection of specially shot images (two kinds of dramatized reconstruction: a gun being made ready to fire and an impressionistic reconstruction of the actual assassination of Martin Luther King). As you can see, each archive has a file number attached to it and a time code because the archive files were lengthy, containing a lot of other material, and the time code reference would help the editor quickly find the footage. Time code references weren't needed for most specially shot images as the files were not very long and each file only contained the images in question.

The right hand column indicates the sound that the filmmaker wants to use in this section. Tracks by a composer called Mitch Dalton are suggested for this opening. This might not be the music you actually use – as the edit progresses you and your film editor are likely to research music libraries to find further tracks that might complement the narrative and you might find something better. But this is a start.

The other sound suggested for this opening is, of course, part of King's 'I Have a Dream Speech' (indicating that the filmmaker doesn't simply want to use the pictures of the speech – but wants to hear the speech itself). Also suggested here are the sounds of a civil rights march and the violence that, at the time in America, often accompanied such marches. The location of these sounds are in the clips suggested in the left hand column. Finally in this sequence, the editor is told that the sound of a gun firing should be dubbed onto the specially shot images of a gun being fired. A fake weapon was used in this reconstruction, with the sound added later on to make it appear as if the gun had really been fired. There is no narration in this sequence. It is a dramatic opening for the film with all the sound (apart from the gun firing and the music track) stemming from archive.

Line 5 This is the title of the second sequence – where we introduce the main protagonist, lawyer Bill Pepper.

Line 6 Left hand column. Bill Pepper is introduced visually by first locating him in New York (Manhattan dusk shots and New York taxi images) then seeing Bill walking down a street and into his office.

Right hand column. The words written in the cutting order are not the script, of course, they are a note indicating the rationale of the sequence. Music is also anticipated as a means of gluing this sequence together – and the editor will find something appropriate from the selection that you and your editor find from music libraries.

Line 7 This is another clarifying note. It is sometimes not clear what clip will work best at a particular point in a film until you hear it, so this is simply a suggestion to try out the two clips – and possibly even cut parts of the two together, if that works best.

Line 8 Left hand column. These two interview clips of Bill Pepper speaking are suggested as his opening comments. Interviews require two kinds of location information: the file number and time code of course, plus the page number on which the clip appears on the transcript of the interview. Also here are suggestions for relevant 'overlay' images that can be used to cover edits in the interview. In this case the overlay suggested is archive footage of Martin Luther King and those specially shot images of Bill Pepper walking down a corridor and entering his office.

Right hand column. The text of the two suggested clips appears here – with a suggestion that two short sentences might be removed from one of them. Don't try to edit down interviews on paper. What works on screen can be very different to what *looks* as if it will work on paper: a downbeat or over-extenuated delivery, a hurried ending to a sentence, an odd glance away from camera at the wrong moment, an interviewer whose incoming question clips the last words of an otherwise great answer, all of these subtle issues can ruin what seems like a strong clip on paper. You have to watch and listen to each clip to judge whether an edit will work. Edits sometimes require a bit of grammar – a 'but' or 'and' for example – pinched from somewhere else in the interview. By giving your editor the page location in the transcript where these clips appear, he/she can search for a nearby connecting word or phrase in the hope that it will be spoken at a similar sound level and speed as the original clip.

Sync Assembly

With your paper cut, you or your film editor can now start to compile what's called a 'sync assembly'. 'Sync' is short for 'synchronized' sound – sound that's synchronized with the movements of an individual's lips: interviews and actuality sequences in which people are speaking. At this stage you don't need to think about pictures or commentary or anything else. Just pull all the interview/actuality clips in your paper cut – including alternative versions – into one continuous file separated by on-screen captions that reflect the building blocks of the film. Continuing the Martin Luther King example, we had these caption titles for the first six building blocks:

1   MLK Opening
2   Bill Pepper Introduction
3   King's First Meeting with Pepper
4   The Sanitation Strike in Memphis
5   King's Last Speech
6   The Shooting

What your sync assembly does, then, is sort your interviews and actuality into an order of thought that reflects the narrative you wish to construct. In an analytical film this will be a journalistic flow-of-thought. In an observational story, it's likely to be a chronology.

Ethical Editing

A word about the ethics of selecting interview clips: when you shorten what someone says, or splice two or three clips of an interviewee together to make it look as if a person said these separate thoughts in an uninterrupted flow, you have to apply the following principle: **The edited version of an interview must be an accurate essence of what the individual intended to say.**

It can be shorter than the original, it can be composed of a combination of thoughts from separate parts of the interview, but it has to remain true to what your character really wanted to express. The best way of deciding whether your edit complies with this principle is to look at the edited clip and ask yourself this question: 'If I played this clip to my interviewee, would he or she be content that it reflects what they really wanted to say'. If you can't honestly answer that question with a firm 'Yes', if you've any doubts, don't do the edit.

Ethical Editing: Three Views

Most of the films I do, I've been invited inside a world – whether I'm following an air-force squadron, or a coastguard. I feel my responsibility is to treat them as honestly and as openly as I possibly can and not abuse the privilege they've given me; not cut an interview, for instance, to make them look stupid. I always feel I have two audiences: I have the bigger audience which is my television, online, cinema audience, whatever it maybe. But I also have always tried to make people who have been the focus of my story, who have let me into their world, comfortable with what I've done.

Leo Eaton, Documentary Filmmaker

I was asked to have a character say a certain thing when, in the interview itself, the character said: 'I will not say this'. And the producer said: 'Well can't you just "Frankenbite" it?'

It's an American term: like Frankenstein. Can you 'Frankenbite' by literally putting syllables together to make somebody say something that they didn't really say. And I actually walked out of that job. I always work so that anytime anybody says something, nothing is taken out of context. I'm always trying to make sure that what they're saying is true to what they believe and how they want to present themselves. I just will never put something together that isn't accurate or untruthful for the sake of the story. If you can't tell your story with what people have said to you in context, correctly, then you don't have a story.

Barbara Ballow, Film Editor

If you take somebody out of context or you change around what they said or you edit them to such a degree that it doesn't represent them fairly, we believe that's journalistic malpractice. We actually review every single edit that a filmmaker makes – because we want to be sure that we think it's ethical and that it represents conversation that the person's actually had. So that's how seriously we take editing practices. With new filmmakers, we spend a lot of time talking about that in the beginning because they're not accustomed to that kind of scrutiny.

Raney Aronson-Rath, Executive Producer, PBS Frontline

Viewing a Sync Assembly

Once the interviews are in the right order, sit back and watch the assembly, with a large time code box on the screen.

- **Don't worry** if this first assembly is double the length of the film you want, it should be much longer to give you room to select out the best material.
- **Don't stop the film** – just watch with a notebook and pen and write down time codes plus a reminder phrase for issues you'd like to discuss at the end.
- **Don't write too much** or you'll miss what comes next in the assembly!
- **Don't get derailed by detail** – yes, the framing of that interview clip is too wide and might need to be pulled in during post-production; and yes, you'll need some colour correction on that rather too blue looking actuality sequence, but these issues are not relevant at this point in the construction of a film.

The only thing that counts in viewing a sync assembly is whether each assembled interview or actuality clip helps drive the narrative forwards at that point in the film.

Ask yourself: is the clip you're watching furthering your task of moving the narrative in a linear fashion (see pages 97–99 in Chapter 5) from A to B – or, is it in fact taking you to G, somewhere you do need to go, but not until later on in the film. If so, note the time code and, when you discuss the assembly, suggest moving this clip to a later sequence. Or perhaps the first part of a clip is just what you need, but halfway through, the speaker swings off at a tangent and goes down a blind alley that's not relevant to the purpose of any part of your film, but then returns on message. The middle of that clip might have to go. This is what you should be noting down.

Once you've watched the assembly and discussed all the points you and your film editor have noted, you begin cutting the sync down to size and adding pictures to the assembly, in line with your paper cut.

Rough Cut

Preparing a Rough Cut

You are now constructing what's called a 'rough cut'. As its name implies, this is not a finished version of your film – far from it. It's an expansion of the sync assembly – containing a rough pull together of the specially shot images, arranged in the cut where you believe they will be most effective. You're not finalizing the images at this stage. You're simply adding relevant pictures to the structure in the right places. Some might eventually be employed to make a music sequence, some simply to add atmosphere and pausing to the film, some used as overlay to disguise edits in interviews. And some might eventually be used as illustration for a written narration. But until the structure and the interviews are agreed, it's a waste of time fine cutting images for sequences that might eventually get junked or radically changed. And it's the same for laying pictures over the edits in interviews: no point in doing this until the clips themselves have been agreed.

If you intend to use stills and archive footage, it's very likely that you won't have all you need at this stage – you may well be researching them as the edit progresses – in which case add a caption that reminds you that this is to come later. It's too early in the edit to write a script, you can't do that until your sequences have been fine cut. You can draft out a guide commentary for the rough cut that will indicate the broad drive of each sequence. But it's only a guide at this stage.

Viewing a Rough Cut with your Film Editor

When you sit down to watch your rough cut for the first time, you'll be taking a step down into the visual organization of your unfolding narrative. Once again, watch the film with time code on the screen and, without comment, note down the times of issues you wish to raise at the end. Be prepared for things not to work – and don't panic! It's completely normal for a rough cut to have significant structural issues that need to be resolved. The iterative process of editing is gradual. Only by watching the cut several times can you refine and adjust the structure to make the most of the sequences, interviews and actuality that you've filmed. Ask yourself these kinds of questions:

- Does that sequence 20 minutes into the cut really work in that position? Or would it make a better first sequence than the one I've currently got after the opening?
- Am I making the best use of my actuality and interview sequences? Do they have sufficient variety to engage my audience from moment to moment – or is the exposition of the film currently much too predictable?
- Do any of the interviews or actuality feel too long?
- Are the visual and sound building blocks of the narrative really doing the right job at the right place in the film – taking the viewer from A to B, B to C, etc.

Once again, don't get derailed by detail; you might hate that sequence of images of your key

> When you watch a rough cut, you need to have a sense that the story is being told in a way that's understandable, and a clear cut sense that the holes in the story are problems you're going to solve. You need to ask: do you have a sense, when you've got to the end, that you know your characters now? I mean it also has to be watchable. You have to be able to sit there and watch your show. If it's a 45 minute show and you can't get through it without checking your phone or fiddling around, then you have a problem with your film – because why should anybody else watch your film if you can't even watch it.
>
> Barbara Ballow, Film Editor

character, but it doesn't matter at this stage of editing; you might think that there should be a reflective pause at the end of a dramatic story, but this is too narrow a point to make at this stage. You are still constructing the 'spine' of your story – ensuring that the narrative is coherent and non-repetitive – running seamlessly from the beginning to the end without detours.

If you find that things just aren't coming together – that the logic of the narrative isn't working, try this: buy a pack of sticky notes. Write the title of each chapter heading on separate notes. Stick them on a wall. Then, also on separate notes, write a title for each interview clip and a one-line description of its purpose in the film. Stick these under the correct chapter headings on the wall. You've now got an immediate visual representation of the current structure of the film – and you can move the order of the notes around until, hopefully, you find a structure that works. Sometimes this sticky note version of the film structure can help break a creative blockage by allowing you to see, at a glance, the connections you've made between each sequence, so that you can more easily identify where the narrative isn't working – and why.

Once you and your editor have discussed any changes you think will be needed, talk about the thought-line for each commentary link. Your editor will have a take on the best length for each link given the available visual material, and you can now start drafting out rough guide commentaries while he begins refining the rough cut, re-ordering sequences and assembling picture sequences. You'll be fast approaching a first viewing of the film with your executive producer

> Working as an editor, you know the film. You know your characters. You know all the footage. You know what's going to happen next because you've cut it. And sometimes it's very hard to divorce yourself from that and remind yourself: 'Oh – another person that's watching this has no idea who these people are or why this is happening'. And that's why it's always good to bring in an outsider with fresh eyes to look at what you've been working on – to make sure that the viewer, the intended audience, is going to understand your story, where you're going with it. It could be as basic as: are they laughing in the right places? Are they keeping up? Where does the story slow down for them when they watch it? That's where the team approach to filmmaking comes in. I mean ultimately you don't want people to be confused or have to work so hard that they either lose the point of your film or they give up because it's too difficult, too labour intensive.
>
> Barbara Ballow, Film Editor

Viewing a Rough Cut with Execs and Commissioners

This is the first test of your creative vision, and first viewings are always an anxious time for a filmmaker. There is a tendency to want to present as polished a film as possible at this viewing. But guard against this feeling. Any experienced exec understands that the rough cut of a documentary is an intermediary stage in which much will be missing, the pacing is likely to be wrong in parts, and the picture sequences are not finalized. So don't get derailed by trying to polish the film when what you should be doing prior to this viewing is focusing on the narrative, on the building blocks of the story and whether they are doing the right job in the right place. That's what your exec will be looking for at this viewing – the structural approach and how well this builds the story you wish to tell. Nothing else.

Rough cut viewings are also the moment in factual filmmaking when the concept of creative collaboration is given a severe stress test. After weeks, sometimes months, of research, filming and editing your idea has progressed from a paper proposal to an embryonic film. You've struggled against the odds to get it to this point: the process of filming is intense. It's success rests on the passion and commitment of a producer/director. But once back in the cutting room, it is all too easy for the very qualities that have delivered a strong set of rushes, to get in the way of cutting them into the best possible story. Your closeness to those rushes – your knowledge of the time and effort that went into filming them – can make you lose sight of the wider picture. Do you really need to spend ten minutes of the narrative on that jungle sequence? Does that eyewitness who took three weeks of negotiations to agree to speak on camera really further your narrative? Wouldn't the film be better without her? Doesn't that sequence inside Congress get in the way of the narrative at the top of the film? Wouldn't it be better placed lower down in the story? And, anyway, where's your explanation of Congress's role in relation to your story – *you* might understand this because you've been working on the story for months, but you haven't given the average viewer anything like enough information to follow the story.

These are illustrations of the kind of issues that can arise during a rough cut viewing, and they are why having an outsider (albeit an informed outsider) look at your film is invaluable: someone who doesn't know the trials and tribulations of getting the film in the can is better able to judge the effectiveness of the cut – from the perspective of the audience – than you.

So don't get defensive. Beware of holding onto what you believe to be cherished notions too strongly, because they might be obstacles on the way to a much better product. More important are the views of those who watch your film for the first time: they are your first audience, after all – and if they feel that something isn't working, take it seriously. Otherwise it will be a much larger audience that eventually has that same feeling! Listen carefully to the feedback and be prepared to adapt the cut. If you disagree with the solution suggested to the problem, find a better one – but don't go into denial and pretend there simply isn't a problem. Certainly don't think that you've failed as a filmmaker just because your exec has suggested changes to the structure. You are simply taking part in a collaborative, creative process that is designed to end up with the best possible film from the rushes you've shot.

Surviving Rough Cut Viewings: Six Views

Younger producers sometimes go into an edit and they cut it for a few weeks, and an executive producer comes in and says: 'perhaps you could do it differently and move the bottom bit up and the top bit down, and redo those bits in the middle'. And the people who are not going to thrive, are those who think they are being told off, or those who think that they've failed, or those who think that somehow it's their job to resist it, that it's their film and nobody should come in and tell them how to do it. I sometimes see people who get completely dejected because somebody has suggested they do a film in a different way. But that is the wrong response. It's not a telling off. It's not a rejection. It is just: here's how it could be better. I think people who are going to thrive in the profession are people who listen to that feedback and then go off and make a better film. And the more feedback the better. Some people I know literally send their rough cuts to their friends, their mums, their husbands, whoever they can and demand their feedback – which must be very annoying for those people, but it's a really useful thing to do because if somebody says: 'I didn't understand that bit in the middle, it was too complicated, it was too dense'. Or: 'I don't understand why I'd even be interested in watching it, you didn't sell it hard enough at the top'. Or: 'you asked this question at the top but you didn't answer it at the bottom – so what was the film supposed to be doing?' It can really help you understand where your film is going wrong. And very, very, very rarely – in fact I would say almost never – do people get it right first time. A structure almost never stays how it started. And it always gets better from watching it and discussing and thinking. So yes, don't be frightened of feedback. In fact totally treasure it and value it.

Diana Martin, Executive Producer, BBC, *Panorama*

One thing I have noticed, is that more experienced filmmakers are usually much better receivers of feedback than first time filmmakers which I find really interesting because you'd think that someone who has made many feature films would feel more proprietary about their work. But usually it's the opposite. Usually the filmmakers that get a little more anxious are the early career ones. As anyone who's worked in film knows, very few people make an entire film from start to finish on their own. It's a group effort. My advice to early career filmmakers would be that most likely the person giving them feedback is doing it in a spirit of trying to make the best film possible and it's not personal, it's really about the work. And so when you're looking at feedback in that spirit, I think that it's the best way to move a project forward. And if you're working with a commissioning editor that you really, truly don't agree with and you think is wrong, maybe ask a friend, run it by them, and if you really still think that they are giving completely wrong feedback and don't understand your project then don't work with them.

Kathleen Lingo, Executive Producer, *New York Times* 'Op Docs'

I do often encounter a certain amount of reluctance in newer/younger filmmakers to understand what we are adding to the project. If they've been taught in an academic atmosphere that is based around facilitating their vision and experimenting, neither of which are bad things, they can be surprised that someone like myself might want to have input to their projects. But what I really, really try to get across is that our contribution to their projects isn't about dictating to them or turning their project around so that they end up with a project that they hate. It's about, I hope, making genuinely positive contributions: helping them to make the film better; helping them to deliver the film that they want to make. And that kind of external eye – that objective eye – from people who are seeing a lot of films coming in all the time, I just think is really invaluable basically. And also we know our audience really in depth. We know what our audience responds to and what's going to connect with them so we want to help filmmakers make a film that our audience are going to watch. It's about seeing the broader picture.

Charlie Phillips – Head of Documentaries, *The Guardian*

The fresh eye is essential because I think we always get too close to our projects. I have resented like hell a network executive telling me that these scenes don't work. But if they're saying it's not working, you'd better goddam listen to them because, if something is not working for key members of your audience, it means something isn't working. You may have to come up with your own solution to it because their solution may be totally off base, but you should always listen. It's one of the reasons why, for me, I always do screenings of rough cuts with as many audiences as I can, just to get that sense of how it's playing to an audience. Often I'll land up locally and say: 'do you want to have a few beers and watch something'. A [filmmaker] who says: 'I want to go in and do this, and this is the way I'm going to do it, screw anybody else and I'm not going to listen': there's no humility there. You should be as open as you possibly can to people who can give you new insight.

Leo Eaton, Documentary Filmmaker

Probably the biggest flaw for younger filmmakers is that they don't share with other people and they don't take the advice of other people. I think it's always really hard to get negative feedback. I mean you always want to go in thinking that everyone's going to say: 'Oh, it's fabulous! If you just did this small little thing it would be the best film ever'. I mean that's what everybody wants to hear, always. And it's almost never the case. You almost never get it right on the first pass and you have to have a Zen attitude about it. You really have to remind yourself that editing is a process and even if you have to make major changes in your show, that is very much a part of the process. And you'll have a better film for it in the end.

Barbara Ballow, Film Editor

It's one of the most important stages of production: the rough cut where you're sitting with someone who knows about the story you're trying to tell, but they're looking at it with eyes that you don't have any more because you've been sitting in the edit. My role is help them tell the best story that they can tell. And sometimes at the beginning of the process that's hard because they think they've already done that. But it's so important because I'm a wider audience and I'm someone who hasn't seen it so it's one of the most helpful junction points. At the end of the day what we've always found is that filmmakers who you trust, and you have a trusted relationship with, there's a way to do it as a commissioning editor in which the filmmaker is part and parcel of the changes. They feel it's still their film. So that's what I try to do.

Raney Aronson-Rath, Executive Producer, PBS Frontline

Fine Cut

You arrive at the fine cut stage of editing once the narrative structure of your film has been approved by your bosses – and you've made whatever changes have been agreed at the last rough cut viewing. So the basic building blocks of your story will be in place, the flow of thought through the sequences and interviews will be decided (but not the final commentary, if there is one); the interviewees will be in the right order (but not necessarily at the correct length); and the picture and actuality sequences will be laid out in a rough form. The process of fine cutting is a process of fine-tuning, one that you hope will transform a caterpillar-like collection of sequences into an elegant filmic butterfly that sucks an audience in at the top and spits them out at the end gasping for more! So it is perhaps the most satisfying part of your production – the moment when that germ of an idea you dreamt up many months ago is finally given a life of its own. Here's what you're likely to be doing at the fine cut stage.

Cutting an Opening

It is usually easier to conceive an opening to a film when you have a clear idea of the narrative and the strength of the different ingredients that go to make up your story. The opening is both a teaser to entice your audience into the show, but also an introduction to the contents. Devising a way of conveying a grabby, accurate essence of the story is much easier when you know exactly what that story really is, than when you first conceived your paper cut. And you don't really get that sense until you've a rough cut in place. You might lay out the basis for an opening during a rough cut – as I did in the start of that Martin Luther King film discussed earlier in this chapter. But that opening will be refined and improved much later in the edit, as the King one was.

Fine-Cutting your Picture Sequences

Until you get to the fine cut, your film editor will have 'blocked out' the picture sequences. By that I mean he or she will not have spent time cutting pictures together – but will simply have added imagery that's relevant to the content of any particular sequence, so that you and others who view the film will know what kind of imagery to expect at any point in the film. But now that you've got the film structure agreed, your editor starts making the picture sequences really work. This is not just about what images are used and how they are cut together, it's also about how they work with music, with actuality and with silence. This is how the pace of your story is designed. So fine cutting is all about making a film *really* watchable – a film that entices an audience into the narrative, guiding them from one thought to the next rather than hurrying them from one point to another, because that's the way to lose their attention. It's about finding a balance, or a harmony, between the different visual and audio ingredients on your editor's palette. In much the same way as an artist works with paints, a talented editor can make as big a difference to a film, by combining these ingredients in just the right way, much as a Picasso might do in a painting.

> The opening and the closing scenes in a film are usually the two hardest things to do because you want to give everybody a good sense of what they are getting themselves into. You want to set-up some excitement or mystery or expectation, and you really can't do that until you've basically got the film told. Sometimes there is a scene that you have and you know it's going to belong at the beginning and it stays there. But if it's a constructed scene, using images from the whole film or bits and pieces from the whole film, you have to wait until you are really far into the cut because you don't know what's really good and what's really working until you are far along in the edit.
>
> Barbara Ballow, Film Editor

If your film requires graphics, these would also be finalized and added during the fine cut – either commissioned from an outside graphic designer or simply cooked up by your editor, perhaps using captions on a filmic backdrop. The final archive and stills you require would also be added at this stage.

Filming – Significant Camera Pieces, Right-to-Replies and Doorsteps

It might sound odd to suggest that you could be filming during the fine cut, but if you are using an on-screen reporter or making an investigative/undercover film, you often have to delay some key filmed sequences until the narrative structure has been agreed. Significant camera pieces, those that introduce or conclude the film, for example, can't always be written until your reporter knows the exact drift of the story

> Basic stand up camera pieces are best done on location because that's when you have your talent and where your story is. What I have found the smart producers do, is they film a bunch of different versions. So it's not like: Ok. I'm only going to say this conclusion. I'm going to have the talent do three or four different ones because that way you have some options. But having said that, there's been lots of times where those scenes have to be re-shot and maybe they're re-shot in a studio or they're shot someplace against a green screen. Sometimes it works out. Sometimes it doesn't work out.
>
> Barbara Ballow, Film Editor

as it appears on film (rather than in your paper cut). I explain this in more detail on page 67 in Chapter 3. Investigative and undercover films also often need a day's filming during the fine cut to allow those criticized in the programme to reply to the claims being made against them – or perhaps to 'doorstep' those who don't respond. You'll also find more on right-to-replies and 'doorstep' interviews on pages 198–199 in Chapter 10.

Writing the Commentaries

Now that the structure has been finalized, it's also time to properly write the commentaries to the pictures you've cut. If your film has a reporter, this will be their job. You'll need to give them a copy of the film, with time code in vision, and indicate where each commentary link sits in the film and how long it needs to be. As a guide you can also give the reporter a paper version of the current cut containing the roughly drafted commentaries. Once the narration has been written you'll record it in the edit and add the commentaries onto the film (or, if time is really short, simply ask your reporter to read them live during the fine cut viewing).

Getting the Film to Length

One last task before the final viewing of your film is to get it close to the agreed length. Broadcasters are much more precise about this than most online outlets since your film has to fit into a live schedule, so you'll usually be asked for a length that can't vary by more than a few seconds if making the film for TV.

Fine Cut Viewings

With the key structural decisions behind you, fine cut viewings tend to be more relaxed affairs than their rough cut cousins. At this stage the feedback you're likely to get from a commissioner will be focused on the content of commentaries (if you are using a narration) – or the actuality (if you aren't) – along with more subtle issues like the length of an interview; the pace of the film – the speed with which you move from one sequence into the next; sometimes music can also be an issue – some commissioners are more fussy than others about the accompanying track. The final camera pieces will also be viewed for the first time. And investigative films which raise significant legal issues often involve a lawyer at this stage – either attending the fine cut viewing or sent a version of the film immediately after.

After the Fine Cut Viewing(s): Final Tasks in the Edit

You'll be very near the end of your edit now – perhaps a day or two at most to do the following:

1. Make the final visual/audio changes agreed at the viewing – for investigative films this will involve responding to your lawyer's comments as well.
2. Get the sound tracks in order before final post-production begins.
3. Re-draft commentaries in line with your commissioner's (and lawyer's) requests.
4. Check the facts in your script and prepare an annotated version of the script.

Accuracy is vital on all factual films – and particularly so on investigative programmes. Without a thorough check, it is all too easy for an inaccurate fact added into a narration when drafting out a rough guide commentary, to make its way through to the final script. If you happen to be making a contentious investigative film that ends up in court, lawyers will use such careless errors to undermine the credibility of your journalism. Figure 6.3 shows an example of what I mean by an annotated fact-checked script. This is the fact check done on the opening two sentences in

VISION	COMMENTARY	FACT CHECK
Jackie drives through the streets of Stamford Hill	Stamford Hill. Home to Europe's largest (1) strictly orthodox Jewish community (2), the Charedi. It's a closed world (3) where outsiders are often treated with mistrust.	**(1)** Hackney Council: The Charedi Orthodox Jewish Community. Hackney is home to the largest Charedi ['pious, religious, orthodox'] Orthodox Jewish community in the world, outside New York and Israel. www.hackney.gov.uk/hackney-the-place-diversity. htm#charedi **(2)** Strictly Orthodox: '**Strictly**' is used by the Jewish Board of deputies (email to producer from JBOD researcher 12.12.1) 'There is no agreed definition of which Jews fall within the description of "Charedi" or "strictly Orthodox" (the latter term usually being preferred to "ultra Orthodox", which some people consider to have negative connotations)'. NOTE: The Jewish Board of Deputies most recent research into Charedim in Britain (2008) says 'We stress that there is no "Charedi community" as such; rather this is an umbrella term to describe Jews who emphasize a strict adherence to Orthodox Judaism'. We have used the term 'community' as an understandable shorthand – the term is used by the Charedi charity the interlink foundation. www.fbrn.org.uk/project%20profiles/ interlink-foundation and publications like The BMJ http://spcare.bmj.com/ content/1/2/247.2.abstract **(3)** – Conversations with contributors and current and former members of the community, – MS describes suspicion of social services looking after children in briefing note with producer. MS '*said the community doesn't like to bring in social services immediately; they are not seen to be sensitive to the culture of the community, and will put the child in a non-religious environment. She stresses that social services don't have religious principles – the instinct, if abuse is alleged, is to remove the child from the family – and they won't care if the new foster family has the same cultural background as the child's family. So the community is not in a hurry to bring in social services*'. – UOHC right to reply statement '*The authorities understand that "unfortunately" some in our community would simply not be comfortable participating in a police investigation.*'

Figure 6.3 Illustration of a fact-checked opening section of a script

the commentary of a documentary made for Channel 4 TV in the UK. As you'll see, this check is extensive. The fact checked version should be sent to your exec but is not normally circulated to commissioners. Its purpose is to ensure that, should any fact in your script be questioned once the film has been screened, you can quickly answer any query without worrying, several months down the line, about where you got the information.

5. *Send the final film for approval.* Your exec and your commissioner (and on investigative films, the platform's lawyer) will need to see this before you start post-production. If time permits you can re-record the changed commentaries in the edit suite and add them on to this version before sending it for approval. If your deadline is pressing, just send the re-cut with time code in vision together with a paper version of the final narration in which each commentary link is also time coded – so that the two can be easily matched.
6. *Prepare your caption and copyright lists.* These tasks must be done before the end of your edit – see pages 177–178 in Chapter 9 for more information.

A Flow Chart of Editing Tasks[1]

JOB	NOTES
Preparation for the edit – the paper cut	An ordered list of the specially shot interviews/actuality sequences plus archive and stills – with indications of the narrative being told in each building block of your film. So this is the story you wish to tell on paper. The preparation often continues after the edit starts.
Editing – Sync Assembly	A pull together of all the interviews and/or actuality sequences in an order that reflects the paper cut.
Viewing – Producer-Director/Editor	Your internal view of the sync assembly. Function: to remove any interview or actuality sequence that fails to further the story you wish to tell at that point in the film.
Editing – Rough Cut	Your specially shot images are added to the sync assembly, roughly assembled in the right places in the structure. Some archive/stills will be added as well if needed.
Rough cut viewing – Producer-Director/Editor	Your second chance to go through the film. Don't get derailed by detail – this is a structural viewing to further refine the narrative, to make sure the sequences you've constructed really are telling the story in a coherent way.
Editing – Rough Cut	Make the changes you've agreed at your second viewing – and prepare draft guide commentaries to either read live at the next viewing or, preferably, record in the edit suite and lay onto the rough cut images.
Viewing 1: Rough Cut with Executive Producer	The first 'outsider' to view the film – in rough cut form. The Exec will know the broad story but will be coming fresh to this viewing – so you'll get your first valuable audience feedback.
Editing – adapting rough cut	Taking your exec's comments on-board, you change the structure.
Viewing 2: Rough Cut with Executive Producer	Your second audience viewing.

Figure 6.4 A flow chart of editing tasks

JOB	NOTES
Editing – Fine Cut	You adapt the cut in the light of the last viewing and fine cut the pictures. Commentaries will be written to picture, re-recorded in the edit suite and added to the sound track.
Viewing 3 – Fine Cut with Commissioner/Exec/Legal	If you're working to an outside commissioner, this is where he/she will give the broadcaster or online platform's take on the film. It's also where a media lawyer may well cast their eye over your film if you are working in a contentious, investigative arena.
Editing – Fine Cut	You adapt the cut in line with the last viewing, re-record in the edit suite any commentaries that have to be amended and add them to the track. If you need big 'page turn' stand ups or, on investigative films, right-to-reply interviews or 'doorsteps', you'll film these at this point in the edit and cut them in. Any missing archive and stills you've ordered should be put in.
Viewing 4 – Fine Cut with Commissioner/Exec	The final viewing before picture lock.
Editing – Fine Cut	Final changes to the film and to the narration are made in line with the last viewing.
Picture Lock	At this point you can't make any further changes to the structure of the film or the images used in the structure.
Commentary fact check	Before the final narration is approved – each fact it contains must be checked for accuracy. The source of each fact is added to an annotated version of the script that's kept as a handy guide to answer queries after the film is shown.
Final cut and final script approval	**The film is at this stage usually sent to the Commissioner/ Exec/Lawyer for a final OK.**
Script Lock	The film is now ready to be post produced.

Figure 6.4 Continued

Note

1 This is an indicative editing/viewing schedule. The precise number of viewings is driven by the kind of film being made and the number of co-producers involved.

7 How to Thrive in the Digital World

Factual Filmmaking for Online Platforms

> **KEY CONCEPTS**
>
> - How to maximize your chances of being commissioned by different kinds of online platforms.
> - Understanding the significance of thumbnails, titles and social media conversations.
> - Why it's not easy to make a living making online films.
> - The skill-set that gives online filmmakers the best chance of success.

The modern media landscape is being transformed by the meteoric rise of online and social media platforms. Factual producers and directors now have greater opportunities than ever before – if they are willing to 'ride the tiger' of change that's sweeping over the market. The statistics in both Britain and America speak of a tsunami of change – driven by young people.

Britain

- TV viewing time among teens and young adults is in free-fall: it's slumped by 40% in seven years. In 2017 alone, young children spent 15% less time watching broadcast TV than the year before. 16 to 24-year-olds' viewing time dropped 12% in this period.
- The average age of TV viewers on BBC One, BBC Two and ITV is now over 60.
- The BBC says that 16 to 24-year-olds spend more time watching Netflix each week than all of its TV services.

America

- Traditional TV viewing among younger age groups is also diving. In five years it's plummeted by 50% among 12 to 17-year-olds; it's 44% down among 18 to 24-year-olds; and 17.5% lower among 35 to 49-year-olds.
- Younger people (25 to 34-year-olds) now spend twice as much time viewing videos on computers or smartphones as 50 to 64-year-olds.
- In 2018 research estimated that Americans were only two years away from spending more time each day on the internet than watching TV.

If young people in both Britain and America continue to move away from traditional TV at this pace, mainstream broadcasters are going to struggle for audience as today's youth grow into middle age. Those who've understood this sea change, and who care about factual film-making, are following the eyeballs online – hoping to re-engage TVs lost audience with digital platforms dedicated to documentaries, current affairs films and newsy shorts. Factual producers and directors with an idea to sell now have a wider range of outlets for their work than ever before: Vice, Buzzfeed, NBCs Left Field, Field of Vision, CNNs Great Big Story, ProPublica, Business Insider, Vox, London 360, BBC Stories and others are all vying for strong factual films. Newspapers have also understood that if the future is online, then video journalism is as much a part of a newspaper as the written word and the still image.

Short news films are commonplace – but some broadsheets, notably *The Guardian* and *The New York Times*, have taken a further step and opened documentary film commissioning departments.

Even radio shows have moved into online film-making. The popular British daily programme BBC *Newsbeat* is aimed at 16 to 29-year-olds, the very age group that's spending more and more time online and on social media. To make sure their young listeners don't jettison the programme, *Newsbeat* is complementing its daily 'ears only' output with a range of films tailored to different

> My attitude with audience is: go to where the audiences are. So the way that people's viewing habits work is: it's hard to tell someone to go somewhere to watch something – but if you put something in front of them where they already are, they're more likely to watch it.
> Kathleen Lingo, Executive Producer of
> *The New York Times* 'Op Docs'

online platforms. Instead of expecting viewers to come to them, enterprising media organizations like Newsbeat are now taking their offerings to the places they hope to find an audience.

The downside of this digitally transformed filmmaking landscape is a lot of insecurity and a noticeable lack of money. There are few full-time paid jobs, aside from those offered to commissioners and a handful of support staff. Freelance producer/directors pitch for low budget commissions – or pre-fund their own projects to get them noticed. It's tough making a living making online films. But what these online platforms do offer is a shop window for the work of enterprising and ambitious filmmakers. A strong film on a credible platform can act as a launchpad to a filmmaking career, a calling card if you like. It's on the site 24/7. It (or a link to it) is also usually on social media as well. Making factual films for online platforms is an important part of the modern producer/director's arsenal. But what do you need to know to thrive in this digital landscape? In this chapter I've spoken to key online execs and commissioners to discover their survival advice.

First – a thumbnail sketch of the platforms they run. You'll find links to their websites in the notes at the end of this chapter. These online content creators fall roughly into two groups: the first three use social media only as a shop window for their films – either posting the full length versions on these platforms or running trailers to drive audience to the film on their own website or on YouTube.

The Guardian Documentaries[1]

A pure documentary strand set in a journalistic context: documentaries are commissioned independently from the rest of the newspaper's news coverage, although there are sometimes tie-ins between a written story and a film. The Guardian documentaries is looking for untold, surprising stories – so it's no good pitching an idea that's appeared in the pages of The Guardian or any other newspaper. Most narration is conveyed by interview and actuality, very little by commentary. '*It's the classic thing of show, don't tell which is one of the first things I ever learned about documentary making*', says The Guardian's Head of Documentaries, Charlie Phillips. Films are pre-funded and range between about 10 and 30 minutes long. Social media is used as a way of building the brand and spreading the audience as wide as possible. Full length films appear on YouTube and Vimeo. Average audience size is 500,000, but The Guardian's strategy is not focused on the number of clicks. '*If you think too much about the numbers you would then just do 60 second puppy videos*', says Phillips. '*And I like 60 second puppy videos but we don't do what we do for any other reason than telling important stories*'.

The New York Times 'Op Docs'[2]

Part of the newspaper's Opinion section – rather than its news output. Executive producer Kathleen Lingo says Op Docs started in 2011 to encourage creative innovation and present information in a new way or with a distinct point of view. The films are always based on real stories and rooted in the truth, but the strand has experimented with virtual reality and used actors. Lingo is precise about the pitches that work for Op Docs: *A lot of times filmmakers will pitch something like: 'here's this problem you should know about'. But that wouldn't work for Op Docs. It has to be: 'here's this problem you should know about – and here's how you should think about it'. It has to have that extra layer. And that can be an artistic approach, the use of animation or virtual reality. Or it can be more overt where the film very clearly has a point of view.*

Op Docs are trailed and shown on social media – you'll even find the full length films in vertical format on *The New York Times* Snapchat feed. Whatever the platform, the films are always shown full length. '*We don't ever make our decisions on what films we take for the series based on viewership*', says Lingo. '*We only choose films based on films that we like and we think are good*'. They range from one minute to 30 minutes.

Field of Vision[3]

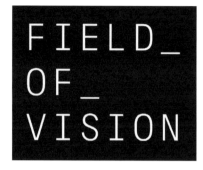

This is an American site that champions what their executive producer Charlotte Cook calls a 'cinematic take' on international news stories – in other words, a more artistic approach, a different perspective. '*A lot of the films that have been the most successful are the more experimental films*', says Cook. '*They are the films that are very different than what is out there currently*'. A big driver behind Field of Vision's films is longevity: they should be topical but also have a long shelf life. One example is a film about confederate monuments in America. '*That was asked to be part of the Legacy Museum which looks at slavery and mass incarceration – and that's on permanent display there now. And for us that is a huge marker of success*', says Cook. Field of Vision fully funds its output, commissions worldwide, subtitles films made in non-English speaking countries in the local language, and has a big presence on social media: full length films on Facebook, trailers and stills on Instagram and stories about the films and their successes at festivals on Twitter. The aim is to drive an audience to the full-length films.

The second group of execs run filmmaking outlets which all create content specifically for social media – as well as for their own sites.

BBC *Newsbeat*[4]

The BBCs flagship radio show for younger 16–29-year-old listeners has followed its audience online and complements its daily radio output with a range of 2 to 30 minute documentary films. '*While we still have around 8 million people listening to us every week on radio, so we're never going to neglect that, there is a much wider audience, and a much wider platform for our work*', says Debbie Ramsay, Newsbeat's editor. '*That's why we've gone digital and very visual as well*'.

Newsbeat creates content for social media – tailoring films to different platforms. One to six minute shorts on Instagram, 12 to 40 minute documentaries on YouTube and on the BBCs own website. It also puts trailers on social media to promote longer films shown on the BBC website or posted on YouTube. Newsbeat stopped posting videos on Facebook after it's algorithm changed in 2018. Ramsay believes that the right subject and the right approach can attract a social media audience to watch longer films. '*They will invest if you get it right, they will invest 20 minutes, they will invest half an hour, but only if it's worth it*', she says. Clicks don't drive content on Newsbeat. If a film doesn't do well, but the

subject is journalistically significant, they'll rethink the approach
to try and get the issue watched.
But success can also be measured
in the number of comments a
story attracts. Budgets are tight –
much less than those offered for
broadcast documentaries at the
BBC.

> Any media organization, has to be on these social media platforms or else you're kind of lost a bit … We know, from our audience, news isn't that kind of old fashioned view of what most journalists are trained to think of news as. The news to our audience is anything that appears in their social feed. So it could be a silly video, that's kind of news to them. They don't think: hard news, soft news, medium news, it's just all news if they learn something new from it or if they find it humorous or if it reflects their lifestyle or explains the world to them.
>
> Debbie Ramsay, Editor, BBC, *Newsbeat*

BBC Stories[5]

This is digital current affairs for the audience the BBC
finds it hard to reach in the UK – young people, women,
poorer and more diverse socio economic groups. '*You've
got to tell stories in ways that* [these groups] *want the stories to
be told*', says BBC Stories and digital current affairs editor,
Jeremy Skeet. Unlike Debbie Ramsay at *Newsbeat*, Skeet
doesn't think that long-form works on social media. '*Most
of the younger age or under-served audience, aren't going to sit
through half an hour or maybe an hour*', he says, '*but they might
sit through seven minutes told in a different way, but using the
same journalism*'. Films on the BBC Stories website and on
YouTube range from around 9 to 44 minutes in length. On
Facebook and Twitter they're much shorter – mostly one
to eight minutes plus trailers for longer films. The social media environment is extremely competitive, says Skeet. If the platforms change their algorithms, it can wipe out the BBCs presence,
so he has a small social media savvy team ensuring BBC Stories maintains a high profile on each
site. '*Six months ago Facebook changed their strategy*', he says. '*So now, to get media into your feed, you
have to have lots of comments. So you're playing to the strengths of each site*'.

NBC 'Left Field'[6]

Left Field is an experimental video unit inside NBC News
that creates content primarily for YouTube, where they
host 3 to 30 minute documentaries. Other social media
platforms – and their own website – are used to drive
viewers to their YouTube output. There are trailers and
short clips on Facebook and Twitter, and behind the scenes photos on Instagram with links
to YouTube films. Cut downs of Left Field's YouTube output also appear on NBCs own news
streaming service, Signal, and three minute square versions are also made for Apple News. Left
Field's experimentation is focused on cinematography, editing and graphics: some films feature imaginative augmented reality with graphics floating in the air around live action; others
use sharp editing or beautiful filming. '*We're meant to collaborate with the whole of NBC News and*

strive to make them stylistically better', says Matt Danzico who launched Left Field 2017. They put out two or three films a week. Around half are made by staffers – the rest commissioned from freelancers. '*The platform dictates the length, the style, and sometimes the dimensions of the video frame*', says Danzico. '*How do people consume it? Then we'll tailor the video accordingly*'.

The last commissioner in my list runs an online platform that straddles the divide between content creators using Facebook, Twitter, etc. as a shop window for long form digital output – and those that create shorts for social media.

PBS Frontline[7]

The flagship news and current affairs strand run by Public Service Broadcasting in America  has also taken its televised investigative journalism into the online world. You'll still find the show in the PBS TV schedules, but it has a big digital and social media presence as well – and tailors content specifically for online platforms. '*That's where we're meeting our new audiences*', says Frontline's executive producer Raney Aronson-Rath. '*So our digital output is quite big now*'. Full length documentaries commissioned from outside filmmakers appear on TV, YouTube and on the PBS website. The show's social media output on Facebook, Twitter and Instagram is made in-house and includes stand-alone short films, shorts that illustrate a text article or trail a long-form film, and more experimental 360 degree and interactive films. For Aronson-Rath, versatility is the key to the survival of journalistically based documentaries in a digital age when strands like Frontline can no long assume there will be an audience ready to watch their output on TV. '*Now we go to where they are*', she says, '*where they consume other media, and we say: "Hey. There's this really important journalism, this really important documentary, that we want you to see". … We have to be always innovating forever now because there are new platforms all the time that necessitate our attention*'.

The Significance of Online and Social Media to Factual Filmmakers

With all the mainstream broadcasters looking for ways of keeping their audiences as they drift away from TV viewing, making films for online and social media platforms is becoming an increasingly significant outlet for factual filmmakers. Yes, the bigger programme budgets are still in the hands of broadcast platforms that operate daily schedules. But all that might change in the next decade or so if on-demand viewing becomes the norm – and if social media is increasingly used as a forum for short form documentaries or a shop window to drive viewers to long-form versions of films. NBC Left Field's Matt Danzico is convinced that the future of factual film-making for younger audiences is online not on TV:

'*I think it's imperative for young people to not only think about digital video – and not broadcast – but to start thinking about what platform in the digital space they want to work*', he says. '*The conversation that is being had in the media industry is all around how in the world are we going to transition all this content into digital spaces – and where are those digital spaces? It's not even how do we save broadcast*'.

The viewing statistics certainly are pointing in the direction of radical change – so the key question for commissioners of factual content is how to ensure that documentaries and current affairs films continue to have wide appeal on whatever platform such content appears.

'I'm not sure what's going to happen to the broadcast landscape', says Raney Aronson–Rath at PBS Frontline, *'or how long that will take. But journalism has to survive. The making of documentaries is only getting bigger and more robust, so I believe that there's a future for the work we do. It may just not be transmitted through a broadcast'.*

Maximizing your ability to get work as a factual filmmaker means keeping a foot in both the broadcast and the online camps at the moment. The advice of BBC Newsbeat's editor, Debbie Ramsay, is forthright: get off your high horse – and appreciate the benefits of social media.

It's about educating yourself on that rather than thinking: 'OK. No. I'm a serious filmmaker, and social media has got nothing to do with me'. It can make your work go global. And yes, it is competition as well, and there is nonsense out there but you've got to think: OK if I do a short version of this film, what would it be to get people to watch the longer version? Or, if I do a short version of this film and it's more successful than the longer version, I'm going to take that as success not actually be deeply offended because there's no point in crafting something amazingly beautiful and the only person who sees it is you and your family. You can't be as indulgent, I think, in today's age.

An Online Survival Guide for Producers and Directors Who Want to Make Digital Films

The approach you adopt has to be driven by the platform – and there's a clear blue line between content creators making films for social media and those using social media to drive an audience to their long-form films. The first three points below are relevant to platforms that create social media shorts.

Follow the Conversations – or Better Still – Start One Off With Your Film

Producers who wish to pitch ideas at platforms that create content for social media must get hooked into what's being talked about on Facebook, Twitter and Instagram. The conversations on social media are a key part of the commissioning process for these content creators. Knowing what interests the audience affects the commissioning process. It's a kind of feedback loop where what's being talked about can be amplified by a relevant film – or conversations provoked by a social media film can themselves spark further films in that area.

'We should be having a conversation with the audience', says Jeremy Skeet. *'And that's something we are experimenting with. The ideal moment is when the BBC starts a conversation and can continue it. But there's other times when you can find out what people are talking about, what their concerns are, and you can reflect that back to the audience. You can be led much more by the audience'.*

So a defining difference between broadcast filmmaking and films made for social media are the data streams that allow content creators to be very audience focused. NBCs Left Field is part of a news outfit, so some of its content is driven by news priorities. But its output also reflects the conversations on social media.

'Digital audiences demand completely different things. It's day and night. It couldn't be further apart', says Matt Danzico. *'There's a conversation happening on Instagram, on YouTube and the videos that do well on these platforms reflect those conversations. And if you were, right now, to search on Google trends, the most popular searches on YouTube, a significant proportion of those searches will have been turned into videos by some of the top new media companies. That is such a huge difference because I don't think story selection in broadcast is being driven by data in the same way as it is on digital'.*

So you've got to be plugged into the discourse on Facebook, Instagram and Twitter to pitch relevant ideas. That's why producers who work on strands that make films for social media are usually young and diverse. Most of the BBC Stories production team are under 30, some are only 19 or 20, precisely because they – rather than 35 and 45-year-old producers – are social media adepts.

Don't Insist on a Stylistic Approach. Be Willing to Adopt House Style on Platforms that Create Content Specifically for Social Media

The structural approach that underpins a successful social media short film has a signifi-cant knock-on consequence for filmmakers who want to work for platforms delivering this kind of factual content: there's no room for 'auteurs'. Factual content creators are experimenting with different editorial and styl-istic approaches, and different lengths of films, to discover what works best on what platform. So producers and directors aiming ideas at these platforms have to be aware of the cur-rently favoured methodology. Some outlets – NBCs 'Left Field' for example – want a specific style for the factual films they aim at Facebook, Instagram and Twitter, because this helps define their output across social media. So it's no good insisting on a particular stylistic approach. You have to adopt a house style.

'*With so many platforms and so many eyeballs looking on from just an incalculable number of spaces, it's hard to maintain brand identity*', says Left Field's Matt Danzico. '*And so one way that we try to do it is through a really punchy logo, really similar cinema-tography, recurring aesthetics and for us, the best freelancers whom we worked with were really interested in trying to meet the style that we're looking for. Rather than coming in and saying no, we want to shoot it this way. You know, for us, you can't have a piece that doesn't look like the rest of the unit anymore*'.

> We're always thinking about what's the story first, and what's the best form to tell it in. So a great example is on Facebook. Originally we thought: everybody's going to turn their phones around, so the 16:9 frame is going to be fine and people [will] enjoy a little cinematic film experience with audio and music. And we found out very quickly: every-body holds their phones upright – and nobody turns their audio on! I think the key for Frontline and for any others who work in the current affairs space, is that the journalism is the same, but the story telling form is different … And when we're translating into digital environ-ments we're definitely looking at how people consume in that environment.
> Raney Aronson-Rath, Executive Producer, PBS Frontline

BBC *Newsbeat*'s Debbie Ramsay also thinks that producers must be willing to compromise on their initial vision of a film because experience has shown what works and what doesn't on a *Newsbeat* social media documentary.

We make that very clear from the beginning: we like this idea, but if we work with you, this is what you need to do. Sometimes there is a lot of push-back. But what we're trying to do is to make it the best it can possibly be, to reach as many people as it can possibly reach. And it is tough and it takes a lot of conversation to actually persuade this person quite often it's not going to happen that way, your vision will not be exactly as you saw it from that very beginning.

Grab Them at the Top to Keep the Audience Watching

Once you've got a viewer to click, you've then got to keep them watching. A successful social media short is underpinned by a significantly different methodology to the approach that works in longer form broadcast or digital documentary filmmaking. Or, to be more precise, it is a more extreme application of the principle of viewability that all documentary filmmakers need to keep in mind. A social media film is structured to retain its audience from the very start. That means the key revelation can't be delayed, it has to be right up at the top.

'*When you're talking about short form on, say, Facebook, that's a very different structure and form than an actual documentary film that we broadcast*', says Frontline's Raney Aronson-Rath. '*So we've learned time and time again, when you grab someone with the editorial insight right away – people will watch … It's just a totally different story telling method than a documentary film*'.

Debbie Ramsay, editor of BBC Newsbeat, believes her film producers have a distinct advantage when making social media video documentaries precisely because they don't hail from a TV filmmaking background and so don't come with traditional TV baggage.

'*The team think in a different way, they shoot in a different way*', says Ramsay. '*There are probably lots of rules that traditional TV makers would say that we are breaking, but they work for social media. On social videos, what we find is you can't leave that crucial bit to the end. They need to know in those first few seconds that, actually, this is what it is about – and, yes, I do want to watch it further. We are very clear on what is right for our audience. It's always thinking of the audience, it's that ruthless focus*'.

Individual Creativity and Directorial Vision are Welcomed by Platforms That Only Use Social Media to Trail Their Long-Form Digital Output

Online platforms like *The Guardian* Documentaries, Field of Vision and *The New York Times*' Op Docs strands have a much more open approach to questions of style and film structure. These are filmmaker-led content creators that shun imposed house styles and instead aim to foster individualistic creative innovation from those they commission.

'*We are very, very much interested in the filmmaker's approach*', says Field of Vision executive producer Charlotte Cook. '*I think that's largely based on the fact that we're run by people who make films. So for us it's really about helping them to tell a story in a way that doesn't dictate changes or shaping the film. It's really about how to help the filmmaker get to where they are trying to go*'.

The approach taken by Executive Producer Raney Aronson-Rath to the long-form output at PBS Frontline's is similar. She insists all her filmmakers have journalistic integrity. But another must-have is individual creative imagination.

'*We're really looking for filmmakers who have great cinematic and directorial vision*', she says. '*And sometimes in journalistic stories it's really hard to find. So that's what we look for, for people who really have a vision about what something will look like and feel like and sound like*'.

Thumbnails and Titles: The Viewer is in Pole Position

Gaining a potential viewer's attention is important to all factual films. But platforms on social media, where attention spans are short and the competition for eyeballs is huge, the design of the 'thumbnail' image and the choice of title used to get that initial click are crucial issues for all the platforms.

'You've got to be so laser focused on the audience', says BBC Stories editor, Jeremy Skeet. *'Who would have thought, 20 years ago, that thumbnails would be one of the key things in story-telling. They are incredibly important. We had a documentary that was just flying on YouTube, really really flying, beating all our metrics. And the commissioner saw the YouTube title … and he thought it was derogatory and demanded that we changed it. And it dived. It literally dived. Do you see what I mean?'*

NBC Left Field's Matt Danzico places the same emphasis on the image and the title that generate the 'click'.

Thumbnails are kind of everything. If you do not have a good thumbnail no-one, I repeat no-one, will watch your video. And if you don't have a good headline, equally so, no-one will watch your video. We're trying to train our journalists, to think heavily about thumbs and headlines for their pieces. And we've learned lessons like: you should use somebody's face within the thumbnail and that person should be clear, but it should be artistic and colourful and not washed out. When we release a video on YouTube, we might actually test several headlines and test several thumbnails to see how they are stacking up against each other.

Online Commissions are Unlikely to Pay Your Bills. You'll be Working on Low Budgets or Even Self-Funding Your Film into the Edit Before You Get Any Money

Money is scarce in the online factual filmmaking world. Whatever platform you are aiming at, budgets are much lower than those on offer from major broadcasters. Most commissioners I spoke to were unwilling to give generic pricing guidelines. The Guardian was more forthcoming and generally pays around £15,000 for a 20 minute film. NBCs Left Field offers one budget for international projects and another for domestic (US based) stories. The New York Times Op Docs doesn't commission from paper pitches at all and expects filmmakers to stump up the cash to get their film to rough cut stage before taking a look, offering a fee for the work they commission.

'Our fees aren't going to cover all the cash costs that it takes most likely', says executive producer Kathleen Lingo. *'I wish that we could but unfortunately we just don't have those sized budgets. A lot of the first time filmmakers we work with are students, so there are films that they make in school and then they have the support to get the project off the ground. But the reason to make an Op Doc is to be part of the New York Times global platform, our award-winning series, and all the promotion we give to the film but also to the filmmaker'.*

So making a living by making online factual films is very tough. For many producers, it has to be a passion project, a side-line that offers exposure on credible platforms that just might kick-start a fledgling career in the industry. But the weekly bills have to be paid by another, regular job.

'No-one makes a living from just doing films for people like us. We don't pay enough', says The Guardian's Charlie Phillips. *'With the younger, emerging filmmakers we work with, they'll often be simultaneously working in a production company as their day job. But it's with a sympathetic company who understands that they might go off and make a film for us for a week. They will often be doing multiple different things at once. It is hard, really really hard to make a living from this'.*

If you can't earn your keep by making online films, if it can only be a side-line to your daily job, and if some platforms can't even cover the costs of your film, then why bother? Kathleen Lingo offers one reason.

I think that young filmmakers need to be realistic. You're not going to start as a director and be able to pay your rent – very few people do that. You have a paid job being an assistant editor or being a production assistant and then you learn from the people around you. You'll also meet more experienced filmmakers who'll not only give you work but also mentor you – which is super important. Some people look at it as a bad thing that you can't just support yourself as a director in year one. I think that's actually totally fine.

Some might find this small compensation for the lack of money in the online world. But it's clear that only the most committed filmmakers, those willing to make big sacrifices for their craft, those with an intense belief in their project and themselves, learn how to successfully navigate this digital ocean. And cultivating the right attitude is key.

Cultivate the Three 'Ps' to Survive in the Online World: Passion, Persistence and Pleasantness

The in-trays on the desks of the commissioning editors I spoke with are brimming with ideas from freelance filmmakers. It's a very competitive environment and fortune undoubtedly favours those willing to go the extra mile to prove their passion.

'[The] *most important thing is enthusiasm'*, says BBC Stories editor Jeremy Skeet. '*If somebody wants to become a filmmaker and comes to me and hasn't made a film, I don't really believe that. They've got an iPhone. Go and make a film and don't worry about the quality. You've got to prove that you're passionate. You've got to keep knocking on the door. That's fair enough, isn't it?*'

So you need to be a little pushy to get a foot in the door. But being too pushy once you're in will ensure the door closes firmly behind you once you've finished that first project. Executive producers want the experience of working with new directors to be a positive one – not an uphill struggle full of tension and conflict. Left Field's Matt Danzico encourages newcomers to adopt an attitude that will foster long-term relationships with commissioners. He says:

When freelancers approach an organization it's so important to approach that relationship professionally and with a positive attitude knowing that it could lead to more work. That first pitch that you send in could possibly be merely the tip of the iceberg. I think that's incredibly important for freelancers to keep in mind when they're approaching folks.

Multi-Skilled Producer/Directors are Highly Valued by Online Platforms

Even more so than the broadcast media where budgets are larger, online commissioners welcome producer/directors who can deliver low cost films by shooting and editing projects themselves. In fact, Matt Danzico thinks the online/social media medium is tailor-made for a new breed of young filmmaker.

'*I think some of the best and most talented cinematographers and video editors we've worked with are right out of under-grad'*, he says. '*If they are passionate about it, they are already video editing and shooting video on their iPhones in middle school. So by the time they reach us, they are, like, ten years in. That's not to say that people who don't have this background wouldn't be able to do it. It's just we find that those are the types that we gravitate towards. The jobs that are opening up all require people to shoot and edit their own pieces. And so we require the same. With kids making their own YouTube videos, throughout their schooldays, I think it's a bit more natural of an ask than it used to be'*.

Think Visually when Pitching at Platforms using Social Media to Promote Their Films

It's always a good idea to offer something visual when pitching a film proposal to anyone – and this is especially important for documentary ideas pitched by newcomers at online platforms using social media to promote their long form films. It's so much easier for a commissioner to see what a filmmaker is suggesting than to read about it on paper. It's not very difficult to do this for little or no cost, using an iPhone and editing on your computer. Offering an essence of what you are suggesting on film, perhaps a compelling character whose strength of personality drives your story forwards or a particular stylistic approach to filming the subject you're pitching, can tip the scales in favour of a commission.

'*It definitely helps if people send us a teaser or some kind of clip from the film*', says The Guardian's Charlie Phillips,'*because if they are not someone I know, I am not going to have any idea about their film-making abilities. I am way more likely to do an emerging filmmaker's idea if they send me something that looks really great*'.

Charlotte Cook, agrees. As a minimum, a proposal aimed at Field of Vision should be accompanied with a self-shot example of the filmmaker's approach.

'*It doesn't need to be a polished trailer*', she says,'*just* [something] *to give us a sense of what they are trying to do visually, is really interesting. So my dream scenario is somebody who can give me even just a couple of paragraphs: this is where I am; this is what I am trying to do; this is the approach I'm taking and here is a couple of scenes or a little bit of footage that I've shot*'.

Ask Why an Audience will Engage with Your Idea when Aiming at Outlets Creating Specific Content for Facebook, Instagram and Twitter

Offering a specific style of filmmaking at platforms that create content tailored to social media is, of course, going to be counter-productive. A more fruitful approach is to show that your idea will resonate with the audience at which it is aimed. And you do that by plugging into the social media chatter to convince commissioners that your idea is both relevant and well timed. BBC Stories editor Jeremy Skeet says:

Now you can find out what people are talking about, what their concerns are, what the conversations are, you can be led much more by the audience, by what they are talking about, and how they want it to be talked about. And you can reflect that back to the audience.

Left Field's Matt Danzico goes one step further. He wants the obvious in pitches for films that inform: who are the characters? Are they good talkers? What's the narrative arc? What's the journalistic reason for doing an investigative story? But pitches for films aimed at entertaining, rather than informing, need a different kind of proof: evidence that it really will interest its intended audience – data that can only come from understanding the interests of the social media audience.

'*There has to be a reason why you want to do this story other than: "I just think it will be cool looking"*', he says.'*… So if we're not delivering hard information that we think will lead to a more informed democracy, then we want to entertain and plug away at tickling people's imaginations and getting them to imagine a greater world. And so if you don't have data to prove that you are going to be able to do the latter, then we're probably not going to commission it*'.

Notes

1 www.theguardian.com/documentaries
2 www.nytimes.com/video/op-docs
3 https://fieldofvision.org
4 www.bbc.co.uk/news/newsbeat
5 www.bbc.co.uk/programmes/p05vxvzp
6 www.nbcnews.com/leftfield
7 www.pbs.org/wgbh/frontline/

Part 3

Planning Skills

8 Reducing Risk

Keeping Crew and Contributors Safe on Research
and Film Trips

KEY CONCEPTS

• How to assess the risks involved in a recce or a shoot – and take steps to minimize the
   likely harms to your production team, your interviewees and anyone else with whom
   you might come into contact on location.

Risk reduction is an important part of preparing for a research or film trip. Producers and directors need to demonstrate that they've done their best to ensure that their crew comes back
safely and without incident, and that any potential harm to contributors or people unconnected
with the shoot have, as far as possible, been minimized. Risk assessment is now part and parcel
of obtaining insurance to cover your research and shooting trips. In this chapter I am going to
look at the methodology behind reducing risks – and offer insights into how best to assess the
potential harm of any trip taken for a factual production. Risk assessment might be a long way
from the creative side of filmmaking, but it is the way in which you lessen the foreseeable negative consequences of your actions on the ground and you must take this seriously if you wish to
keep your team safe and your filmmaking reputation intact.

The Principles of Risk Assessing a Shoot

Risk assessing a trip is not a box-ticking exercise or an informal process. For each trip that you
take, you complete a form that forces you to consider the potential harms involved in your
recce/shoot and indicate the ways in which you intend to minimize these risks. The form is then

circulated to all those travelling so that they can take its advice on-board. It is also sent to the insurance company covering the production, and a failure to provide an RA might affect the cover being offered – especially if you plan to be travelling to a hostile environment or doing anything hazardous. If things go really wrong, your risk assessment could be used in court to demonstrate that you acted with appropriate forethought. Without it – lawyers would have a field day undermining your claim to have acted responsibly.

> [Risk assessments] are hugely important and I think they are not given enough thought in general. They are done for really good reasons. If you have a Google at things that have gone wrong on shoots – where people have been sometimes really quite seriously injured – it's things generally that could have been easily avoided with a bit of forethought.
>
> Lareine Shea, Production Manager

I am going to explain the kind of information you'll need to consider in order to complete a risk assessment to help you understand the process of harm reduction. On the website, you'll find an interactive version of the risk assessment discussed below containing my comments. You will also find a downloadable pro-forma version for your own project. **If you've been commissioned by a broadcaster or online platform, check before using this because they might want you to use their own RA form**. However, they all cover similar ground.

There are usually two sections to an RA form. The first (Figure 8.1) contains crew and useful location contact information. Once you've glanced through this part of the form, I'll explain the reasoning behind many of the entries.

RISK ASSESSMENT FORM	
This form must be completed and signed before the recce or filming can go ahead.	
SECTION A: BASIC INFORMATION ABOUT THE TEAM, THE PROJECT PLUS LOCAL CONTACTS	
PROJECT TITLE	
COMMISSIONING OUTLET (if any)	
PROJECT SUMMARY	
COUNTRIES TO BE VISITED (if project involves foreign travel)	
OVERALL RECCE/FILMING DATES	

Figure 8.1 The contacts section of a risk assessment form

RISK ASSESSMENT FORM					
1	**LOCATIONS TO BE VISITED** (with dates)	**ADDRESS**	**CONTACT**	**PHONE EMAIL**	**DATES OF VISIT**
2	**LOCATION CREW CONTACTS**				
	NAME	**MOBILE**	**E MAIL**	**SKYPE OR OTHER ONLINE GROUP CHAT LINK**	**NEXT-OF-KIN EMERGENCY CONTACT**	**BLOOD GROUP** (if known)
3	**PRODUCTION/COMMISSIONING OUTLET CONTACTS**				
	NAME	**MOBILE**	**OFFICE**	**HOME**	**E MAIL**	**SKYPE**

Figure 8.1 Continued

RISK ASSESSMENT FORM					
4	LOCAL EMERGENCY CONTACTS				
	NAME	**PHONE AND CONTACT**		**ADDRESS**	
	Nearest Hospital (with Accident and Emergency facilities)				
	Police/Ambulance				
	Embassy (if working abroad)				
	Local branch of TV channel/online platform (if working abroad and project has been commissioned by an outlet that has a local presence)			**Have they been alerted to your presence in the country?**	
				Who has been contacted?	
				Date of contact?	
	Other contacts				

Figure 8.1 Continued

Risk Assessment Form – Section A

Section A contains basic information about the team, the project, its purpose, the commissioner, the production company, the dates of the trip and the locations being visited. Also here are the following contacts – with explanations of their purpose:

Line 2 Location crew contact details – If anything should go wrong, it is really important that information can be passed swiftly across the team members even if they are separated from each other. So a complete list of on-the-ground contacts is vital: hotels, mobiles, emails, etc. It's also worth adding online contacts like Skype or setting up a group chat on WhatsApp. Contact information should include next-of-kin details so that relatives can also be quickly informed of any incident.

Line 3 Production/Broadcaster/Online platform back-at-base contacts – Key people back at base are added to this list so that the location team can get vital back-up during an incident without wasting precious time looking for phone numbers and email addresses. On a budgeted production these are likely to be the production manager and executive producer plus your commissioner. If you're not funded, then ensure there is someone back at base who can act as your back-up in an emergency.

Line 4 Local emergency contacts – Emergency services: police, ambulance, hospitals. When things do go wrong you need to be able to react quickly. In your own country, you'll know how to reach the police to investigate a robbery in which all your camera kit is taken. Or call an ambulance to take someone to hospital. But abroad you'll be floundering without some prior knowledge. So list the contact numbers that will enable you to contact the emergency services. Similarly, if you're working in a nation that lacks an effective ambulance service, or you're in a remote district, you might have no choice but to drive an injured colleague to hospital. So list the location of the nearest hospital with an accident and emergency department.

Line 7 Embassy (if working abroad) – If one of your researchers gets kidnapped by rebel fighters or arrested by the police or detained by soldiers, you're likely to need support from people with their ears to the ground and good political contacts. So it is important that your team back at base has the ability to contact your Government's embassy in the country, should they feel this is the appropriate course of action. The embassy might be able to apply pressure to get you released.

Line 8 Local branch of TV channel or online platform – If you are working abroad and your project has been commissioned by a broadcaster (or large online platform) that has a local office in the country, then tell a relevant person in the local branch that you'll be in the area researching and filming. If they find out by a back-door route that you are in their patch it can cause internal problems, especially if your team gets into some kind of difficulty and the newspapers

> The risk assessment should be done by the most senior person on location [because] that person is most likely to have recce'd it or to have a clear understanding of what you're going to find when you get there. I know some people might think: 'well, of course, you can just think about it when you get there'. But that's not good enough in law and, if there is a bad accident on your shoot, the health and safety executive these days will want to see your record of risk assessments – not just the risk assessment for that shoot. There's a wealth of information online and actually it shouldn't take very long to do one.
>
> Lareine Shea, Production Manager

come knocking on the channel's door and they know nothing about what you're doing. The only situation in which you might consider not mentioning this is on a particularly sensitive story where you fear alerting the channel could lead to a leak.

Line 9 Other contacts – If you're filming on a boat off the coast you might want the coastguard's contacts in case of an emergency. If the story takes you into a mountainous region, it might be the mountain rescue team. Use your judgment here.

Risk Assessment Form – Section B

The rest of the form contains the 'meat' of your risk assessment. This is normally completed by the film producer or director. It offers a list of likely hazards followed by a section where you detail the actions taken to minimize the risks. The items on this list are always wider than you'll need so only fill in those that apply to your shoot/recce. But it's not exhaustive either. Each trip has its own unique set of issues so be prepared to add to this list if you consider something significant is missing.[1]

Figure 8.2 is the second part of the risk assessment – where you identify the risks and show the steps you've taken to minimize them. Beneath this form is explanatory information for each section – the numbers in these explanations refer to the numbers in the first column of the form.

RISK ASSESSMENT FORM			
SECTION B: TO BE COMPLETED BY THE PROJECT PRODUCER			
	RISKS TO CONSIDER	**TICK RELEVANT RISKS**	**MEASURES TAKEN TO MINIMIZE RELEVANT RISKS**
1	**Medical risk** (including vaccination if abroad)		
2	**Terrorism** ★		
3	**Public disorder** ★		
4	**Conflict** (including impact of past conflict e.g.: mines) ★		
5	**Crime and criminal violence** ★		
6	**Kidnap** ★		
7	**Areas of cultural or religious sensitivity.**		
8	**Climate** (heat/cold/desert working etc.)		
9	**Travel** (i.e. cars, vans, planes & helicopters, boats and using vehicles off road or in hostile environments)		
10	**Secret Filming**		
11	**Weapons** (for example, for reconstructions)		
12	**Special filming equipment**		
13	**Lighting and camera equipment**		

Figure 8.2 The second part of a risk assessment form – containing the risks and the steps you'll take to minimize them

RISK ASSESSMENT FORM			
14	**Dangerous or derelict buildings**		
15	**Fire Safety**		
16	**Working alone**		
17	**Individuals with special needs**		
18	**Filming children**		
19	**Long hours**		
20	**Working at height**		
21	**Security of filming kit and other equipment**		
22	**Heavy loads**		
23	**Other risks**		
I am satisfied that the contents of this form adequately assess the risks involved in the planned activities and the measures taken minimize those risks.			
Signature of Producer		Date	
Signature of Executive Producer		Date	

Figure 8.2 Continued

Risks to Consider

You must research these risks thoroughly. A good starting point is the travel advice sections of the US and UK government websites.[2] Both contain a broad range of helpful advice and information for travellers covering visas, vaccinations, embassy locations, safety and security, local laws and customs, health, travel and transportation. But you can't just rely on these sites. You also need to keep in close touch with news developments, and speak with a locally-based experienced fixer (see below) who knows the areas that you'll be visiting.

1. Medical Risks (Including Vaccination if Abroad)

In this section you detail the risks and the measures you're taking to minimize any medical harm to your team. Do they need to be vaccinated when travelling abroad? Consult a doctor to discover what vaccinations are advised and plan the trip with sufficient time to allow the vaccine to become active. You must also protect against illnesses that can't be vaccinated against, like Malaria – and equip the team to deal with medical problems. It's always prudent to carry a medical kit containing plasters, bandages, antiseptic ointments, etc.

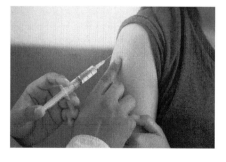

But if you're travelling to a remote region or a location where medical facilities are basic, it's also worth considering bringing antibiotics, sterile needles and syringes. Take the advice of a doctor to find out the most relevant medical kit for the trip.

2–6. Terrorism, Public Disorder, Conflict, Crime and Criminal Violence, Kidnap

General thoughts. You'll need an explicit green light from your commissioner before working in areas made unsafe by conflict, public protest, crime or terrorism – and you won't get that without a careful consideration of the risks involved and the ways in which they can be minimized. Before working in a conflict zone, for example, most reputable broadcasters will insist that you attend a hostile environment training course where you'll be taught how to survive in extreme environments, what to do if you're kidnapped, plus the basics

of first aid in a war zone. These courses are expensive – some last up to a week. If your project is funded, your commissioner will pay for you to attend. If you're thinking of going it alone, these courses prepare you for the dangers you're about to experience and can be a life-saver – so are well worth the money they cost.

The importance of a local fixer. A vital step on the road to risk reduction is to work with a know-ledgeable local fixer who lives and works in the areas you'll be visiting. Their understanding of local customs and danger spots can guide you into safe working practices and get you out of a tight fix. I was making a documentary for the BBC in Palestine some years ago about human rights abuses being committed by the Palestinian Authority (PA). We'd stopped to film a grave-yard in Gaza, the burial place of a victim of the PA. We were accompanied by the relatives of this individual who'd agreed to let us film his grave – but suddenly found ourselves surrounded by a large group of angry men, very unhappy about our presence in the cemetery. The situation became extremely tense. The local journalist working with us knew the area and the people well. He told me they felt we were disrespecting their dead and they weren't going to let us leave until we'd been hauled in-front of the head man in the village. My fixer told us to keep calm, forget the tight filming schedule, and go and speak to this man – otherwise things could get violent. On our own we might have tried to persuade the men to let us carry on filming. But our fixer was adamant: we had to speak to the boss. So we went to see him at his home. The fixer explained what we were doing there, reassured him that, far from wanting to disrespect anyone alive or dead, we wanted to respect the opinions of people who felt aggrieved by the actions of the PA. We drank tea and, after an hour and a half, the tension evaporated. He said: 'Go ahead and film the cemetery, you have my blessing'. So I had my Palestinian fixer to thank for getting us out of that hole. The lesson here is: do not attempt to cut costs by trying to research or film on your own in areas where there is conflict, terrorism, public disorder, crime or kidnapping threats or areas in which political sensitivities are raw, especially if you're abroad. A local fixer can be a life-saver when the unexpected happens.

Completing this section of the RA. Once you've understood the risks from your research, from conversations with the fixer etc., you draft out a plan for conducting your trip safely and add the information into the form. This can range from avoiding certain areas of a city after dark to providing protective equipment: anything from flak jackets and helmets to armoured vehicles depending on the situation.

It is not possible to offer general rules about the steps you need to take – but it is vital that you understand the need to take these risks seriously, research them thoroughly and be prepared to argue for extra resources if you feel they really are needed to keep your team safe. And if you can't get those resources, then abandon the trip: no story is worth dying for.

7. Working in Areas of Cultural or Religious Sensitivity

Some religious communities resent the presence of outsiders, especially film crews. One investigative documentary I made for Channel 4 TV was partly filmed in Stamford Hill, an area of London where many members of the Strictly Orthodox Jewish community live. We didn't want to be insensitive to religious traditions and so avoided filming on Holy Days, like the Sabbath, and other religious festivals. So when working in countries or with groups that have particular cultural and religious sensitivities, you must

research these and add restrictions onto your risk assessment that you feel will help reduce the chance of arguments or worse on the ground.

8. Climate (Heat/Cold/Desert Working, etc.)

You have to keep your crew – and contributors – safe and comfortable in environmental extremes. If you're travelling to an arid region you must consider how to protect against dehydration and sunstroke. So you might need to supply protective clothing, hats, water bottles, re-hydration salts, etc. You'll also need a code of conduct when visiting a very extreme environment: how long it's safe to stay outside in the arctic, for example, how much water must be drunk each hour in the Sahara desert. To complete this section of the form,

speak to others who have visited the region before and take their advice on the kind of kit you need to provide.[3]

9. Travel (i.e. Cars, Vans, Planes and Helicopters, Boats and Using Vehicles Off Road or in Hostile Environments)

The potential harm involved in hiring or using any vehicle is now a part of the risk assessment process. The aim is to minimize the risk of injury, to ensure the validity of any insurance cover you might have taken out to protect yourselves, and ultimately to prevent civil court actions against you or your production company for negligence should anything go wrong. So you need to be sure that any vehicle you use is in a serviceable condition and covered by insurance. This won't be a problem if you are hiring from a reputable company

like Hertz, Europcar or Avis – or local affiliates. You still need to read the small print to make sure passengers are in fact covered by the insurance, and to see exactly what your excess costs will be if the vehicle gets damaged. But what about hiring your fixer and his/her car? Is it roadworthy? Does the insurance cover accidents to passengers? Does the fixer have a current driving licence? Does the vehicle have seat belts? You must ask for, and check, relevant documents and note

> It's sometimes hard to think of all the hazards in an environment we are unaware of. But if you go online a quick bit of research will flag up that there's lots of other stuff that you wouldn't necessarily think about. If you can think about it a couple of days before your shoot, it gives you more time to rectify any health and safety issues you might not have realized about. Give it sufficient time so that you're not scrapping around at the very last minute and possibly jeopardising your shoot.
>
> Lareine Shea, Production Manager

down on the risk assessment what you've done. This ensures that your crew – and contributors – are being carried in safe vehicles, by someone who can drive and that they are covered by insurance in case of an accident.

Add warnings to the risk assessment that might seem obvious to you: no driving under the influence of drink or drugs; only using a hands-free mobile phone when at the wheel; what to do in the event of an accident. These instructions cover you (and your company) in the event of an accident. If your driver crashes while holding a mobile, it's likely to invalidate any insurance cover you've taken out – and if passengers are hurt, without this kind of explicit warning, it might also open you to a civil court action for damages.

The same principles apply to hiring, or being offered the use of, helicopters, private planes, small boats, etc. You need to obtain copies of documents that demonstrate the condition of the vehicle and the competence of the pilot/captain. You might also need to take out separate insurance cover to protect those who are being carried in this way.

10. *Secret Filming*

Risk assessment is inevitably a major part of planning an undercover shoot. But covert filming raises significantly different harm issues, so your assessment is completed on a separate undercover filming permission form. Simply state here that a separate risk assessment exists. The risks of secret filming are covered in Chapter 10.

11. *Weapons (For Example, Used in Reconstructions)*

You can only be certain that a real weapon is unloaded or loaded with blanks if someone trained in their use provides the weapon and tells you so. And having such an individual on a shoot is costly. Instead find a replica that cannot be fired (and dub on the firing effects in post-production). Your risk assessment details where you got the replica and how you can be certain it is a replica rather than a weapon that's been disabled. I have done effective reconstructions using replica guns bought from toy shops. Unless you're planning detailed close-ups these will usually work well.

12. Special Filming Equipment

If you are working on a well-budgeted show, you might want to use more specialized kinds of filming kit – anything from a camera car mount, to a dolly and track, a camera harness, or a camera crane. Some of this equipment needs trained personnel to operate it – and all will have guidelines on safe use. These must be detailed here. Drones are a cheap way of getting lovely aerial shots – but they also have to be used responsibly – and your risk assessment must demonstrate compliance with the regulations governing their use. See pages 42–43 in Chapter 3 for more information about drones.

13. Lighting and Camera Equipment

There are issues to consider when using professional kit. Many years ago, I went to film one of the people who helped develop the Bell X1 – the first plane to fly faster than sound. We began filming an interview. Suddenly there was a loud bang, the lights went dark and a shower of hot glass flew across the room, burning holes in a lovely carpet. A bulb in one of the lights used by our camera operator had blown – and we were lucky that no-one was injured. Our lighting kit had been checked prior to filming, and the bulbs were meant to be immune from such dangerous behaviour,

so our insurance replaced the interviewee's carpet. This is unlikely to happen today as most lighting kit uses LED light bulbs that don't get as hot as their incandescent cousins.

But using lighting equipment does raise other risks that need to be minimized: for example, cables run across a floor should be taped down (or placed under cable trunking) so that people cannot trip over them; and lighting stands used outside should be weighed down with sandbags to prevent them blowing over in the wind. You also have to guard against certain harms when using camera equipment: a camera operator working hand-held and walking backwards to follow a contributor, needs someone walking behind them to prevent a fall. Safety precautions need to be detailed if there are trip hazards, or if the filming is taking place near to dangerous machinery or a busy road. Your camera-person must also be given regular breaks when working hand-held – as this can be very tiring.

Your risk assessment must indicate how you will protect camera equipment from the elements. It must remind the crew to check that the kit is in working order before the shoot day; and to review all rushes on a monitor after the day's filming to check for any technical problems. You make all this explicit to comply with your insurance cover. If there is a technical fault in the camera, for example, and you shoot several days of rushes before noticing that every file is unusable, your production insurance is likely to only pay for one day's re-shoot. They'll argue that you have behaved irresponsibly in not minimizing likely risks – saying that you should have picked this up at the end of the first day's filming. But it might not be an insurance company asking difficult questions. It could be a barrister in a court of law if something really serious happens. So take these risks seriously.

14. Dangerous or Derelict Buildings

These are high-risk areas for obvious reasons: rotten floors, dangerous ceilings, sharp debris, staircases that lack railings, unfenced roofs and so on. You need to take extra care and record your preparations in this section. It might be as simple as ensuring that your team wear strong shoes. But if you need to film from an unfenced floor on a derelict building, you might need to hire a harness for your camera operator, tying it to a nearby structure to prevent a fall.

15. Fire Safety

If you are filming inside a building, you need a basic fire safety procedure just in case the worst happens during the shoot. Your RA should appoint one member of the team – usually the director – to be responsible for determining the evacuation route, ensuring the crew exits the building rapidly in the event of a fire and checking that everyone has got out safely.

16. Working Alone

You must be aware of the potential dangers of working alone in areas where crime or violence is rife. Some districts can be relatively safe during the day but become very risky at night. You need to research these dangers, using local knowledge, and then implement a safety code. It might mean ensuring that team members never work alone, or that a female researcher is accompanied by a male when visiting a potential interviewee at night in a rough district. In some areas, you might also need a contact protocol, so that someone back at

base is called before the team visit the area, told how long they are likely to be there, and then phoned again once they have left. You must, of course, also have a list of the people being visited, their addresses and phone numbers.

17. Individuals with Special Needs

If you're working with an elderly person or someone with physical disabilities, they might tire easily and need regular rests. If they are in a wheelchair and there's no easy access to the building in which you wish to film, they might need to be carried in. But you'll need to be certain you can do this safely. A contributor might suffer from an illness that requires specific medical

attention while with you. These are the kind of risks you need to detail here – with an assessment of how you plan to minimize them.

18. *Filming Children*

The rules that govern how filmmakers work with children differ in America and Britain – and risk assessments should detail the way in which the production intends to comply with such regulations.

FILMING CHILDREN IN THE UK

Ofcom, the communications regulator, oversees the participation and portrayal of children and young people in programmes made for broadcast.[4] Its rules state that, irrespective of any consent obtained by a parent or guardian:

> *Due care must be taken over the physical and emotional welfare and the dignity of people under eighteen who take part or are otherwise involved in programmes.*
>
> *People under eighteen must not be caused unnecessary distress or anxiety by their involvement in programmes or by the broadcast of those programmes.*[5]

So if you are thinking of including someone under 18 in a film made for broadcast in the UK, read the relevant sections of the Ofcom broadcasting code and the guidance notes on these sections[6] first. The rules are very detailed and the advice I offer here is only a broad summary. Your risk assessment needs to demonstrate how you intend to comply with these two rules at all stages of production and after the programme has been shown. Ask yourself the following questions:

Is it appropriate for a child to contribute to my film? Ofcom says that each case of a child taking part in a programme must be judged on its own – taking into account the nature of the programme and a child's 'age, maturity and capacity to make judgments' about the consequences of taking part. Because the regulator places the welfare of the child above their participation in any programme – you might need to ask a medical or psychological expert about the impact of speaking about intimate matters. A survivor of the Islamist bombing of the Ariana Grande concert in Manchester, for example, could be re-traumatized by talking about what happened to them. Or it might prove to be a positive, cathartic experience. You will not in a position to judge this and the advice you have taken to understand the likely impact of your plans needs to be detailed on your risk assessment. There might be situations in which you decide not to film a child even if they and their parents are giving the green light to their participation.

What permission do I need to film the child? You need to obtain formal informed consent for a child or young person to participate in your film. What that means depends on the age and maturity of the person – and the nature of their contribution. I explore this in more detail in my explanation of release forms on pages 171–172 in Chapter 9.

What impact will the experience of taking part in the filming have on the child? Your risk assessment needs to demonstrate that you are placing the child's welfare above the requirements of your film schedule. So you have to consider whether the process of the filming could have an adverse impact on the child. Filming can be a little intimidating to those not used to it – so having both a single point of contact on the team for the child and a close friend or family member who can accompany them to the shoot can be helpful.

Have I considered what is likely to happen after the film is shown?   The broadcast of a film dealing with sensitive personal issues might, for example, provoke a social media storm that could have consequences for the contributor: they might be bullied. Your risk assessment should detail the preparations you've made to anticipate this.

FILMING CHILDREN IN AMERICA

There is no Ofcom-type regulator in the US and so no official guidelines telling filmmakers how to behave when filming children – which makes filming young people in public spaces much easier than in the UK. In a public place someone who is under 18 years old can, legally speaking, be treated in much the same way as an adult: no permission is strictly required so long as they are portrayed accurately. But if you pre-arrange filming with a younger child, it is good practice never to do so alone, to have a parent or guardian present. You shouldn't have any physical contact with the child, or film during school hours, and one member of your team must be responsible for ensuring that all these rules are adhered to. If you are filming more than a one-off interview with a child, you should also make sure you are complying with federal and state child labour laws. US TV networks sometimes impose their own regulations that filmmakers have to follow if they are using children – for example, some insist on signed consent forms co-signed by a parent.

Filming Children: the Lawyers' View

Britain

In many countries nowadays there is, understandably, a sense that some filmmakers in the past have perhaps played fast and loose with the duty of care required towards contributors. The duty of care owed to an adult contributor is one thing. But the duty of care owed towards a vulnerable contributor, particularly a child, is absolutely imperative in terms of the potential repercussions for them in future years of having participated in your film. Your responsibility is to ensure that you have obtained their informed consent. It essence the contributor must fully understand the nature of the film, their intended contribution and in the case of vulnerable contributors that they are able to give their informed consent. It is a matter of good practice that you would obtain parental consent as well as the child's consent, being mindful that there are parents out there who have a vested interest in their children contributing to films which may not be in the best interests of their children. You also need to be alive to the fact that certain children can be older than they appear, so they can be quite articulate, and others who are older, can actually be more vulnerable. Understanding the complexities of dealing with children and how you film them, I think is essential.

Prash Naik, UK Media Lawyer and Channel 4 TV General Counsel 2014–2017

America

From a practical point of view, it is always good to get parents to sign a consent form, and some networks require it. But from a strictly legal point of view, there are not as many problems as most people think. If you're filming a group of kids playing a basketball game in a public place, the rules are pretty much the same as filming adults: there's nothing that says you have to go get their permission or their parents' permission to use that in a documentary programme. Of course, it's always going to be subject to legal review. They have to be portrayed accurately. You can't say: 'these drug using gangster children are hanging out at the park'. You still can't defame them. And you wouldn't want to knock on somebody's door and say to a minor whose parents aren't home: 'Hey. Can we come in and film you?' This would cause all kinds of problems. For one, a minor does not have legal capacity to give you consent to enter the home and film. So, you have to pass all the other legal tests but there's no sort of special legal requirement that when filming in public, just because they are minors, you must have them or their parents sign a written release form.

Where you have pre-arranged filming with children you need to be aware of state labor laws, especially if the filming is continuous over a period of time and/or the child is being taken out of school. And protocol should be put in place where no member of your crew is ever alone with any minor, and, preferably, a parent or guardian is always present.

Mike Cleaver, US Media Attorney

19. Long Hours

To keep budgets in the black, producers inevitably want to make the most cost effective use of filming time. There's always too few hours in the day to complete what needs to be done and there's often a temptation to squeeze a crew to do as much as possible when scheduling a shoot. But you have to realize there's a point at which the need to keep costs down crosses over into unsafe practice. That happens when you push people so much that they are too tired to make effective judgments. When scheduling your shoot you must consider whether the next day's plans are really practical or whether you are, at best, compromising creativity – at worst risking people's safety – by asking them to do too much. It might be cost effective to drive four hours to the next location after a 12 hour shooting day, but it's certainly not going to be safe. It's also not going to generate much goodwill if you work your crew to the bone. Camera operators, like the rest of us, are much more creative after a good meal and a decent night's kip.

20. Working at Height

Filming from the top of a tall crane, on a cliff or on the roof of a skyscraper each pose different safety issues. How do you ensure that your camera operator can climb to the top of that crane without dropping her kit or, worse still, falling off while trying to take a shot? Can you be sure that the path you've decided to take up to the top of the cliff with a fantastic view, really is safe? Perhaps you need special climbing equipment? And how safe is that skyscraper roof when the wind is blowing hard? You'll need expert advice on these issues  that's detailed in this part of the risk assessment. You might also need special insurance cover to film at any of these risky locations.

21. Security of Filming Kit and Other Equipment

Most car insurance cover will only pay up for items stolen from a vehicle if they are kept locked and out of sight. Your team might not be aware of this limitation – and flagging it up on your risk assessment is a good precaution. If you are filming on the streets, it's very easy for kit to vanish – stolen or forgotten when attention is focused on the shoot rather than on the equipment left on the ground. So add a warning that someone must always be responsible for looking after the kit while filming takes place. Your insurance com-  pany is likely to want to see evidence of the precautions you've taken to avoid loss before paying out if there's a theft.

22. Heavy Loads

Professional camera, lighting and sound recording kit packed into protective cases can be very heavy. A film crew that works well together is usually one in which specific roles and responsibilities are forgotten when it comes to clearing up at the end of a shoot. But you don't want any obligation to creep into end-of-shoot activities, particularly if someone suffers, or has in the past suffered, from back pain. Publicly excusing anyone who has a history of back problems from lifting heavy kit will avoid this likelihood. You can go further, and  offer advice to help avoid the possibility of future back problems: keeping a straight back while holding the load close to the body and using leg muscles to achieve lift, for example.

23. Other Risks

Filming can involve a range of other risks – working with animals, diving, stunts, aerobatics and a lot of other dangerous activities. Here you can detail anything else you consider to be relevant and list the actions taken to minimize any likely harm.

Sign off Section

Finally there's the sign off section. The filming can't go ahead until this form has been signed by those with responsibility for the production – usually the producer and executive producer. If you're working on your own, then it's down to you. In signing, you and they are agreeing that they've read the form and acknowledge that it has addressed the risks of the shoot as far as possible. So this is not a mere formality. You really do need to be happy that risks have been minimized.

In summary: don't take this form lightly. If anything should go wrong on your research trip or shoot, it provides the basis of your evidence that the risks were handled responsibly.

Notes

1 Try googling the risk to see what is already online about it. There's helpful information about risk assessment in the film industry here: www.hse.gov.uk/entertainment/theatre-tv/film.htm

2 UK: www.gov.uk/foreign-travel-advice
   US: https://travel.state.gov/content/travel/en/international-travel.html

3 There's also helpful information here: www.hse.gov.uk/temperature/outdoor.htm

4 At the time of writing, Ofcom doesn't have the power to regulate online content, although creators of such content do have to comply with legislation that protects children who might appear in a programme, or who might be involved in family court legal proceedings. However, in 2020 the UK Government announced plans to extend Ofcom's remit to cover social media sites - to ensure that illegal material (mainly terrorism and child abuse) and content that companies themselves deem to be harmful (self-harm for example) is quickly removed.

5 www.ofcom.org.uk/__data/assets/pdf_file/0017/24704/section1.pdf – rules 1.28 and 1.29 on pages 12–13.

6 www.ofcom.org.uk/__data/assets/pdf_file/0016/132073/Broadcast-Code-Full.pdf – sections 1.28; 1.29; 7.4; 7.5; 8.20 to 8.22.
   www.ofcom.org.uk/__data/assets/pdf_file/0017/24704/section1.pdf – pages 11 to 19.

9   Planning a Production

How to Organize Yourself Before, During and After a Film Shoot

KEY CONCEPTS

- How to prepare an effective call sheet.
- How to keep track of your rushes.
- An explanation of release forms and their importance.
- How to organize translations and transcripts on a fast-turn-around film.
- An overview of the time-critical tasks prior to post-production.

Factual filmmaking is driven forwards by creative inspiration – but however much flair you have, imagination must be underpinned by rigorous organization or you'll end up flailing around, overwhelmed by irreconcilable demands on your scarce time and resources. Creativity is just a part of the struggle to bring home a successful film. A systematic approach towards the logistics of your production allows you to create a space in which your vision can be executed. You have to prepare yourself for the task of filming with great foresight; be meticulously organized during the shoot and have had the foresight to make time-sensitive and methodical preparations for your edit and for post-production. If you fail to do this, your filming and editing will over-run and the stress of this happening will prevent you from being able to craft a strong programme. In this chapter I am going to offer some practical suggestions to help the process run like clockwork. For those of you working on a well-budgeted film, with a production manager on board, he or she will be responsible for some of the practicalities outlined in this chapter. But a producer *must* understand the processes and keep a watching brief over them. There are key times – particularly during your edit – when certain tasks have to be completed to ensure the production runs smoothly and your production manager won't necessarily be at your side reminding you what to do. Producers on low budgets or self-funding their films will be managing all these organizational issues themselves – and a project that runs effortlessly is absolutely vital where there is a lack of cash.

Preparing For Your Shoot: The Call Sheet

It is always a struggle to prevent a film schedule from over-running – because there are many variables beyond your control that can knock the best laid plans off course. You might arrive at an interview location only to find that several workers have turned up unexpectedly to repair the road – and the sound of their drill makes filming impossible for an hour. Or your interviewee has forgotten to tell you that they live underneath an airport flight path and the filming has to be done slowly, once the noise of each aircraft has subsided. Or a torrential downpour forces you to abandon those beautiful sunset shots you'd planned. You can't prevent every problem, but you can place yourself in the best possible position by ensuring that the details that are within your control are *really* practical when working out a day-by-day schedule

The Call Sheet

It's the one document that pulls everybody together. And it's good to have an overview of what everyone's doing. So it's your kit. It's your travel. Who's doing what. Who's responsible for what. You've got to be safe on a shoot. You don't want anyone to have an accident. I think it's proven that after 14 hours in a day people start to make stupid mistakes that nobody wants to have on their conscience, an accident that could have been avoided. And insurers like to see a call sheet, occasionally they will spot check them to see if anything high risk [is] on there that the insurance isn't covering.

Lareine Shea, Head of Production

for the filming. That means preparing a daily schedule – known as a call sheet – containing all the information needed by your crew to keep them in the right place, at the right time with the right kit and not so tired they can't perform effectively. If you over-run your planned schedule, costs can rack up quite quickly, especially if you are working with a camera-operator who charges overtime by the hour.

The golden rule to remember is this: **Filming invariably takes longer than you think it will – so bear that in mind when planning your schedule.**

Take a close look at the call sheet in Figure 9.1. This is a fictitious shoot but will show you the level of detail needed to make things run smoothly. Many of the entries are obvious and need no introduction – but I have annotated some with helpful comments to explain their rationale.

There is an online interactive version of this form containing my comments on the website, where you can also download a clean call sheet for your own project.

	CALL SHEET				
1	DATE:			CALL SHEET NO:	
2	WORKING TITLE:				
3	PLEASE DO NOT LEAVE CALL SHEET WHERE IT CAN BE READ BY ANYONE OTHER THAN MEMBERS OF CREW				
4	CREW CONTACTS ON LOCATION				
5	**NAME**	**JOB TITLE**	**E MAIL**		**PHONE**
6		Producer/Director			
7		Reporter			
8		Camera Operator			
9		AP/Researcher			
10	CREW CONTACTS BACK AT BASE				
11		Production Manager			
12		Executive Producer			
13	LOCATIONS IN FILMING ORDER				
14	**AREA**	**CONTRIBUTOR**	**PHONE**	**ADDRESS**	**DIRECTIONS**
15	Finchley	John Haskins	(H) 020-3000-3000 (M) 07777-800000	79 Ableton Road, North Finchley, N12 2ZA	See Map 1
16	Primrose Hill	Julia Johnson	(H) 020-7000-8000 (M) 07999-600000	Meeting at Primrose Hill – NW1 4NR entrance at end of Elsworthy Terrace.	See Map 2
17					
18	INSURANCE – CONTACT PRODUCTION BEFORE SPEAKING TO INSURER				
19	**NAME**	**POLICY NUMBER**		**EMERGENCY CONTACT NUMBER**	
20	Hiscox	SB245-HR-762		020-7140-6332	

Figure 9.1 An example of a call sheet

21	SCHEDULE		
22	**TIME**	**ACTION**	**NOTES**
23	0730	**Hire car picked up by producer**	Avis, 145 Battersea Park Road, London, SW8 4BX Tel: 0344-544-7033
24	0730	**Camera operator packs crew vehicle and travels to first location.**	See Map 1
25	0800	**Producer travels to first location in hire car**	Address: 79 Ableton Road, North Finchley, N12 2ZA
26	0830	**Arrive at interviewee's house**	Parking: Plenty of room to park in driveway at house.
27	0845	**Unpack gear and set up for interview**	
28	0915	**Film interview**	
29	1015	**Move camera, set–up lights**	
30	1045	**Film interior images with interviewee working at desk**	
31	1130	**Move camera into garden**	
32	1145	**Film exterior images with interviewee (in garden)**	
33	1230	Travel to Lunch	Location: Park Café, Southside, Primrose Hill.
34	1245	**Lunch**	Table booked for 1245
35	1345	**Crew travel to Primrose Hill**	See Map 2 Parking: pay and display only in Elsworthy Road. £2.40/hour. 4 hours maximum. Free after 6-30pm. Permission to film given by Royal Parks PRO Julian Barnes Phone: 020-3380-1522
36	1415	**Julia Johnson being picked up by taxi**	Taxi booked by Production Manager. Taxi Cab contact: Vision Express 020-7742-7777
37	1445	**Crew and Julia Johnson arrive at Primrose Hill**	Meeting at entrance to Primrose Hill at end of Elsworthy Terrace
38	1500	**Set up for interview on bench with view of London**	
39	1515	**Film exterior interview**	

Figure 9.1 Continued

40	1615	**Film establishing images with interviewee and park images**	
41	1715	**Move to cityscape view at top of Primrose Hill**	
42	1745	**Film London cityscape**	
43	1815	**Pack gear**	
44	1830	**Location wrap**	
45	1930	**Camera wrap**	

46	**MEALS, PARKING, PETROL** **Please keep all receipts and submit expenses for food.** Maximum lunch allowance is £15 per person to include all soft drinks, tea, coffee, etc. during the day. Parking and petrol to be claimed via receipt. Any parking, or speeding fines are the responsibility of the driver and will not be paid by Production
47	**BACK-UP DRIVES** Each day's rushes must be backed up onto two hard drives. Producer to leave drives at post-production house for ingesting at end of shoot. 2 x 2TB hard drives supplied by production company. Return these to post-production suite at end of shoot.
48	**CAMERA, SOUND AND LIGHTING KIT** Supplied by ………… [Name of Camera operator if self-owned or Company if hired in, plus address, phone] For hired in kit: Delivering to ……………………………………………..……… Time: Picking up from ……….………………………………....…… Time: Full kit list will include: • 1 x C300 with tripod, batteries, rain hood etc. • 1 x 16-35mm lens • 1 x 24–70mm lens • Basic sound kit including top mic, 1 radio mic with back up in case of failure, spare batteries • 2 x 1x1 LED light panels • 2 re-usable 32Gb flash cards supplied with camera kit.
49	**LOCATION AND CONTRIBUTOR RELEASE FORMS** Supplied by production manager. Please ensure all releases are signed and dated, along with a brief description of the location or the individual filmed, noted on release form.
50	**HEALTH AND SAFETY** **Risk Assessment – To be sent to all by the morning before the shoot. This must be read by each member of the crew.**
51	**MAPS/DIRECTIONS** **Map of location 1** **Map of location 2**

Key
Line numbers in the explanations that follow refer to the numbers in the left-hand column.

Figure 9.1 Continued

Line 1　*Date, call sheet number* – Each day on a shoot should have a different call sheet, hence the date at the top to avoid mistakes. Each person on the shoot should get a copy before they leave for the location. And key individuals back at base also get one – the executive producer, for example. If you are working with a production manager, they prepare this. If not, it's the producer's job.

Line 2　*Working title* – The title of your film is likely to be a 'working title' at this stage – the final film title will be agreed with your commissioner much further down the line. On a sensitive investigation, you might disguise the film title with something anodyne, to minimize the possibility of anyone outside the crew and contributors finding out what you are doing.

Line 3　*Please do not leave call sheet where it can be read by anyone other than members of crew* – This warning note will not be necessary on most films, but information security is important, for example, where a contributor will only agree to appear in silhouette and you clearly don't want to risk anyone outside the production team discovering their identity. On such films you might decide only to add an address, and omit the name of the contributor from the call sheet.

Lines 4–12　*Crew contacts on location* – These contacts ensure everyone on the shoot and back at your base can rapidly contact each other.

Lines 13–17　*Locations in filming order* – List these in the order in which you'll be visiting them so that, at a glance, your crew knows where they will be travelling.

Lines 18–20　*Insurance – contact production before speaking to insurer* – Your team needs to know who to contact in an emergency, especially if working abroad and in need of urgent repatriation. If you are working with a production manager, it's best to speak to them before contacting the insurance company.

Line 23　*Start of the day* – On this shoot the filming day begins at 7:30am when your producer picks up a hire car. Thirty minutes has been permitted for that task – to allow for a wait, the paperwork, and for the car to be driven round to the customer. If you don't anticipate the likely real time it will take to do a task, you'll start the day behind schedule.

Lines 24–25　*Travel time* – Realistic travel times that allow for rush hour traffic, are vital in a film schedule otherwise you'll arrive late and knock the rest of your schedule out of line. The number of hours in a filming day becomes a critical costing issue if you are working with a camera operator and/or sound recordist. Their fee covers a working day of either 10 or 12 hours in length, agreed in advance, and timed from the moment they start work (by packing gear into their vehicle) to the time they arrive back at their base with the gear unpacked. If you exceed the agreed length, you'll be charged overtime at an hourly rate. So the call sheet must include travel times for your camera operator (and sound recordist) at both ends of the day – allowing you to plan a schedule the keeps within your filming budget.

Line 26　*Politeness time* – You have to allow some time to say hello, possibly even drink a cup of tea or coffee with your interviewees. If you simply barge in and set up the camera kit without such niceties, you're going to have a jumpy, nervous contributor once you start filming. So allow a little time for chit chat to keep the schedule on track. Also here are parking instructions because you don't want your team to waste time looking for a place to park and, if they have to pay for it, find that they don't have any change for the meters.

Line 27　*Set-up time* – It takes time to bring in the kit, unpack the camera and lights and get everything ready to shoot. How long you allow depends on the situation and on how perfectionist you want to be about the image and the lighting. So consult with your camera operator if you're working with one, to estimate how long you'll need to allow. If not, take some advice from a more experienced producer.

Line 28 *Film interview* – The time needed for any interview will of course vary with the number of questions and the content of what's being discussed. So make sure your allowance is realistic.

Line 29 *Move camera, set-up lights* – It also takes time to wrap your interview set – and then move to another room and set up lights and camera ready to film some establishing images of your interviewee. Allow for this in your schedule.

Line 30 *Timing a sequence* – How long will it take you to film a picture sequence with your interviewee? It is easy to underestimate the time needed. If you are working with a professional camera operator, it's worth describing what you want to achieve, to find out how long to allow. If not, ask someone who has done a lot of filming.

Line 33 *Travel to lunch* – If you are planning a lunch break at a local café, find out how long it takes to get there from your filming location and add this to the schedule.

Line 34 *Lunch timing* – If you are self-shooting, you can decide when to have a break, when to eat and when to stop filming. But if you are working with a camera person, you have to plan for lunch. The financial and time pressures on a producer are severe and can make you want to skimp on lunch. But a camera operator doesn't work well on an empty stomach and it's no good saying: 'Sorry, we've overrun our schedule and you'll have to forget about lunch'. That's going to sour your professional relationship – and creativity suffers when there's discord on location. Or empty stomachs. So make sure you have planned a lunch break: it could be sandwiches from a nearby take-away if time is really pressed – or a sit-down lunch at a café but book a table in advance, as you don't want the crew to be standing around using up precious schedule time waiting to get a meal.

Line 35 *Directions, parking, permission to film* – Exterior locations like parks, train stations, shopping arcades require formal filming permissions to be in place before you arrive. Your crew needs to know the details so that they can respond to any queries. That might simply be the phone number of the authorizing person – but it often means giving the crew a more formal written permission obtained from the relevant authority. If you are parking a vehicle, add information about the nearest location and the costs, if any.

Lines 36–37 *Transport contacts for guests and meeting location* – When your crew moves to a new location, they'll most likely be driving in a vehicle equipped with a sat nav. They'll need the address of the location, of course, as indicated in line 16 in this schedule. But add driving directions and a map as a back-up. If interviewees are travelling separately to a location by cab, as in this fictitious example, then add the phone number of the taxi firm to the sheet so that you can quickly track them down if they don't appear when they should. If they are driving to the location, tell them where they can park, with directions if necessary. If they are coming by public transport, add the details of their trip, the bus number, the train arrival time, etc., onto the sheet. Don't forget to add a reminder of the meeting location.

Line 43 *Pack gear* – These 15 minutes allow the crew to walk back to their vehicle and pack up the filming kit before leaving.

Line 44 *Location wrap* – This is the time at which you leave your last filming location.

Line 45 *Camera wrap* – The time at which your camera operator has arrived home and unpacked his/her kit. That's when their working day ends. If you are working with a sound recordist you'd also add a sound wrap time onto the schedule.

Lines 46 *Meals, parking, petrol* – To keep on budget, the crew needs to know how much they can spend on food and drink. You can either give them a daily cash allowance – or set a maximum limit and insist on receipts to claim back what they've spent. Petrol and parking costs will also normally be refunded via receipts. This line should also include a disclaimer about speeding and parking fines.

Lines 47   *Back-up drives* – In this example, two re-usable 32Gb flash cards are supplied with the kit (listed in the next section) and, at the end of each day's filming, all the rushes have to be copied onto two hard drives – a master copy and a safety – freeing up the flash cards for the next day's shoot. This saves having to buy (or rent) enough flash cards for your entire shoot. Some companies insist you keep the day's rushes on the flash cards after downloading onto a hard drive. Either way, you'd indicate this here.

Lines 48   *Camera, sound and lighting kit* – List the kit that's being supplied and where it is coming from. If it belongs to your camera operator, he or she will bring it to the shoot. But if you are hiring in, you'll need to indicate the supplier, plus how, where and when it is being delivered to the shoot – and what happens at the end of the day.

Lines 49   *Location and contributor release forms* – Broadcasters and online platforms require you to obtain 'release forms' for each location in which you film – and each contributor that you interview. You or your production manager must ensure there are enough pro-forma releases on location for this purpose. Release forms are explained in more detail later on in this chapter.

Lines 50   *Health and safety* – A reminder that the risk assessment for this shoot will be sent round the evening before filming begins and must be read by all. Risk assessments are discussed in detail in Chapter 8.

Line 51   *Maps/directions* – Sat navs avoid the need for detailed driving instructions – but it's worth attaching a map of the locations to your schedule, just in case the crew has trouble finding it.

During The Shoot: Organization on Location

Shot-Lists: Keeping Track of the Contents of Your Rushes

Unless you are cutting the film yourself on your own computer, editing is costly – more than £2,000 a week if you're using an editor and working in a facilities house. So you really can't afford to waste precious time searching for that magic panoramic shot of London or Los Angeles. Neither should you be struggling to find that incriminating clip of the Justice Minister that occurred somewhere in the middle of a two hour interview. You avoid this by creating a log of the contents of the files recorded by the camera.

To do that you need to understand how the camera identifies each file – and the location of any image on each file. When you start filming, the camera records a file that is given a number. When you stop the camera, that file is complete and the next time you begin filming, a second file is created with a sequential number – and so on.

During the recording of any file, the camera lays down a time code track – which is vital for accurate editing. This track records hours, minutes, seconds and frames. There are 25 frames to the second in the European standard PAL recording system – 30 in the US NTSC system. So the time code track is accurate to 1/25th second for Pal and 1/30th for NTSC. Normally you won't see this time code, but you can opt to see it during the shoot.

> No-one ever has enough time in the edit, so why waste some of that precious time by having your editor looking for things that you could help him with in the first place. You need to be keeping at least what I would call a sequence list of what you are doing. Note down on your list any problems: [for example] that the lady in your shot doesn't want to appear on film so please make sure you crop her out. You might think at the time that you'll remember it, but you never ever will.
>
> Lareine Shea, Production Manager

With this information, you can log your rushes. How you do this depends on whether you are filming interviews or images.

Image Shot-Listing

On a factual shoot, there's normally no need to log each shot you film. That would be too time consuming. What you do need is to log each *sequence* of shots into your shot-list. For example, if you're filming establishing images of our fictitious Primrose Hill interviewee Julia Johnson walking across the park and sitting down on a bench, your shot-list for this sequence would look much like Figure 9.2 – however many shots of this sequence you take. In this case, the sequence covers 16 different shots.

Date	File no	Description
20/1/19	0001 to 0016	Julia Johnson walking on Primrose Hill.

Figure 9.2

But if you then walk to neighbouring Regents Park to film her throwing bread to some ducks on the lake, a different sequence of images, you'd add a new line, as in Figure 9.3.

Date	File no	Description
20/1/19	0001 to 0016	Julia Johnson walking on Primrose Hill.
	0017 to 0022	Julia feeding ducks in Regents' Park.

Figure 9.3

So long as your film editor knows which files the images are on, he/she can retrieve them efficiently.

Interview Shot-Listing

During a long interview, unless you stop the camera between each question (not very prac-tical as it will interrupt the flow of thought), the entire interview will be covered on one file. To find clips from the interview easily, you need the number of the file on which the interview is recorded, of course. But you also need to log the time code recorded by the camera for each question. Two kinds of time code can be recorded – the camera allows you to choose which one to use:

Record run TC. The time code laid down into the files you shoot continually mounts upwards. So when one file ends, the time code in the next file will begin one frame after the last file. To dis-cover the time code for each question means looking at the camera display or asking your oper-ator for the read out. This simply isn't practical when filming an interview without disturbing the camera operator. There are two ways to avoid this problem. One of them costs money: you can hire what's called a digi slate – a portable time code reader that syncs up with the camera and displays the time code it's recording. But an easier, no-cost, alternative is to instruct the camera to record a different time code track.

Free run TC. The time code track laid down is the same as the time of day at which the images have been recorded. That of course means that the time code will jump upwards from file to file because if you stop filming for five minutes, the time of day will have advanced by the time you start filming again. So this time code is not continuous. The advantage of recording 'free run' time code is that, if you synchronize the time on your watch with the time showing on the camera at the beginning of your filming day, you only have to look at your watch to know what time code is being recorded. In other words, there's then no need to look at the camera viewfinder, or ask your camera operator.[1]

A free run TC track is handy during a long interview when you either don't have the time or the money to transcribe every answer once it's filmed.[2] By logging the time code at the start of each question into your shot-list you'll be able to find the good answers in a hurry, saving considerable time once you are back in the edit suite. If you are filming the interview yourself, or asking the questions, you'll have to ask someone else to do this job. So my developing fictitious shot-list would now look like Figure 9.4.

Date	File no	Time Code	Description
20/1/19	0001 to 0016		Julia Johnson walking on Primrose Hill.
	0017 to 0022		Julia feeding ducks in Regents' Park.
	0023	11-10-00	Julia Johnson interview start.
		11-10-15	Q: Tell me what happened to the $4 million that should have funded a new health centre in the town?
		11-12-30	Q: Describe your feelings when you discovered this.

Figure 9.4

By keeping a careful log of the files containing each of your picture sequences and the file number plus time code for each question during the interviews, you'll be able to retrieve your images and sound clips in an efficient and cost effective manner.

Release Forms

These are formal agreements signed by interviewees permitting their contribution to be edited and included in the programme, or by the owners of locations giving their permission for the filming to take place on their property. Broadcasters and online platforms insist on having these 'release forms' for the films they commission. Although this might seem overly bureaucratic, by formalizing the agreement to participate in the film or the filming, they help avoid misunderstandings later on and make it easier to obtain Errors and Omissions (E&O) insurance (see pages 236–237 in Chapter 11) to protect the producer against the cost of defending a legal action for defamation or breach of confidentiality/privacy once it's been screened. Without a release form for a contributor, an insurer might exclude that individual from the policy.

Contributor Release Form

Figure 9.5 shows an example of a UK contributor release followed by an explanation of some of the less obvious entries and terminology. There is an interactive version of this form that includes these explanatory comments on the website, together with a clean downloadable version. **If you're commissioned by a broadcaster or online platform check whether they need to agree the wording before using the release form. Some do. Releases for the American market might vary significantly from the example given here.**

	CONTRIBUTOR CONSENT FORM **(Agreement for use of contribution)**	
1	Production company	Address
2	Working programme title	Description of programme
3	Commissioning outlet	
4	Producer	
5	Contributor name	Description of contribution
6	Contributor address	Date of contribution
7	Telephone	
8	Dear	
9	Thank you for agreeing to contribute to the above programme. This form gives (*Name of Production Company*) the right to use the whole or part of your contribution in all media and markets throughout the world.	
10	• We very much hope to use your contributions, but we cannot guarantee to do so.	
11	• You assign to (*Name of Production Company*) the copyright and all other rights in your contributions for use in all media now known or which may be developed in future	
12	• You confirm that your contributions will not infringe the copyright, or similar rights, of any third party.	
13	• You agree that (*Name of Production Company*) may edit, adapt, or translate your contributions	
14	• You waive irrevocably any 'moral rights' you may have in your contributions.	
15	• (*Name of Production Company*) will be liable for any loss or damage to you, or your property, but only if it is directly connected with this engagement and caused by our negligence.	
16	• You agree that your contributions will not bring (*Name of Production Company*) into disrepute or be defamatory but you will not be liable in respect of defamatory material which is included without negligence or malice on your part.	
17	• The personal data you provide in this contract will only be used to fulfil our obligations under this contract in line with the Data Protection Act 2018. For further information, visit our privacy policy at _____[3]	
18	• This agreement shall be freely assignable by us and shall be interpreted in accordance with the laws of _____.	
	If you agree with the terms set out above, please sign the form below and return it. A copy is attached for you to keep. If you are unsure of the meaning of any of the conditions set out above, the production team will be able to explain them to you. Thank you once again for your assistance. I agree these terms Signed .... Date	

Figure 9.5 An example of a contributor release form

Line 2	Description of programme – America and British media lawyers have a different view on the amount of information to be given in the programme description. See text box on this and the next page.
Line 9	Tells the contributor that their interview might be shown on any media platform in any part of the world. This gives the company the right to sell the film.
Line 10	Makes it clear that in giving the interview, the contributor cannot assume that it will eventually be screened at all. It might not get in the final cut of the film.
Lines 11–12	The contributor agrees to give all the rights in their contribution to the production company. So the interviewee can't later on claim that the interview was in any way owned by them. And they agree that their contribution doesn't violate someone else's copyrighted material. For example, an interviewee who reads out someone's poem claiming it to be their own.
Line 13	Gives the production company full editorial control over the interviewee's contribution – the contributor can't later on request the right to have a veto over how they appear in the film.
Line 14	The contributor gives up their right to be recognized as the author of the contribution and therefore their right to object to its use in your programme.
Line 16	The contributor agrees that their contribution won't deliberately bring harm to the company.
Line 17	In the UK, individuals or companies that collect personal data have to use the information in a way that complies with the Data Protection Act 2018, a law that implements the EU General Data Protection Regulations. So a release form – which contains personal information – contains a statement indicating that this data will be handled in a manner that is compliant with this 2018 Act. It also tells a contributor where they can read the company's privacy policy outlining in detail how their information will in fact be handled. The precise wording of this statement (and the privacy policy itself) would need to be agreed with the lawyer advising your production to ensure full compliance with the 2018 Act. In the US, there is no single law regulating the collection and use of personal data. Instead a mixture of federal and state laws are involved. So filmmakers working with American citizens do not need a similar data protection statement in a release form – and the collection and processing of personal data during their work should not violate any US law so long as they comply with any company data protection policy and take reasonable care not to release personal data to unauthorized people.
Line 18	Permits the production company to give the rights and obligations of the agreement to a new owner – and states the country whose legislation governs the agreement.

Written Release Forms – The Lawyers' View

Britain

There are producers who feel that this is a complexity that only results in contributors being deterred from taking part in films; that it's often a legalese-type document which they find difficult themselves and contributors often struggle to understand the legal implications of signing. I think the reality is, that informing your contributor of the nature of the project that they are to participate in, is a matter of good practice that all filmmakers should do. Differences of opinion can arise, and having something in writing which sets out clearly why they are participating, the nature of the project, and the fact that they have consented is important to ensure that there is no misunderstanding later. And I think, having that evidenced in writing is essential, because it shows that actually you've entered into a relationship with your contributor – whether you want to call it a legal one or an ethical one – that it's important to have dotted all the 'I's and crossed all the 'T's. I also think it is important to have an agreed programme or film description which is a fair and accurate description of the film so there can be no dispute later as to the nature of the project that the individual or individuals have contributed to.

Prash Naik, UK Media Lawyer and Channel 4 TV General Counsel 2014–2017

America

It's always in your benefit to have a signed release form from everyone who's featured in your programme or film. It's going to make everything for you moving forward a lot easier, from obtaining E&O insurance to delivering to the network to defending against any potential claim. In situations where that's not possible, or for whatever reason it wasn't done and you cannot go back and get one, it's not automatically detrimental to your project, because it's not always strictly required from a legal point of view. I don't want people to think: 'Oh – we don't need a release form. We can just go and film and do whatever we want'. That's not the right approach to take. The right approach is to do whatever you can within your power to get one – but know that where that can't be done, that doesn't mean that there is no possibility of using the footage, or an automatic requirement to blur.

A lot of UK producers want to put a description of the programme on all release forms, but it's not something that we are as concerned about in the US. Sometimes there is a concern that it could actually cause issues, if the programme ends up being different to what you initially intended, in which case the contributor could argue he or she was misled. For that reason, we generally will not include any sort of detailed description, and instead just include a working title which leaves more flexibility with what it is you're doing. That's not to say there's never a situation where we wouldn't say: 'OK, we need to make sure everybody's on the same page about what we're doing here'. Where we're revealing some truly private facts about somebody or if we're trying to expose something, we might approach it differently, and include language to specifically address that.

Mike Cleaver, US Media Attorney

Verbal Release Agreements

Producers working in some countries sometimes find there is considerable resistance to signing written release forms – even if you have gone to the trouble of translating them into the local language. In nations run by oppressive regimes, for example, people can be scared of signing any official document. One way round this problem is to obtain a formal verbal release on camera just before you begin filming. You'd need to agree the principle of doing this, and the actual wording, with your commissioner. Before the interview begins, and after the camera has been switched on of course, your reporter says this verbal release to the interviewee – and asks the contributor to give their assent to the wording before beginning the interview. This will be a shorter, simpler version of the written release.

Verbal Release Forms: The Lawyers' View

Britain

Consent on camera I think is a very important alternative tool if a written release cannot be obtained. A clearly articulated explanation of a project, a clear verification from the contributor that they understand what they are being told, can get round language difficulty, literacy issues, as well as the sensitivity around contributors that are happy to participate but are reluctant to put anything into writing.

Prash Naik, UK Media Lawyer and Channel 4 TV General Counsel 2014–2017

America

What we would advise really depends on the circumstances of what it is you're filming. It could be as simple as: 'Hey, we're filming this programme about X, is it Ok if we film you and include you in the programme?' In that scenario, 'X' would be a broadly defined term, such as 'the police'. If it's something more controversial, we might try to sneak in a little more language that could be helpful to you, but still practical to use in the field.

Mike Cleaver, US Media Attorney

Children and Release Forms

To include a child under 16 years old in your film in the UK, you have to comply with rules introduced by the communications regulator Ofcom (see pages 153–155 in Chapter 8). These say you should obtain informed consent from the child's parents or guardians – and you must do this if the child is being asked about private matters. How you explain the contribution and its implications clearly depends on the age and maturity of the child – but a child should never be pressured into taking part; the likely negative consequences of participating should be pointed out along with the positive, and parents and child should be given time to make a decision. If the parents do decide the child can take part, they sign a release form agreeing to the contribution in the film.

Whether older children also need to sign is a matter for the legal/compliance team of your commissioning platform. Ofcom says 16 and 17 year olds are, in principle, able to give consent by signing a release form on their own to appear in a programme. But the agreement of parents or guardians is still required if the young person 'is not in a position to give consent' or if the contribution 'infringes privacy'. What that means depends on both the maturity of the individual and the kind of contribution being sought. You might not require parental permission for a non-contentious interview about football, for example, but might decide it's sensible to get it for an interview about a 16-year-old's problem with dyslexia. Each case has to be judged on its merits. **A pro-forma example of a release form suitable for a child can be downloaded from** *The Insiders' Guide* **website.**

In America a child (in most states that means under 18-years-old) lacks legal capacity to agree any contract they sign – including a release form. But in some states, courts hold the view that a child can give general consent if they are capable of understanding the nature, extent and likely consequences of what they've agreed to do. And this view has allowed filmmakers in those states to rely on a child's consent in the face of a claim that the child did not have the legal capacity to give it. But this doesn't mean that filmmakers can ask any child in these states to sign a release form. Each case should be treated individually, and it's always best practice to get a parent to co-sign a child's release form.

Location Release Forms

A location release performs a similar function to a contributor release – offering a production formal reassurance that the images they've shot at a location can be used in the way they desire. Figure 9.6 shows an example of a UK location release followed by an explanation of the less obvious terminology.

There is an interactive version of this form on the website that includes my explanatory comments, together with a clean downloadable version.

Once again, clear the wording with your commissioning department before using this form.

LOCATION AGREEMENT			
1	Production company		Address
2	Working programme title		Brief description of programme
3	Commissioning outlet		
4	Producer		
5	Location contact name	Address	
		Email	Phone
6	Dear .... Re: *(Add Name, address of property)* **(referred to as 'the Property' in this agreement)**		
7	You hereby grant to us and persons authorized by us the sole and exclusive right during the Period to enter upon the Property and to film, photograph and record all or any part of [the interior, the exterior and the contents of] the Property and, for such purpose, to bring onto and into the Property such persons and equipment as we may deem appropriate.		
8	'The Period' shall mean (i) *(add dates of filming)* and (ii) such other days or half days as we may mutually agree.		

Figure 9.6 An example of a location release form

9	All rights in the films, photographs and recordings made and/or taken by us at the Property shall vest in us and we shall be entitled to assign, license and/or exploit the same by all means and in all media as we may at our absolute discretion elect.
10	We shall be entitled to refer to the Property by its true name or by a fictitious name or not to refer to the Property by name.
11	We shall have no obligation to you to include any or all of such films, photographs, recordings or transmissions in any films or programme or to exploit the same or any film or programme in which the same are included.
12	You agree that we have the right to make changes, additions and alterations in and to the Property but such shall be of a temporary nature only and we undertake after our final use hereunder to restore the Property to its condition immediately prior to the Period.
13	We shall indemnify you up to a maximum of *(add value of insurance cover)* in accordance with the terms and conditions of our insurance cover against any damage which may be caused to the Property as a direct result of a negligent act or omission by ourselves or our agents, employees or invitees provided that you notify us immediately in writing of any such claim.
14	In full consideration for all rights and benefits hereby granted by you to us we shall pay to you the sum of *(add fee if being paid or delete this line)* in total.
15	This agreement shall be freely assignable by us and shall be interpreted in accordance with the laws of _____. Kindly indicate your acceptance of the foregoing by signing and returning to us the enclosed duplicate of this letter. Yours faithfully Read and agreed by _____ _____ for and on behalf of *(add name of production company)* for and on behalf of the Owner

Figure 9.6 Continued

Lines 9–11   Ensures that any images filmed at the location are owned by the production company that is given the right to use them, or not use them, as it sees fit.

Lines 12–13   Reassures the owner that the property will be left as the film crew found it; and that the production company has sufficient level of liability insurance cover to pay for any damage for which it is responsible.

Line 14   This line is only included if you are paying a facility fee for the use of the property.

Line 15   As in the contributor release, this sets out the country (England and Wales – or the US) whose legislation governs the agreement.

Transcripts/Translations: For Fast-Turn-Around And Low-Budget Films

Fast Turn-Around Films

If your deadline is not pressing and you're on a decent budget you can finish filming, organize transcripts and/or translations of your interviews and prepare a paper cut of the film before the edit starts. But tight deadlines will most likely leave no such thinking/prep time. This is a very pressured way of working and to survive, you'll have to send your interview files over the internet to a transcription typist (or translator) during the shoot so that you can make a start on your paper cut.

> These days people are just too busy to take time to stop and think. Schedules are tighter. There's less money or the director's still shooting while the edit is starting and therefore isn't there to set things off properly. What generally happens is, edits that are booked for four weeks, then over-run to five or six weeks anyway because you're not giving yourself time to plan – and it costs them more in the long run. Planning is key. If you can, don't finish filming and then go straight into the edit. Have some time to stop, to review your material, to think about it and then go into the edit. Then your edit will be shorter.
>
> Peter Zacaroli, Managing Director,
> West Digital Post-Production

You can simply record the interview sound on a phone and upload the file. But it's very easy to forget to do this on a pressured shoot. Alternatively you can copy the recorded sound of the interview from the camera onto a laptop or phone voice recorder – and upload the resulting sound file via one of the many large file transfer sites.[4] But an hour-long interview will take an hour to copy. To avoid that, you can upload the video file itself to one of these transfer sites after reducing its size to speed up the process. Most hotel internet connections are much too slow to manage the very large file size of raw footage. It will just take too long. But you can downgrade the file size by converting to mp4 format using a free video converter on the net.[5] The sound quality will be fine, and it can be uploaded in a reasonable time span. If you are concerned about using a commercial upload site, most post-production suites have an ftp (file transfer protocol)[6] site that you can use instead. This is a part of their own website where you can upload/download files that might be too large to email.

Getting some transcripts/translations back during the shoot lets you make a start on the written version of your film story – the cutting order or paper cut. That means working some evenings instead of enjoying those long boozy meals. But sometimes you have no choice. You don't need to work out the entire cutting order during the shoot, just enough to occupy your film editor for the first few days of the edit while you then work on the rest. Read pages 110–113 in Chapter 6 for advice on the layout and information you need to put into a cutting order.

Low Budget Films

If you are really pushed for cash, and have to transcribe interviews yourself, you won't be able to do this until filming is over – or you'll exhaust yourself directing a shoot during the day and transcribing at night. So you'll have to build transcription time into your scheduling estimate. As a rough guide, you'll be able to transcribe about ten minutes of interview in an hour. So a 30 minute film with 7 x 30 minute interviews would take around 21 hours to transcribe. It's time consuming. But if money is the issue, then your own effort is preferable to paying for transcription typists. For translation, there's no easy way round the problem. If you are bilingual in the language in which your film is being made, then do it yourself – but be certain you really can pick up the nuances of language and accurately convey their meaning in English. If you are making a contentious investigation the last thing you want is a row about the accuracy of a particular comment. Another option is to find a translator abroad, in the country in which you've been filming or in another country where the language is spoken. Translation costs can be much cheaper than in the UK or US, and if you transfer interviews over the internet during the shoot, you'll avoid any impact on your overall schedule. But you will have to be convinced that their command of English is sufficient to do the job accurately – and that they really do understand the dialect in which your interview has been recorded.

After The Shoot: Preparing For Your Edit

The four edit prep tasks (viewing rushes, reading and marking up transcripts; preparing a cutting order and researching archive, stills and music) are covered on pages 108–113 in Chapter 6.

During The Edit: Preparing For Post-Production

Towards the end of the edit, once your film structure has been finalized, you have to gather together the information that allows final post-production to run smoothly. You'll be in listing mode: the smooth running of post-production and the task of accounting for third party material used in your film rests on the timely preparation of five lists.

Information Needed for Post-Production

At the end of your edit you need to prepare three lists containing the information for all the captions that will appear in your film.

Interviewee list. This is still sometimes called an 'Aston' list in the UK – and a 'Chyron' list in the US – because in bye-gone TV days these lists were prepared by character generators made by Britain's Aston Broadcast Systems and the American Chyron Corporation. The list contains the correct spellings and job titles of anyone whose name will appear in the film, in the order in which they appear. You'll need approval from your commissioner for this list – so leave yourself enough prep time before final post begins or you run the risk of misspelling a name or adding an incorrect job title with all the embarrassing consequences that such a mistake can bring.

Credit list. Containing the names of all those who have contributed to the film, plus all the archive/still sources. Many outlets for factual films have a precise format for the order, length and sometimes positioning of credits – the information will be in the commissioning specification for the film, so check before putting them on-screen. You'll also need your commissioner's approval for the credits.

Subtitle list. If your commissioner wants you to use on-screen translations to make foreign language interviews intelligible, you'll need to create an accurate list of subtitles and have them placed on-screen at the right points in the dialogue. The subtitles do not have to be

If your caption list is a half-arsed thing that you've done on a piece of paper the night before, and you haven't checked it you waste a phenomenal amount of time in the online doing that. It's things like mis-spelling people's names. It's things like finding out what somebody's job description is. You know, we're doing the online, it's the last day we've got, and at three in the afternoon we start putting the captions on and then somebody realizes that they don't know if this person is a professor of something or a doctor of something. And they go on Google and they find three different versions of what the person does so they either end up making it up or they end up trying to contact the person. You are making it a lot harder on yourself if you don't have a caption list when you go into the online. So that is something I think is really important.
Peter Zacaroli, Managing Director, West Digital Post-Production

accurate word for word, but they must convey an *accurate essence* of what the interviewee is saying. You usually need to abbreviate what a contributor is saying to make the subtitles fit – especially if you are also going to add their name onscreen: you risk overwhelming your viewer with too much information if you have both subtitles and names appearing at the same time. You should always bring a bilingual translator into the edit suite, once your structure and interviews have been agreed, to check the accuracy of the subtitles and their timing. They'll also check that your foreign language edits are sound and that what you think a person is saying (according to your original translation) is in fact what they really are saying.

Contributor name captions, credits and subtitles should all be correctly placed and timed before the end of your edit. They can be given in electronic, time coded form to your online editor. This preparation minimizes the time needed for adding this on-screen information during expensive post-production.

Information Required for Copyright Holders and Commissioners

Once your film structure is agreed, when there are no more changes to be made to pictures or sound, you have to prepare a detailed record of all the music, stills and archive footage you've used. This accounting is vital – the production company you're working for and the broad-caster/online platform will want confirmation that what you'll be paying to rights holders for their material matches with what you've actually used in the film. The information will be included with the 'Programme-as-Completed' (PasC) paperwork that has to be delivered with each commissioned film.

Music cue sheet. Films made for many major broadcasters and some online platforms in the UK and US now use a web-based system called Soundmouse to report on the copyrighted music used in their programmes. Producers either fill in an online music reporting form manually – or upload the film and let Soundmouse's automated system do the work by comparing the tracks used to its large database of music and automatically creating a cue sheet.

If you are not using an online reporting system, you'll need to prepare your own cue sheet for copyrighted music. Figure 9.7 shows an example of one. **There is a pro-forma version on the website that can be used for your film.**

All of the information you require to complete this form should be provided with the track downloaded from a music library or on the disk cover. If your budget stretches to a specially composed score, then you'd list the tracks one by one along with the musician's name and any other performers who might have been used to record the music.

Archive/stills cue sheet. Films made for major broadcasters in the UK use a similar online system called Silvermouse to complete the rest of their post-production reporting requirements – and this includes a detailed list of archive and stills used in the film.[7] In the US, broadcasters tend to use their own reporting systems. If you're not using this system, take look at Figure 9.8 that shows an example of an archive and stills cue sheet. A pro-forma, version can be downloaded from the website.

Preparing all these lists cannot be left until final post-production has started because the precise details of exactly which clip of archive, which still or which track of recorded music you've used at any point in the film is held in the edit computer. It will be too late (or much more costly) to obtain it once you've begun final post.

MUSIC CUE SHEET

Film Title		Episode		Production company	
Broadcaster/Online Platform		Production ID		Production contract	

Rights requested

TRACK NO	MUSIC TITLE	PUBLISHER	COMPOSER/ ARRANGER	PERFORMER	RECORD LABEL + CATALOGUE NO	USE: S or F	MUSIC ORIGIN	TIME CODE IN FILM	DUR
1									
2									
3									
4									
5									
6									
7									
8									
9									
10									

Key

Track No: An ascending chronological list of the tracks used in your film.

Use: S or F: Is the track used in the film as signature music (i.e. as the main title or over the credits) or just featured (used elsewhere in the film).

Music origin: Does the track come from a live performance, a film sound track, a music library, specially commissioned, from a video, or from retail use or a commercial.

Time code: The start and finish time codes in your film between which this particular track appears.

Dur: The length of the track.

Figure 9.7 An example of a music cue sheet

ARCHIVE – STILLS CUE SHEET

Film title	Episode	Production company
Broadcaster/Online commissioning department	Production ID	Production contract no.

Rights to be cleared

CLIP NO	TITLE	DESCRIPTION	ARCHIVE OR STILLS?	SOURCE AND CONTACT	COPYRIGHT OR ROYALTY FREE?	COPYRIGHT OWNER	COST	TIME CODES	DUR	RIGHTS AGREED
1										
2										
3										
4										
5										

Key

Rights to be cleared:	The rights your commissioning department wants you to clear. Add this information here. For more information about rights and clearances see explanation in schedule 9 in the budget spread sheet on pages 227–230 in Chapter 11.
Clip No:	A sequential numbering of each archive clip or still used in the film.
Title:	The title of the footage or still as it appears in the source library.
Description:	Your description of the content of the footage or the image.
Source and contact:	The name of the company which holds the footage or still – and their contact information.
Copyright owner	This can be different to the source of the material for copyrighted archive/stills.
Time codes:	The start and finish time codes in your film between which this particular footage or image appears.
Dur:	The length of the footage or image in your film.

Figure 9.8 An example of an archive and stills cue sheet

Chapter Summary

Key Organizational Tasks at Each Stage of Production

1   Pre-Production
   • Preparation of call sheet for the shoot
2   Production
   • Shot-lists
   • Contributor and location release forms
3   Production: fast turnaround or low budget films
   • Arranging translations/transcripts while filming or doing them yourself after the shoot.
   • Preparing start of cutting order
4   Pre-edit
   • Viewing rushes
   • Reading and marking up transcripts
   • Preparing cutting order (often continues into the edit)
   • Researching stills/archive (ditto)
5   Edit
   • Compiling interviewee, credit, subtitle lists
   • Compiling music, archive and stills cut sheets

Notes

1 Your editor can distinguish between one day's rushes and the next when recording free run TC because the date of recording can be set in what are called the camera's 'user bits'. So the user bits need to be re-set at the start of each day with the correct date.
2 Free run time code is also useful for finding matching shots when you're filming an interview on two cameras – because each camera then lays down the same time code at any point in the interview.
3 This line is only required in UK release forms.
4 Try https://wetransfer.com or www.transfernow.net/en/ or www.dropbox.com/transfer.
5 This site suggests ten video converters for use on a PC: https://videoconverter.wondershare.com/video-converter/free-video-converter-windows-10.html
   This site has the same for use on a Mac: https://videoconverter.wondershare.com/mac/free-vidco-converter-mac.html
6 While in transit to the ftp site the files will be encrypted. But if you are really concerned about security, once they arrive and have been downloaded to the post house server, make sure you get the ftp copy deleted.
7 As well as archive/stills, Silvermouse also includes information about on and off-screen contributors; diversity; copyrighted archive and stills, and transmission details. Some broadcasters also ask for production contracts and confirmation that the programme complies with broadcasting standards about violence, sexual content and bad language.

Part 4

Undercover Skills

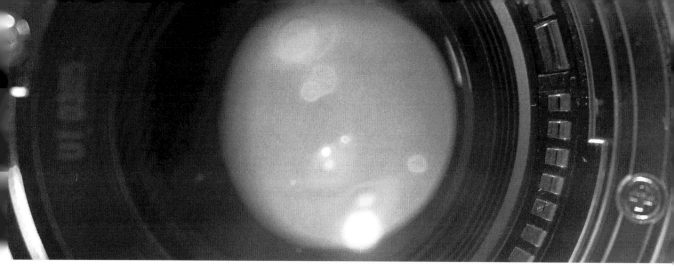

10 Secret Filming

Evidence, Ethics, Safety and the Law in
Undercover Filmmaking

KEY CONCEPTS

- How do you get the green light to expose wrong-doing with secret filming?
- How do you manage an undercover shoot safely, ethically and legally.
- The issues that must be considered before your exposé is shown.

Investigative journalism plays a key role in our democratic culture. Electors need accurate information about the health of the body politic on which to base the decisions they take in the privacy of the polling booth. By shining a search-light on corrupt, criminal, anti-social or unethical actions, journalistic investigations underpin an informed democratic process. Fearlessly telling the truth about rich, famous, or powerful individuals who'd rather keep such behaviour under wraps, is vital to a healthy democracy and filmmakers can do this better than any other medium because secret filming shows – rather than simply talks about – these negative activities. Filmed undercover investigations have caught hypocritical and venal politicians red-handed; exposed horrific abuses of vulnerable people in care homes; brought misogynistic and hateful comments by religious preachers into the open and shown out-of-control prisoners high on drugs and drink – to name just a few notable successes.

Modern digital technology has made undercover approaches easier than ever before. Correctly used, secret filming is a hugely powerful tool. Incorrectly used, covert techniques can backfire and leave you, the filmmaker, facing accusations of unethical behaviour, invasion of privacy or, worse still, it can lead to serious physical harm to filmmakers and their contributors. So this approach has to be used responsibly and with great forethought.

This chapter will guide you on the basic issues to consider before embarking on an undercover project. These cover the evidence needed to persuade a commissioner to approve an undercover project; the legal aspects of your investigation; the safety of your production team and your contributors; and the judgment the outside world is likely to make about your actions once news of the film reaches a wider audience – in other words, the ethical dimension of your approach.

What I'll be saying here is not an exhaustive account of the issues involved in undercover investigations. Each film comes with its own unique risks that need to be addressed. But I'm hoping that, by reading this chapter, you'll develop a mind-set that will naturally want to address the risks. For more detailed information on specific topics, two very good sources are the BBC[1] and Channel 4 TVs[2] editorial guidance pages for covert filmmaking.

The very intrusive nature of undercover filming requires an understanding of – and clear answers to – the following questions before you embark on any covert project.

Can I Film Undercover and Keep Within the Laws that Protect Privacy?

There a different answers to this question in America and Britain. In the US, although the First Amendment of the Constitution provides great protection for the broadcasting of truthful, newsworthy stories, it doesn't offer any defence to an undercover journalist accused of physically invading someone's privacy – by trespassing, for example, or by illegally intruding on their privacy. Privacy laws vary from state to state but, in general, the more private the space in which undercover filming takes place the higher the risk of a valid claim. Privacy rights are dramatically reduced, and the risk drops, if the filming takes place in areas where the public has access – like a park, public street, railway station – or even an area within an otherwise private place to which many people have access, like a common area of a large company. So in America, whatever the journalistic merits of the story, secret filming must always take into account the laws of privacy – as well as other laws that the circumstances of the filming might bring into focus.

In the UK there is a different emphasis. Privacy is protected by the Human Rights Act 1998 which balances the right to privacy against the right of freedom of expression and, in general terms, uses a public interest test to determine whether private information should or should not remain private. In other words private behaviour should remain private *unless there is a compelling public interest justification* in letting other people see it. So your justification for invading someone's privacy by filming them covertly is anchored in the wider good to society – the 'public interest' – that can result from bringing certain behaviours into the public domain. The broadcasting regulator, Ofcom, is very specific about this: it says that justifying an infringement of someone's privacy by claiming it is in the public interest, entails showing that the public interest outweighs the right to privacy.[3]

So in the UK, what's meant by 'public interest'? The BBCs editorial guidelines offer a clear explanation.[4] To justify invading someone's privacy, you have to ensure that at least one of the following facts is true about the individuals at the focus of your investigation:

- They are breaking the law.
- They are behaving in an anti-social manner.
- They are acting corruptly, incompetently, negligently or in an unjust way.
- They are making misleading statements.
- Or the information you expose about an individual helps people make decisions on issues of public importance.

In short, your subjects have to be bad guys – or, as indicated by the last in this list, public figures who's actions might not be illegal but which expose incompetence, negligence or hypocrisy that would offer a legitimate public interest justification. Even if you can answer yes to one or more of these facts, the strength of your justification for secret filming will vary with the circumstances of the filming itself – and the person under investigation. For example: covert filming at someone's workplace, is likely to be less intrusive than covert filming at their home, with children likely to be present – and this latter would require an exceptionally strong justification before any responsible broadcaster will give you the go-ahead. Conversely, there can be a lower bar to secret filming of individuals with public profiles than other people – because higher standards are expected of those in the public eye, especially individuals who are responsible for public money.

Privacy, Proportionality and the Public Interest

You have to make a strong case that there is evidence of wrong-doing being done. And that case will be scrutinized. People will ask: how do you know? And how can we trust your source? And how do they know? So all of that will be scrutinized. There will also be another question asked of you, which is: do we have to go undercover? Could we actually film this overtly? And is it essential to the story that you go undercover? And then people ask: Is it worth risking our reputation? Is it worth the risk to the undercover reporter and any whistleblower? Is it worth invading these people's privacy? Is it in the public interest for this to be revealed? So there is a very strict process, and it is very tried and tested, and you just have to fit into it.

Diana Martin, Executive Producer, BBC TV, *Panorama*

You would want to be absolutely confident that, if you are going to be infringing an individual's privacy, it is warranted by the weight of evidence against that individual or company. So it's a balancing exercise. It's a proportionality test. And you'd need to demonstrate that the level of wrong-doing is serious enough to warrant that infringement. You don't want to be naming and shaming someone who owes, hypothetically, a £750 debt to society and is only 20 years of age. Naming and shaming them – that's not going to be justified by covert filming. On the other hand, there's a more compelling public interest in a company involved in the manipulation of the electorate by the use of voter suppression tactics, and therefore the infringement of their privacy balanced against the wrong-doing is more justifiable in those circumstances.

Prash Naik, UK Media Lawyer and Channel 4 TV General Counsel 2014–2017

There is a very fundamental issue here – a really important issue for everyone to grasp which maybe isn't taught as clearly as it should be – which is this thing called the public interest, which is a slightly nebulous and scary sounding term. It sounds quite pompous, obviously. But in the end you are breaking the law if you start filming people undercover without their permission. It's a breach of privacy which means that you have to have prima facie – i.e. sufficient first-hand – evidence to be allowed to break the law in the public interest. People go: 'oh no, journalists don't break the law'. We break the law all the time – in the public interest. The law allows us to do that, but we have to prove that there is criminal behaviour, anti-social behaviour, in the case of politicians – grossly hypocritical behaviour, that allows us to breach people's privacy in the public interest. And obviously if you are filming undercover, you are doing that.

Tom Giles, Controller of Current Affairs, ITV

I am going to illustrate the rest of the questions you'll need to address to obtain permission for covert filming, by looking at how the BBC was persuaded to give the green light to an undercover film that I produced some years ago. The aim of this hour-long film was to show on camera the kind of anti-social and illegal street behaviour about which many people had been complaining in two districts in the UK – Tower Hamlets in London and Glasgow in Scotland. We wanted to send a reporter and a director to live for a few weeks in each area, asking them to walk the streets wearing an undercover filming kit, recording what they saw. As you'll see, the task of obtaining formal covert filming permission was significant and time-consuming. It entailed offering clear answers to the following questions.

Can I Get the Story Without Recourse to Secret Filming?

To justify a covert approach, there must be no other realistic way of showing the problem you've identified. In our undercover documentary, the open presence of a camera in both Tower Hamlets and Glasgow was likely to inhibit people from acting as they might normally do – or it could even incite behaviour that would otherwise not occur. To capture the problems on film, we had no choice other than to film secretly. So the next task was to convince the BBC that we had a strong enough case to justify this.

How do I get the 'Green Light' from a Commissioner to Film Undercover?

Because of its intrusive nature, permission for secret filming is not given lightly by reputable broadcasters and online platforms. It requires in-depth justification and very careful consideration of the practical problems it raises. In the UK, covert filming has to comply with the regulations of the broadcasting regulator, Ofcom.[5] In the US, there is no equivalent Ofcom-like regulator. Instead key legal risk issues raised by the filming need to be assessed. I've already mentioned illegally intruding on someone's privacy. Also in the mix will be fraud (lying about who you really are when working undercover) and state laws governing secret sound recordings – which I outline more fully on page 192 and 194 in this chapter.[6]

Major broadcasters in the UK that run investigative strands have systematized the process of obtaining permission to make an undercover film. There's a lengthy form to complete covering the following key issues:

A. The prior evidence you've obtained of the problem you wish to expose.
B. The technique you'll be using to obtain the undercover footage.
C. The cover story your undercover team will use.
D. The safety of your crew and others involved with the project.
E. Guidelines to ensure your team act ethically on location.
F. The legal aspects of your investigation.

A significant level of detail is required to answer these questions, as I'll demonstrate by outlining some of the information needed to persuade the BBC to green light the undercover filming in the Tower Hamlets part of the documentary.

The Prior Evidence You've Obtained of the Problem You Wish to Expose

You have to produce compelling evidence that the criminal, violent, anti-social or corrupt behaviour does really exist and is a significant problem. Let's first look at the kind of evidence that *won't* be acceptable.

No Second-Hand Information

You can't offer information gathered from second-hand sources to justify secret filming. Our request to film undercover in Tower Hamlets couldn't have been based on information from someone who'd told us they know there's a lot of violence in this area because they they'd spoken to a friend who lives there who says they've seen this for themselves. This 'hearsay' evidence is not enough to justify such a serious invasion of privacy. The same principle applies to newspaper reports. They might alert you to the existence of an issue – and you might use such reports to back-up the case you are making – but you can't rely solely on someone else's reportage to make a case for undercover filming. You must get as close to the evidence of illegality as you can.

No 'Fishing Trips'

You also can't use secret filming to gather evidence of bad behaviour. That's putting the cart before the horse. Imagine this scenario: you run a care home for disabled children and offer a compassionate individual a job as a carer. On their first day a colleague catches sight of the new 'carer' in a bathroom switching on a small video recorder attached to a pinhole camera wired into her shirt. Her cover's blown before she's filmed a frame: she tells you she's an undercover reporter sent in to expose the physical abuse of the children. If you believe you are running a decent care home, you'd be outraged at this invasion of the privacy of residents and staff. You'd ask the programme's commissioner and the filmmakers to justify such an intrusive approach. They'd face significant legal problems unless they have compiled sufficient evidence of the abuse *prior to* sending in the undercover reporter. You have to journalistically prove the need for secret filming with hard evidence gathered using basic research techniques. So no undercover 'fishing trips', as we call them – no use of covert cameras to gather evidence of criminal, anti-social or other behaviours that you think warrant investigating.

> If you're working with a British broadcaster, there are specific rules on secret filming which have to be complied with in accordance with the statutory regulator code issued by Ofcom. The cardinal rule is: you cannot go in and film in a place undercover unless you have prima facie evidence of wrong doing. You can't go in on the basis of a 'fishing expedition'. It's simply not permissible. And one thing that's guaranteed to put off a broadcaster is, if you turn up saying: 'We think X is doing this. We've managed to inveigle our way into the company. We don't have any real evidence but we just hope we might get a chance of catching them on camera while we're there'. That's not going to encourage a broadcaster to go with you.
> Prash Naik, Media Lawyer and Channel 4 TV General Counsel 2014–2017

So what counts as sufficient proof that bad behaviour is actually taking place and is of sufficient concern that it would be in the public interest to expose it with secret filming?

First-Hand – 'Prima Facie' – Evidence Essential

There are a range of possible sources: first-hand eye-witness testimony from people who've experienced the problem for themselves; official documents or letters; and reports from individuals – academics, social workers, pressure groups, authors and local representatives – who have studied the problem or have knowledge of the issue from working in a relevant field.

Getting the green light to film undercover in the Tower Hamlets part of the documentary required the following kind of evidence.

LOCAL PEOPLE'S TESTIMONY

One store manager told us about daily visits from teenage thieves and violent thugs in his shop. Another told us about four incidents of abuse in 18 months, two involving violence. One of his drivers was attacked in his shop by a large gang and needed hospital treatment. Residents in a tower block also described the estate as dangerous and threatening thanks to drug takers and violent gangs.

TESTIMONY FROM EXPERTS, ACADEMICS AND LOCAL REPRESENTATIVES

> Obviously we have to justify every piece of undercover filming we do. But actually, it's got to be more than just: we have one piece of prima facie evidence, that there's some wrong-doing here. Do we have enough recent evidence? It can't obviously be evidence from a couple of years ago. Is it still happening? Where have we got that evidence from? Is it from a potentially disgruntled whistle-blower whose got an axe to grind? So the bar for getting undercover off the ground is incredibly high. Quite rightly. And I think PDs, especially newer PDs, can often be incredibly frustrated with the level of paperwork and the level of the burden of proof that we have to get to in order to do undercover.
>
> Louisa Compton, Head of News, Current Affairs and Sport, Channel 4 TV

One councillor told us of a recent gang-related shooting and said the violence had got worse with the introduction of hard drugs into the area. The local Crime Reduction Service had received complaints from women bothered by kids throwing stones at them and blocking pavements so that they can't pass. They'd issued 100 'acceptable behaviour contracts' – which commit offenders to stick to a set of behaviour rules. And a recent survey of the Bangladeshi restaurant trade found that 60% of respondents had witnessed or been involved in distressing incidents in the last 12 months.

THE EXPERIENCE OF OUR PRODUCTION TEAM

One of our researchers witnessed a large group of teenagers trying to overturn a caravan on an estate. Another saw a man rolling around on the ground with his shirt covered in blood, either very drunk or drugged up. And a teenager walked up to our reporter and deliberately stepped into him, hitting him with his shoulder.

PAST EXAMPLES OF GANG VIOLENCE

From news reports and conversations with shopkeepers, we compiled a list of more than 70 examples of gang violence, stabbings, muggings, gang fights, drug dealing or vandalism in the past 12 months.

We had to do the same kind of in-depth research to persuade the BBC to let us film undercover in Glasgow.

The Technique You'll be Using to Obtain the Undercover Footage

You have to demonstrate that you've considered the practical problems of using a hidden camera in a responsible manner. First, questions about the camera itself.

What Kind?

There is a wide range of covert camera kits on the market. They can be hidden in almost any common household article from pens, to air fresheners, plugs, smoke alarms, clocks, computer mice, thermostats, children's teddies – the list is endless. They can record onto flash cards or send the video wirelessly over Wi-Fi. Or they can be worn on the body with a miniaturized pinhole lens concealed behind a shirt or coat button, in a pair of glasses, in a tie, or carried in a bag. The reporter and the director in the Tower Hamlets undercover filming used a concealed pinhole camera lens, with a wire connecting the camera to a miniature flash card recorder held in a pocket.

When will it be Switched On?

You only want to invade people's privacy where relevant and necessary. If you are filming in a hospital, for example, you wouldn't want your camera switched on all the time because you'd be filming patients without their consent and without good reason. You'd only switch on when you got a hint that abuse was about to take place. In the Tower Hamlets filming we decided the cameras would only be turned on in situations that appeared to be threatening – or where illegality or anti-social behaviour was occurring – to minimize the intrusiveness of the filming to innocent passers-by.

Communications Test

This might seem obvious – but we had to make sure our team checked that everything was working properly before each film trip and make that intention clear to the BBC. There's nothing worse than coming back with what you think will be the best sequence in the film only to discover that your battery ran out just before it started.

Hidden Camera Training

Neither the director nor the reporter knew how to use a digital camera. The lens in covert cameras is wide angle, maximizing the field of vision and therefore the likelihood of capturing the behaviour you hope to see. But positioning the lens in the garment, and the way in which users carry themselves, can make the difference between recording the action and recording the ceiling. So practice sessions with the undercover kit were vital preparatory work, and this had to be detailed on our secret filming permission form.

The Cover Story Your Undercover Team Will Use

You need a relevant and practical cover story for your undercover operative – to let them respond appropriately if they get asked who they are and what they are doing. If they're posing as a member of a violent gang, for example, the cover story is absolutely vital to their safety and the success of the project. The cover story wasn't such a significant issue in the Tower Hamlets covert filming as the team would be walking the streets rather than infiltrating a group. But we still felt they should have a convincing cover so as not to arouse suspicions in case they got into conversations with people. There are some general principles you can apply when constructing the story.

The Deception Should be Minimal

You must be aware of the possibility of the deception damaging innocent people (i.e. applying for a job as a carer of elderly or disabled people when you've got no caring experience).

Work Out a Credible Story – and Stick to it

Our reporter, a northerner, was to be a builder who'd come down to London to look for work and to join his girlfriend, the director. She was to be a student. They moved into a short-let flat (rented for the purpose of the filming) in the area to add to their credibility.

Don't Carry Anything that Could Conflict with Your Cover Story

If the reporter strikes up a conversation with local lads, tells them he's a builder but then pulls out his wallet to buy them a drink that still contains his BBC ID card, he could be in for a difficult time. If he says he's single, but has a photo of his wife and children in the wallet, that will also compromise the fake ID. So you have to be meticulous about your pre-planning of a cover story. In some situations a simple mistake could be life threatening.

Rehearse and Memorize the Cover Story

In the Tower Hamlets shoot this wasn't too difficult because the story didn't need to be very detailed. But if you are trying to infiltrate a criminal gang or get work in a company you wish to expose, then the details of the new identity are critical and need rehearsing until they trip off your tongue without undue thought.

The Safety of Your Crew and Others Involved with the Project

You cannot take uncalculated risks with the welfare of anyone. You can take risks – but only those that you, your production company and the platform for which you are making the film have agreed are acceptable and that have been minimized as far as possible. So health and safety is a key issue to address before going out with an undercover kit.

The BBC undertakes many undercover investigations – and has institutionalized the process. An entire department, its Health and Safety High Risk team,[7] is devoted to keeping staff safe – and making a covert project for the BBC inevitably involves detailed discussions with this team. We took their advice on how to keep our reporter and director safe while filming undercover on the streets in potentially hostile situations. This is what we arranged.

Security Back-up

Two security men – with considerable experience of providing protection to people – would accompany our undercover team on each covert filming trip: one keeping within eyesight on foot, one in a car that could be used as an escape vehicle in case of difficulties. We agreed a detailed protocol with them: keeping mobiles free during filming, an emergency evacuation key-word and a panic alarm to be carried by the crew as a back-up means of contacting the security team.

Stab Vests

Our reporter and director each wore a protective stab vest on every undercover filming trip because there were real risks in what they would be doing. We did our best to protect the crew.

But it's not possible to guard against every eventuality and, despite our well thought-out plans, one night-time covert trip nearly ended in disaster when they inadvertently walked by a group of aggressive teenagers in a park. One took exception to the reporter's presence in their 'territory' and threatened to stab him saying: 'I'll shanks in your face' ('shanks' is prison slang for being stabbed with a homemade knife) just because he looked at him. The reporter was lucky – the incident ended without violence. But had he been slashed in the face there was nothing he, his stab vest or our safety team could have done to prevent this. So you can't remove risk entirely from a film shoot. But you can evaluate the likely harms of your project and guard against them in a realistic way.

Familiarization

Before filming commenced, we also insisted that the back-up team got to know the areas in which we expected to be working – getting to know the layout of estates and the entry and exit points.

Clothing/Safe Zones

Clothing/footwear had to be suitable for a quick escape – so no high heels. We instructed the team to be aware of the nearest 'safety zone' (i.e. the location of their back-up vehicle or the nearest public building like a fire station that could provide safety) and the route to it.

Emergency Contacts

Our reporter and director carried a list of emergency contacts – like the nearest police station and hospital, plus contacts for the producer who was the first call in case of queries or problems. So someone responsible from the team who was not on site had to be on call throughout the undercover filming.

Restraint Training

The crew were both given a day's training by an expert in physical restraint to learn ways of extricating themselves if physically attacked, in a way that would enable them to run for help.

Guidelines to Ensure Your Team Act Ethically on Location

We had to ensure that the undercover crew behaved in a way that would not be seen as unethical. And that meant anticipating situations in which they might find themselves, thinking through the most appropriate responses – ones that would not invite criticism.

We had many discussions with the BBCs Editorial Policy advisors, whose job is to offer advice to filmmakers wanting to embark on difficult investigative projects. We put together an ethical protocol to guide our team while they were filming undercover. It covered the following issues.

> Everything we do should be ethical. Everything we do should be fair, and it should be balanced, and without any pre-conceived ideas. And I think often people who end up working on the story become so convinced that [their] position is correct, they end up not seeing fairly. The direction we would give to any undercover reporter is obviously: don't ask leading questions; don't assume that something's going to happen just because you think it is; go there and be eyes and ears into a world without any pre-conceived ideas. And that's a really key message for undercover: no way can you try and influence or change people's behaviour because obviously ethically [that] totally destroys a piece of undercover journalism.
>
> Louisa Compton, Head of News, Current Affairs and Sport, Channel 4 TV

You have to work out a way of behaving if and when the targets of the undercover are doing the bad stuff that you went into film. You obviously can't participate in it, but you can't really be seen to criticize it too much in front of those abusive colleagues because they might smell a rat and kick you out, or they might turn against you. So there are really interesting ethical questions there. What do you do when you see somebody hit somebody and you're filming it? Do you stop them hitting? Do you suddenly say: 'right, undercover's over. I'm going to the police, it's too outrageous?' It is ethically very, very tricky and sensitive and needs a huge amount of care and thought. In each of those cases, we do a whole series of scenario plans. What if this happens, what will you do? What if someone says this, what will you do? So a huge amount of thought goes into these things and hopefully somebody will have thought of the scenario before it happens.

Diana Martin, Executive Producer, BBC TV, *Panorama*

What Do You Do if You See Someone Being Attacked?

An undercover crew has obligations as citizens – alongside their role as filmmakers and just passively filming someone being attacked would be immoral. So we decided it was OK to capture evidence on film if the act of doing this didn't delay an intervention that could have stopped someone getting hurt. Otherwise they should stop filming and intervene – but only if they believed it was safe to do so. There was no point in getting themselves hurt in the process. If they thought it was too dangerous to go to a person's aid – they should call the police.

What Do You Do If The Police Ask For Your Name And Address? Or If They Ask What You Are Doing?

There's what the law says (and this will differ from country to country) and, as above, how filmmakers balance their professional obligations with their duties as ordinary citizens.

In America, you should never deliberately lie to the police or provide them with false documents as you could be prosecuted for doing so – and being an undercover operative would not be a defence. So potential encounters with the police would need to be carefully assessed for each undercover trip. There are ways of avoiding an outright lie: for example by making innocuous but technically true statements, like 'I am taking a walk' or 'I am meeting a friend'.

In Britain, the legal position is not clear. As a citizen, you are under no obligation to answer police questions at all, or tell them what you are doing, if you are stopped while filming in a public place.[8] But if the police suspect you are doing something illegal they may have the power to arrest you, and being obstructive or evasive could create the suspicion that you're hiding something from them and give them a reason to do this. Equally, if you give misinformation you also run the risk of opening yourself up to a prosecution for wasting police time or interfering with process of justice. We decided that the Tower Hamlets undercover crew must

It's important to have your own moral compass. If you feel that something you're asked to do is beyond the pale or doesn't sit comfortably, you should stand up and express your view – you might be the only dissenting voice in the room, but you might also be the voice of reason in the room.

Prash Naik, UK Media Lawyer and Channel 4 TV General Counsel 2014–2017

give the police their real names and addresses if they got into a situation like this, and tell them what they were doing. But we advised them to do so out of earshot of any local people so that their cover was not blown.

Mustn't Act as an 'Agent Provocateur'

Undercover filmmakers mustn't be seen to be inciting the behaviour they want to film. If our reporter had deliberately encouraged people to mug him by carrying an expensive phone and waving it around in a rough area, that would be acting unethically. On the other hand – making or receiving a call seems a normal way to behave wherever you are. This was not a black and white issue, rather something that should be driven by common sense. In our covert filming, the team were told not to overtly invite violence.

Carrying Self-Defence Aids That Could be Seen as a Weapon

In America, state laws govern the possession and use of weapons – and these vary widely from state to state. So you'd have to check the legal position of the state in which you're planning to film undercover – as well as consider the ethical dimension of carrying an item for self-defence that could be considered a weapon.

British law recognizes two types of weapons: items that are defined in law as weapons such as flick knives, machetes, guns – and it is an offence to carry them – and normal household objects (like a rolling pin or a kitchen knife) that you are carrying and which the police could view as being an offensive weapon. They'd have to prove this in court so there's a risk in carrying any object that could be perceived in this way. Our undercover team was not allowed to carry anything that could be construed as a weapon.

Secret Filming in Places like Shopping Arcades, Railway Stations – Privately Owned but to which the Public has Access

We could film here, but we had to leave if asked to do so. We'd need to editorially justify the need to go to such a place before deciding to film there. It couldn't just be on a whim.

Secret Filming in Private Homes

In Britain, it would be very difficult to justify undercover filming in a private house when the covert approach is being used for social research purposes – as in Tower Hamlets. It might be OK if you are exposing crime (i.e. drug dealing) but such filming is very intrusive and you would need to show a strong public interest justification to get permission to do this. Any plans to film covertly in someone's home also can't be a spur-of-the-moment decision: we'd have had to get prior clearance from the broadcaster. For the position in America – see the explanation of privacy on page 184 in this chapter.

The baseball bat 'sexed up' filming row: an example of the importance of working within an ethical framework.

Despite all the preparation and care that we took not to attract unwelcome attention while filming this project – we awoke one morning during the Glasgow part of this undercover shoot to some very unwelcome front page headlines. In one local newspaper the council leader was demanding an explanation from the BBC after a claim that our film crew 'encouraged youths to run around a city park with baseball bats' and re-enact gang violence. Another Scottish daily said the BBC had been accused of asking young men to stage a mock gang fight to 'sex-up' their film.

Other papers picked up the story. Glasgow Council sent an indignant complaint to the BBC's Director General. The negative publicity persuaded two key interviewees to pull out of the film.

It wasn't a very good day for the production team. We hadn't, of course, staged a mock fight or encouraged anyone to run around holding weapons. But Glasgow's reputation for violence was a politically charged issue – and some sections of the community were very suspicious of the media. So it was particularly easy for innocent actions to be taken out of context and used to discredit the film. This is what had actually happened.

We'd obtained the permission of parents to interview five teenagers. We filmed them walking in a park. There were no baseball bats or hockey sticks. One lad was carrying a golf club. But there was no aggression offered or requested. The story was completely false. But this firestorm started when someone approached the crew while they were filming and asked what they were doing. Their explanation fell on deaf ears. This individual was very antagonistic towards the BBC. He was convinced we were exploiting the young people who didn't have any understanding of how the media worked and, seeing a golf club, wrongly assumed we'd asked the lads to stage a mock fight. He made a complaint to the council – which sparked off this 'fake news' firestorm. The council had spent years struggling to overcome Glasgow's 'hard-man' image and the last thing they wanted was a programme focusing on the city's dark side.

Our bosses reviewed the unedited footage, looked at the ethical guidelines we'd developed to guide our crew on the ground, read our reports of the day's filming and backed our story publicly. In a letter to one national newspaper, our executive producer said that the council's complaint was based on a: 'completely unfounded charge. We stand by the programme'.

In the end, we didn't use the interviews in the final film – for editorial reason unconnected to the row. But what this incident shows is that, by starting out with a clearly worked out ethical approach to your filming, you put yourself in the best possible position to weather any unjustified media storm that might hit you. Without such guidelines, our team's approach would have been more open to question. With a well worked out protocol, it's much easier to convince a commissioner that your team not only intended to act in an appropriate manner, but did in fact do so.

The Legal Aspects of Your Investigation

Undercover producers need to consider what the law in the country in which they are filming, says about what they are planning to do.

Is Secret Filming Illegal?

In the UK, you can film undercover for journalistic purposes for a broadcaster, so long as you abide by the rules laid down by the regulator Ofcom. These rules don't apply to on demand programme providers[9] but they are considered to be 'best practice' and lawyers advising such online providers are likely to tell producers to follow them anyway. With no equivalent to Ofcom in America, producers who want to film covertly have to assess the risk of being prosecuted for illegally intruding on someone's privacy, as I explained earlier in this chapter. They also have to assess the eavesdropping law that applies in the state in which they are filming: the law that governs the consent that's required when a conversation is secretly recorded. Most states only require one party to consent to a recorded conversation – paving the way for covert sound recordings (and filming) with bad guys. But in 12 US states, the law insists that both parties must consent to a recorded conversation – which makes secret filming more difficult, but not impossible in these states (see the text box on the next page). It's important to take the advice of a lawyer in the country in which you plan to film covertly to guide you in both the criminal law risks, if there are any, and the civil law issues of what you're planning.

Even if a covert approach is legal under the country's criminal codes, the broadcast of secretly filmed images can sometimes contravene the law. Some years ago the BBC commissioned my company to make an undercover documentary in Jordan about the abuse of disabled children living in care homes. We'd compiled sufficient evidence of verbal, physical and sexual abuse to secretly film in two of these homes. This was a very sensitive issue – as it necessitated filming children. So we knew we'd have to blur the faces of any who appeared in the film. We didn't want to disguise the faces of any carers caught on camera abusing children, but asked a Jordanian lawyer what the country's law said about secret filming and about identifying the culprits. He told us that secret filming was legal in the country if what we were doing was in the public interest. So, much as in the UK, we'd have a defence if the owners of the care homes decided to sue and we ended up in court. But we had to be very careful about identifying care home workers on camera: Jordanian law said that if the workers were employed by the Government, it was illegal to identify them, whatever they were doing. Fortunately for us, the care homes were privately owned and the final

> ## Eavesdropping Laws in America
>
> Although 12 states require the consent of all parties to a conversation, there are ordinarily exceptions based on reasonable expectations of privacy. So, for example, if it's a conversation that's happening on the street or in a public place where somebody else could easily overhear, then in most of these states you should not be required to obtain everyone's consent. However, if it's a telephone call or a conversation inside somebody's home or some other place where there is an expectation of privacy, then in those states, you must have consent of all parties prior to recording. If one person is in a one-party consent state and the other person is in an all-party consent sate, we would ordinarily apply the more conservative law, as it is possible that either state could exercise jurisdiction.
>
> Mike Cleaver, US Media Lawyer

film did identify several workers filmed abusing children. Such legal codes differ from country to country, of course, so you must establish your legal position at the start.

Have I Sufficient Detailed Evidence to Defend a Libel Action in Court?

You can of course be sued for libel after your film is shown – always a risk for investigative filmmakers. In the UK an individual who believes that a statement in your film is defamatory, only has to show that it refers to them and has been published. He or she does not have to prove that the statements are false. Instead the filmmaker has to prove the truth of what was said. If the complainant is a company, it only has to show that a statement is about its business and has caused or is likely to cause serious financial loss. So in the UK it's quite a high bar for journalists.

In America, the situation is reversed: it is the aggrieved individual who has to prove the falsity of a statement. In fact, if the statement is about a public figure or a government official, he or she has to prove it's been made with actual malice, that is, made with an awareness of its falsity or with a reckless disregard for the truth. Even if what a journalist says is ultimately proven to be false, they only have to show that they had legitimate reasons for believing it to be true, to successfully defend the case. So US journalists have much more protection in law than their British equivalents when covering people in the public eye. For private individuals, the standard of proof required to win a libel case is a matter of state law, although the US Supreme Court has ruled that, where an issue of public concern is involved, as a minimum, negligence must be involved.

Whenever you work undercover, then, you have to ensure that your team compiles the evidence needed to defend their actions in court should the subjects of your investigation sue for damages. You're likely to be heavily cross examined by a lawyer whose aim is to show that you have either set-up the filming, faked-it, or that what you filmed has a less problematic interpretation. So your command of the detail and context of any contentious event is critical – and our Tower Hamlets undercover team obtained this detail by doing the following during their covert filming.

KEEPING A DAILY LOG OF THE RUSHES

The director had to view each day's filming as soon as possible after it had been filmed, noting down the significant events, where they appeared on the file, and what time they occurred. The producer also reviewed the rushes.

WRITING A DETAILED DAILY DIARY OF WHAT'S BEEN WITNESSED

Accurate and reliable note taking was essential: documenting what's been captured on camera, how it was filmed plus any relevant contextual events that might be important for validating the filming. These notes had to be written as soon as practical after the events had occurred.

Making Sure You Can Defend Your Investigation in Court

A Lawyer's View

When people do undercover, they naturally assume that: because I've got it on camera, I'm there, I don't need anything else. The camera can't lie. But of course, the camera can lie. And that's the problem. Sometimes you catch only snippets of information or the camera sometimes fails to record at a crucial moment. There have been a number of cases where the filming was fairly compelling but the subject matter of those undercovers pursued a complaint, either to the regulator or attempted to sue. Those producers who were successful in defending themselves were wise enough to ensure that, from the very outset, they were scrupulous in the way they collected the evidence. Because in those situations, the most common accusation will be: that I was entrapped; that the undercover reporter put words into my mouth; that the footage has been unfairly edited; that the footage only shows part of the story and the comments made off-camera have been omitted to conceal the truth of what really happened. It's a complex area but there are ways of working which can protect you in the event that a claim is brought. First of all, it is important that the production operates under an agreed secret filming protocol which sets out the dos' and don'ts of filming undercover – some broadcasters have their own guidelines which can be followed. Such protocols include how your undercover reporter should be briefed so that they know the difference between asking open questions and questions that are leading and might be perceived as an attempt to entrap the subject; making sure that the rushes are logged every day, that the logs are reviewed by someone senior to make sure there are no things that the reporter hasn't inadvertently missed or said that might give rise to an issue later on; keeping a contemporaneous written record. These are just some examples of the types good practice procedures which are encouraged.

Prash Naik, UK Media Lawyer and Channel 4 TV General Counsel 2014–2017

Can I Commit a Criminal Offence?

In America, with no 'public interest' defence as there is in the UK, the need to break the law to reveal a story is a question of risk assessment: how can you get the footage you want without exposing yourself to a significant legal risk of being prosecuted? Each case would be judged on its merits – balancing the value gained by breaking a particular law against the risks of being arrested and/or prosecuted and the potential consequences if that were to happen.

In the UK, breaking the law to get a story can be approved in some situations but needs specific high-level permission from your commissioner. You'll only get the green light when the public interest in breaking the law to expose wrong-doing greatly outweighs the criminal act that will be committed (see the text box). The producers of a BBC investigation about dog fighting, for example, were allowed to attend a dogfight, a criminal offence in Britain, in the interests of exposing this cruel sport. They got the OK to import a banned breed of fighting dog to show how easy it was to get them into the country. Permission was granted in the wider public interest of exposing the weakness of the laws on importing dangerous dogs and several gangs of men who were illegally fighting dogs as a sport.

Breaking the Law to Reveal an Important Story

The Lawyers' View

Britain

In the aftermath of the phone-hacking scandal, the crown prosecution service revised its guidance to crown prosecutors on the application of what's known as the 'public interest test' in the case of media defendants. This is a published document – it's freely accessible. Whilst it does not give journalists immunity from prosecution, it recognizes that some public interest journalism may carry additional weight when considering whether to initiate criminal proceedings. The guidance allows crown prosecutors to weigh up the public interest in what was exposed and how that relates, in proportionality terms, to a breach of the criminal law, and whether there are certain circumstances where it may be justifiable to not commence criminal proceedings because the revelation outweighs a breach of the criminal law. However, the best advice is to always seek legal advice at the earliest opportunity before you venture into potential breaches of the criminal law.

Prash Naik, Media Lawyer and Channel 4 TV General Counsel 2014–2017

America

Yes, sometimes filmmakers do things that could technically be considered illegal, but the risk is considered very low and all involved are on board and say: we all agree that risk is acceptable. But this is certainly a rare exception to the rule, and you should never knowingly violate any law without very careful legal supervision and a clear understanding of the potential consequences. On the other hand, sometimes filmmakers propose things that are technically legal but create a high risk of a claim that's probably not worth what the filmmaker is going to get out of it. Any claim is expensive to defend, whether or not it has a valid basis, so we're always trying to avoid the risk of any claim, balancing risk v. reward. It's important to remember that filming something that's in the public interest is not a defense to a legal claim and the fact that it's a news-worthy story isn't a 'get out of jail free' card. The First Amendment provides a lot of freedom in what you broadcast, but it does not generally provide greater access to stories. You have to look at the relevant laws surrounding the filming – because every situation will be very different, depending on the circumstances, depending on the locations where you're filming, depending on the state that you're in. It's always an assessment of risk.

Mike Cleaver, US Media Lawyer

In a film that I made about HIV/Aids in Russia, where the virus was being spread by drug addicts, I wanted a sequence showing the problem: addicts making and then fixing up an illegal home-made drug that was behind the HIV epidemic then sweeping the country. Could we do this in a way that was legal? Our advice was: don't set the sequence up specially for the camera or we'd be seen to be inciting illegality and might be held responsible should something go wrong. However, if drug making and taking was already planned, we could go along and film it. But what if the police raided the premises while we were there? To avoid any suggestion that we were involved in taking or supplying drugs, we carried a letter from the broadcaster stating who we were and what we were doing.

In our Tower Hamlets covert filming there was no need to even consider committing a criminal offence. We might witness illegal drug taking or anti-social and violent behaviour, but we wouldn't have anything to do with it.

If you think you need to break the law to make your film – do it with your eyes open – and with your commissioner's consent. If you don't, and things go wrong, at best you'll be on your own in facing the inevitable public row that will follow. At worst you might end up in jail.

The precautions I've highlighted here are aimed at reducing the risk of any negative consequences of the filming of an undercover investigative project. They can't, of course, remove risk entirely. Exposés are never completely free of risk – but your can maximize your chance of achieving your aims by thinking through the risks and taking legal advice before embarking on the project.

Pre-Screening Issues

Getting permission to *film* undercover is the first step in getting an undercover exposé on the air. You also need to obtain your commissioner's agreement to show the undercover footage to your audience. So it's a two-step process because filming the images and actuality and showing them on the TV or on the internet raise different issues. Here's examples of the kind of pre-screening questions you'll need to address.

Right-to-Reply

Any individual or company subjected to criticism in a factual film in the UK has a right, under the Ofcom Broadcasting Code,[10] to know what's being said about them prior to the film's transmission and be given a right to reply to the accusations. This is basic journalistic fairness. Without a right to reply, you would be unlikely to have a public interest defence if your programme was sued. So you have to give the subject of your covert filming an accurate written account of the allegations in the film (there's no need to give them the actual footage) – sufficient information for them to understand the claims and enable them to give an informed response should they wish to do so. They also need enough time in advance of the transmission of the film to consider the claims and give their response. How much time varies with the

> Everybody who is the target of an investigation has the right to give their point of view and they have the right to know what you're going to say about them. And they have a right to defend themselves. And they have a right to have enough time to defend themselves. And that can cause problems because people can seek legal injunctions and try and stop us putting programmes out. But again we have lawyers and where appropriate we'll fight those cases.
>
> Diana Martin, Executive Producer, BBC TV, *Panorama*

nature and complexity of the issues. They might reject your invitation to be interviewed and instead offer a written statement – and you have to reflect an accurate essence of what it says in the film.

In Britain, only if the subjects of your undercover film have been given the information about the allegations made in the film, and have ignored requests for a reply, will reputable broadcasters or online platforms allow you to 'doorstep' them, to force an on-camera response. And the decision to do so must be taken in consultation with your commissioner and their legal advisor. There might be over-riding reasons why a bad guy who has failed to acknowledge your letters and phone calls should not be door stepped – for example, if you know he or she has a heart condition or is very old and the shock of being confronted by a film crew might be too much for them.

The situation is very different In America. With no comparable Ofcom regulator there is no similar duty to offer a right to reply to the subjects of criticism in a film. Neither does US law require a 'right to reply' and a failure to give one cannot be used as sufficient evidence of malice in a potential defamation claim. In fact the US Supreme Court has ruled that any law designed to control editorial judgments would conflict with the free press guarantees of the First Amendment of the Constitution. Despite this, when producers make allegations about an individual or a company that are not 100% verifiable, they may decide – after taking legal guidance – to offer a right to reply, in the interest of producing a fair and accurate documentary.

Do You Hide the Faces of Bad Guys?

This is not always an easy question to answer. The point of an undercover film is, of course, to expose people behaving badly – breaking the law, acting in an anti-social manner, being hypocritical, etc. So, of course, you'd want to show the faces of your intended subjects rather than hide them from public gaze. But the decision is sometimes muddied by circumstance and each case has to be considered on its merits. Here's two examples.

In the Tower Hamlets undercover shoot, our director came across a group of younger lads boasting that earlier on they'd stolen a motorbike. Do you show their faces? After some debate, we decided to hide them because they were still children and we felt it was not in the public interest to show their faces and identify them as criminals at such a young age. We also did not have first-hand evidence that they had done what they claimed they'd done. It might have been bravado.

In the Jordanian care homes undercover exposé mentioned earlier in this chapter, one of the workers we'd filmed abusing a young child wasn't wearing a headscarf. In the very conservative Muslim culture from which she hailed, in which a woman is meant to cover her hair at all times when in public places, identifying her in the film risked reprisals from her family – she might be kicked out of her home or worse. So we decided to blur her facial features to prevent such a fate.

What Do You Do About Innocent Bystanders Caught on Film?

When you're filming in the streets, it's sometimes impossible to avoid filming people who have nothing to do with your programme. Overlaying a commentary about criminal behaviour with images of people who have nothing whatsoever to do with your investigation can set up a negative association in the minds of viewers. In the UK and the US, that can lead to a civil action for damages from someone who feels their good reputation has been sullied. In the Tower Hamlets undercover sequences we needed to blur out the faces of people inadvertently captured in this way but who were not involved in anti-social/criminal behaviour. Because blurring out people's faces can be very time-consuming and costly in post-production it's advisable to minimize filming in locations where there are large numbers of people unless the sequence is absolutely vital.

Pre-Transmission Legal Issues

In America, the protection that the First Amendment of the Constitution gives the media the right to comment on any issues it desires, extends to on-going criminal legal cases. The only time that the US media can't comment on an on-going criminal case is where comment is banned by a gagging order issued by a judge. This is extremely difficult to obtain because it is considered a serious violation of the First Amendment. But in Britain, the law is very restrictive. Generally, once someone has been arrested or charged with a criminal offence, all that can normally be reported before the case comes to court are the basic facts of the arrest, the charge against the person and the date of the trial, information that must be carefully checked with the police. The aim is to prevent publication of anything that might unfairly influence the jury that will eventually decide the individual's guilt or innocence. Publishing any details of an ongoing criminal case that have not been revealed in court is a serious offence – journalists and broadcasters can face prosecution for contempt of court. Following a judge's ruling in a high profile civil case between the BBC and a British celebrity in 2018, the British media is now likely to take a cautious approach to even naming anyone under investigation by the police until they've been formally charged.

Some of the stories featured in Tower Hamlets were legally 'active' in this way. The manager of one store featured in the film had in fact been assaulted by a gang of young men – but there had been an arrest and a court case was pending, so we asked him only to speak in general terms about the situation in his shop, not about the specific incident. We also had to make repeated checks with the police right up to transmission to make sure there were no arrests and no-one had been charged in the incidents he did speak about.

Chapter Summary

Key Issues to Consider Before Filming Undercover

1 **Your justification for invading someone's privacy. They must be:**
   - Breaking the law.
   - Behaving in an anti-social manner.
   - Acting corruptly, incompetently, negligently or in an unjust way.
   - Making misleading statements.
   - Exposing information that helps people make decisions on an issue of public importance.
2 **Can you get the story without secret filming?**
   - If you can, don't do it.
   - If you can't, move onto point 3.
3 **Getting the 'green light' from a broadcaster to film undercover. You'll have to consider:**
   - The prior evidence you have of the problem you wish to expose- it must be first-hand evidence.
   - The equipment you'll be using to obtain your footage – and how you'll be using it.
   - The cover story your undercover team will use.

- The safety of your crew and others involved with the project.
- Guidelines to ensure your team act ethically on location.
- The legal aspects of your investigation.

4   The issues to consider before your film is shown publicly.
- Right-to-reply.
- Do you hide the faces of bad guys?
- What do you do about innocent bystanders caught on film?
- Pre-transmission legal issues.

Notes

1 www.bbc.co.uk/editorialguidelines/guidance/secret-recording/
2 www.channel4.com/producers-handbook/c4-guidelines/secret-filming-guidelines
3 Ofcom Broadcasting code, rule 8.1 www.ofcom.org.uk/__data/assets/pdf_file/0005/100103/broadcast-code-april-2017.pdf
4 www.bbc.co.uk/editorialguidelines/guidelines/editorial-standards#13thepublicinterest – section 1.3
5 www.ofcom.org.uk/__data/assets/pdf_file/0016/132073/Broadcast-Code-Full.pdf – section 7.14 and 8.12 to 8.15.
6 There may also be other laws to take into consideration, like the 1996 HIPAA Act safeguarding medical information if filming in a health care facility and what are known as 'Ag Gag' laws that in some states protect the agricultural industry from whistleblowers.
7 More information can be found here www.bbc.co.uk/safety/security/productions-on-location
8 There is one exception to this – if you have knowledge of past or future terrorist offences, or the funding of terrorists. In this case the Terrorism Act 2000 obliges everyone – including filmmakers – to inform the police of such information. Failure to do so is a criminal offence subject to a penalty of up to five years in prison or a fine or both.
9 Some on-demand programme providers do have to comply with Ofcom rules governing harmful content and commercial references, but the undercover filming regulations don't apply to them.
10 www.ofcom.org.uk/__data/assets/pdf_file/0016/132073/Broadcast-Code-Full.pdf – see sections 7.11 and 7.12.

Part 5

Financial Skills

11 Counting the Cost

Budgeting a Factual Film

KEY CONCEPTS

- A line-by-line demystification of a typical production budget – with easy to understand explanations of the more complicated categories.
- Advice about the hidden costs of making changes to your schedule.
- How to design a budget that allows you to respond to a crisis without breaking the bank.

Becoming adept at making scarce resources stretch as far as possible is a critical skill that producers need to cultivate – especially if you wish to run your own film productions. Filmmaking is an expensive business, and if you overspend on a commissioned project you're unlikely to be given a budget for another one. So it's worth taking some time to understand the requirements of a typical production budget. If you're costing a factual film for the first time, the detail required can look intimidating: a budget is really just a categorized shopping list, albeit a sophisticated one – but it's not always immediately obvious what some of the categories are for, whether you need to include them and, if you do, what the costs might be. So I am going to demystify the production budget by deconstructing it line-by-line. I will explain the more obscure, technical or complicated spending categories and suggest what you need to consider in order to complete each one. My comments will be addressed to reasonably budgeted films – and to those being made on low budgets.

Budget Design

Producers of all but the most well financed factual films always face the same conundrum: how the irresistible demands of production can be served by a fixed budget that often appears too small for the task at hand. Squaring this circle needs careful thought to stop a production falling into the red under the sometimes unpredictable demands of filming, editing and post-production. I am going to suggest two issues to keep in mind when creating and working with a budget to help ensure that your costs don't run out of control.

Maximize Cost Estimates when Preparing a Budget

How can you know at the start of a project exactly how much to allow for airfares and other transportation – before you know precisely where you will be filming? How do you know exactly how much shot footage you'll have to look through and then edit? Or how many hours of overtime your camera crew will work – before you've tackled all of the problems that arise when out filming? The short answer is that you can't know the precise costs of your film in advance. But by planning your budget estimates with care, you can leave enough slack in some categories to let you move money to where it is most needed. There is a skill to this: add too much slack and your commissioner's cost controller will become suspicious and raise questions about your costing assumptions. Add too little and you won't be able to respond to a crisis. It's a fine line to tread. Here's two pointers to designing a budget that will let you cover the unforeseen while giving your commissioner the kind of costs they're likely to approve.

Maximize Costs

The sums allowed in each section of a production budget should reflect the maximum cost of any item. For example: you need a camera for a seven day shoot and you find that a kit suitable for a self-shooting producer/director will cost you £200 per day to hire. But you also know that the facilities company is willing to offer you a four-days-paid-for-seven-days-used deal – cutting your hire charge from £1,400 to £800. Your budget should reflect the full daily £200 hire charge not the deal you strike. You then have a £600 'slush' fund stashed away for emergencies. A cost controller is unlikely to question this because the logistics of your shoot might, of course, require you to hire out two separate kits in two different locations, one for four days the other for three – and then you'd lose your four days for seven discount. The same principle applies when budgeting for airfares, hotel rooms, post-production facilities and post-production rates. The budget reflects the *maximum* price you might have to pay – not the discounted deal you're offered after bargaining with your suppliers. Do this and you are likely to have sufficient spare cash stashed away when the going gets tough.

Maximize Staffing Time

Similarly, your budget should reflect the maximum time that you think people are going to be needed on the payroll. You might decide to budget a freelance production manager for two days a week throughout a ten week schedule. But you know there will be times in the schedule when their services won't be in great demand (for example, the first part of pre-production when little travelling is being done; or the first half of your edit when there is often little to do outside the edit suite). So in reality, you might decide to reduce your production manager down to one day a week during the less pressured parts of production, saving more cash for that rainy day. But your budget would reflect the maximum cost.

Be Aware of Hidden Costs

When designing your budget – or if you're considering a schedule change once production starts – you have to be aware of indirect costs that can have a big impact on the real bottom line cost of your film. These require an understanding of a producer's legal and financial responsibilities and the technical processes of production and are best explained with an example. Production is underway and you decide to extend filming by two days to capture an unexpected sequence and have time to conduct relevant interviews. You're working on a reasonably well-budgeted film. What are your possible extra costs? The principles will be the same if you are working on a low budget – even if the costs are less than indicated here.

ITEM	EXPLANATION	COST
Producer/ Director	If you've been careful, you'll have negotiated a buy-out deal with your producer/director – meaning that she can't charge overtime for doing more hours during a working week. So she will do the two extra days filming at the weekend, fitting within your existing schedule. The overall schedule doesn't rise and there's no extra fee to pay her.	£0.00
Camera operator and kit	Camera operators won't strike that kind of a deal because their pay on a project is measured in days not weeks. So you have no choice but to pay two extra days for the camera person and their kit.	£1,500.00
Food, hotel, transport	The two extra days require your producer/director and camera operator to stay for two more nights in a hotel (£80 per person per night), be fed during this period (£20 per person per day). You'll also need two more days in the crew vehicle (£40 per day).	£480.00
Edit over-run	Your film editor says it's just not possible to cut this sequence without having extra time in the edit – so you allow two more days. You'll have to pay your editor for those extra days (£560) as editors don't normally agree a rate for the job irrespective of its length. And you'll have extra costs for the hire of the edit suite (£240).	£800.00
	Expected overspend	**£2,780.00**

Figure 11.1 Direct financial costs of two extra day's filming

Two extra edit days extend your overall schedule by two days, so you also have to pay more for the other staff on your production at that time – as shown in the following table.

ITEM	EXPLANATION	COST
Producer/ Director	They buy-out deal covers the hours she works during any week while on the project, but not an extension to her overall time working on the film. And 2 days extra on the edit means two days extra pay.	£600.00
Production Manager	Working part-time at this stage of production –you agree an extra half-a-day.	£125.00
Executive Producer	Doesn't ask for an extra fee because the extra edit time doesn't involve her in extra work.	£0.00
Assistant Producer	He has found the interviewees but it's his good relationship with them that guarantees their presence on the day. So you need him during the filming. In the UK you'd have to comply with tax rules stating that certain professions, Assistant Producers among them, have to be given a tax-deductible contract. This covers a five day working week – so the two extra filming days have to be paid.	£360.00
Holiday pay	In the UK, lengthening the schedule by two days means adding 10.77% extra for statutory holiday pay for the editor, PD, PM and AP.	£177.17
National insurance	Employers of staff on tax-deductible contracts – the AP here – also have to pay a 13.8% contribution towards their National Insurance payments in the UK.	£49.68
Pension contribution	Again, in the UK, you might also have to pay a 3% contribution towards the workplace pension of all of those employed on tax deductible contracts on the project – once again, the AP.	£10.80
	Indirect staffing costs overspend	**£1,322.65**

Figure 11.2 Indirect staffing costs of two extra day's filming

So you're racking up costs with that extra two days filming! But the reckoning isn't over yet. There could also be several other indirect technical costs to consider.

Transcription	Some of the extra shooting was spent on interviews – which will need to be transcribed. You'd allowed £1,200 in your budget for this – but find it has grown to £1,450.	£250.00
Hard drives	You are using flash cards, downloading the material to two hard drives after each day's filming and re-using the cards. Your producer/ director has already filmed much more than you expected and the extra two days (mainly filled with interviews) will more than fill the two drives. So you have to buy two more.	£150.00
Ingesting time	Altogether your producer has shot 650 minutes of rushes, not the 500 in your budget. So with 150 extra minutes of rushes to download into the edit computer you'll have to find some more money.	£65.00
Online time	Two of the new interviews have asked for anonymity. You'll need to pixellate out their faces – a process that extends your online by 30 minutes – with machine time costing £150/hour.	£75.00
	Indirect technical costs overspend	**£540.00**
	Total indirect (staffing and technical) costs overspend	**£1,862.65**
	Total overspend (direct and indirect costs)	**£4,642.65**

Figure 11.3 Indirect technical costs of two extra day's filming

What might have appeared like a £2,780 overspend caused by extending filming by two days – ends up 67% higher when you add on the indirect costs.

So give your schedule and your budget a lot of thought. Take advice from people who are used to working in factual programming. You will always feel you don't have enough money to make your film, but by being aware of real costs and by careful budget design, you can usually find a bottom line cost that your commissioner will pay – and that you feel confident to work with.

The Production Budget for a Factual Film: A Line-By-Line Deconstruction

There's no set format for a budget but they all follow similar principles. It is a guide, a way of grouping together similar items and you can add or delete lines to suit your project. In what follows I have split the budget into sections: a summary page followed by the detailed spending categories themselves. You can either read the explanations here – or go onto the accompanying website where you'll find an interactive version of this budget and the explanations: simply click on cells that are highlighted to obtain relevant information that will help you complete your own budget. You can also download a clean budget spread sheet for your own project. Commissioning departments sometimes have their own they ask producers to use – so ask before adopting the one here or making up your own. The advice offered is targeted both at funded films and at producers working on low budgets.

Budget Summary

The first page or two of any budget is a summary sheet. Here we find an overview of the film, and the totals in each costing schedule.

		BUDGET SUMMARY		
1	Programme Title			
2	No. of Programmes:			
3	Duration:			
4	Commissioning Dept.			
5	TX date (if known)		**Date:**	
			Prepared by:	
	COST SCHEDULES – TOTALS	**SUMMARY**		
6	DEVELOPMENT			0
7	PRODUCTION STAFF			0
8	OTHER STAFF			0
9	PRODUCTION: CREW			0
10	PRODUCTION EQUIPMENT			0
11	EDITING: CREW			0
12	FLASH CARD STOCK			0

Figure 11.4

13	POST-PRODUCTION				0
14	ARCHIVE				0
15	TRAVEL/TRANSPORT				0
16	HOTEL/LIVING EXPENSES				0
17	LEGAL/INSURANCE				0
18	PRODUCTION OVERHEADS				0
19	**TOTAL-DIRECT COSTS**				0
20	PRODUCTION FEE	PERCENTAGE OF DIRECT COSTS	0		0
21	CONTINGENCY				0
22	**TOTAL BUDGET**				**00.00**

<u>Key</u>

▓▓▓ Cells containing calculated totals　☐ & ☐ 0 ☐ Cells requiring your input

Figure 11.4 Continued

The line numbers in the following explanations of the budget categories refer to the numbers on the far left of the spreadsheets.

1– 5 – Programme Information

These cover the working title of the film; the number of programmes if it's a series; its duration, its broadcast date if known and if commissioned by a TV channel; the commissioning department; and the date the budget was prepared – and by whom. The date is important since it will distinguish between budget revisions that can occur as you negotiate for your cash.

6–18 – Cost Schedules – Totals

Costs on a film budget are broken down into different kinds of spending – and each kind is called a schedule. Lines 6–18 contain the total sums budgeted for each of the detailed schedules that appear later on in the budget.

19 – Total Direct Costs

This is the total production costs of making your film – but not the total bottom–line cost, as there are two further sums to add in the next two sections.

20 – Production Fee

This is the 'mark-up' or profit margin that an independent production company takes for the responsibility of managing the project. There's no set percentage mark-up. It's usually agreed by negotiation and varies with the size of the budget and the organization that's paying for the film but is generally somewhere between 10% and 15% of the direct costs of production on factual commissions. It is reasonable for a company to charge a production fee: it takes all the risks of production and if the film goes over-budget, it is usually the company's responsibility – not that of the commissioning platform.

21 – Contingency

The difficulty or the very nature of some films makes it hard to estimate certain costs. There might, for example, be significant uncertainties in the length of time needed to research an investigative film; or it might not be clear whether you will be offered filming access to a particular observational sequence with the police – the film doesn't fall without it, but it will need several days extra filming if you get it. In these circumstances, a contingency sum is added. This extra amount is outside the main budget – it can only be used for the specific purpose for which it is included and is generally not included when estimating your production fee.

22 – Total Budget

A summation of the direct costs of production plus the production fee and any contingency. In other words – the final bottom-line costs of your project.

Schedule and Staffing

The next lines in your budget offer a commissioner a handy overview of the project's duration and staffing.

	PROJECT SCHEDULE SUMMARY			
	STAGE OF PRODUCTION	FROM	TO	TOTAL WEEKS
23	DEVELOPMENT			0
24	PREPRODUCTION			0
25	PRODUCTION			0
26	POST-PRODUCTION – EDITING			0
27	FINAL POST-PRODUCTION			0
	TOTAL			**0**

	STAFFING SCHEDULE SUMMARY							
	ROLE	DEV	PREPROD	PROD	EDIT	POST	TOTAL DAYS	TOTAL WEEKS
				DAYS				
28	EXEC PROD	0	0	0	0	0	0	0
29	DIRECTOR	0	0	0	0	0	0	0
30	PRODUCER	0	0	0	0	0	0	0
31	ASSISTANT PRODUCER	0	0	0	0	0	0	0
32	RESEARCHER	0	0	0	0	0	0	0
33	PRODUCTION MANAGER	0	0	0	0	0	0	0
34	FILM EDITOR	0	0	0	0	0	0	0
35	REPORTER	0	0	0	0	0	0	0
36	PRESENTER	0	0	0	0	0	0	0

Figure 11.5

37	CAMERA OPERATOR	0		0	0	0	0	0	0
38	SOUND RECORDIST	0		0	0	0	0	0	0
39	LOCAL FIXER	0		0	0	0	0	0	0
40	OTHER STAFF	0		0	0	0	0	0	0

Key

▨ Cells containing calculated totals   ☐ & ⟨0⟩ Cells requiring your input

Figure 11.5 Continued

23–27 – Schedule Summary

These lines detail the precise dates (if you have agreed them) of each stage of production and their overall lengths.

28–40 – Staffing Summary

Although these cells repeat the information that will be contained within several different schedules lower down on the budget, it is useful to be able to see at a glance one list of the key staff employed on your project with the times they are on-board during each stage of production. Laying the details out in visual form helps to focus your mind on this task. There's no need to add staff provided by your post-production suite as their fee is rolled into the hire cost of the equipment.

Costing Schedules

The rest of the budget is a detailed breakdown of individual costs that, once added up, are summarized on the opening page. First – take a broad look at the layout, then read on to get more information about the spending categories. You'll see that there's an item 'rate' or 'cost' column (depending on whether you are detailing staff fees or equipment and other non-personnel costs) and then columns for the amount of time you'll need each person or item, measured either in days or weeks during each stage of production. One week = five days. Where an individual is not working a full week you'd put a fraction in here – so 0.2 for someone working one day a week. If an item/person is missing from any schedule, simply add another line and include it.

The final column in each category – the total cost of the relevant line in the budget – is calculated automatically by the spread sheet.

In what follows, some costing lines are obvious and need no explanation. Others are explained in detail.

		RATE	DEVEL TOTAL COST	PRE	PROD'N	EDIT/POST	TOTAL
	SCHEDULE 1						
	DEVELOPMENT						
41	**DEVELOPMENT COSTS**		0	×	×	×	0
						Total:	**0**

Key

▨ Cells containing calculated totals ⟨0⟩ Cells requiring your input ☒ Item not required

Figure 11.6

41 – Development

Only complete this line if you have received and spent a development budget, because however much you've been given has to be paid back from your final production budget – so it becomes an expenditure line in the budget. You only add the total cost in here because you will already have submitted a detailed breakdown of your costs to obtain the development budget in the first place. A funded development is a bit like a grant that's only repaid if you get a commission.

	SCHEDULE 2						
	PRODUCTION STAFF	RATE	PRE WEEKS	PROD'N WEEKS	EDIT WEEKS	POST DAYS	TOTAL
42	**EXECUTIVE PRODUCER**	0	0	0	0	0	0
43	**PRODUCER/DIRECTOR**	0	0	0	0	0	0
44	**RESEARCHER**	0	0	0	0	0	0
45	**ASSISTANT PRODUCER**	0	0	0	0	0	0
46	**PRODUCTION MANAGER**	0	0	0	0	0	0
47	**FIXER**	0	0	0	0	×	0
48	**REPORTER**	0	0	0	0	0	0
49	**ARCHIVIST**	0	0	0	0	0	0
50	**PRODUCTION ACCOUNTANT**	0	0	0	0	0	0
51	**NATIONAL INSURANCE (UK) – MEDICARE/ SOCIAL SECURITY (US)**	0	0	0	0	0	0
						Total:	**0**

Key

| | Cells containing calculated totals | 0 | Cells requiring your input | × | Item not required |

Figure 11.7

Schedule 2: Production Staff

42 – Executive Producer

Executive Producers are not budgeted full-time (they often work on more than one film at a time). Their time is counted in days.

- *Budgeted films:* will most likely schedule an EP at 1 day a week during pre-production, production and the edit.
- *Low budget films:* an experienced EP is a good use of money because, alongside editorial and directorial advice, they'll also be able to help advise on the best ways of keeping your costs down. But you'll have to strictly limit an EP's presence on the payroll. For a 40 minute

film you might consider one or two days during pre-production for advice on turning a treatment into a visual narrative and on devising a practical filming schedule; one day during production to help with problems on the shoot, and two or three days during the edit for advice on the paper cut and to cover the viewings.

43 – Producer/Director

A producer's responsibility for determining the editorial content of a film necessarily involves him or her from the start of the full production schedule to the end. When a director joins a project varies with the kind of budget.

- *Budgeted films*: directors are usually taken on board a week or two before the end of pre-production, once the research is coming to an end and the editorial line of the film is clear. This gives them time to work out a visual approach to the narrative. They'd then work down to the end of post-production. Many factual films employ producer/directors to save money and to unify the editorial and visual approach.
- *Low budget films*: it's best to combine the producer and director roles into one person. But you'll need that person on the project throughout your production schedule.

44–45 – Researcher and Assistant Producer (AP)

They have different roles during pre-production, production and the offline edit.

- *Budgeted films:* on well-funded films, a researcher or AP will be on the schedule throughout most of pre-production – and often also during production. They'll have had the closest contact with your interviewees, so their presence during filming is reassuring for contributors who can sometimes be intimidated by a film crew. On a sensitive investigation, your researcher or AP can make the difference between an interview and a 'no show'. You have to balance this need against the extra cost to your budget. You might be able to have your cake and eat it by choosing a researcher or AP who can shoot. That way you can keep them on board during production, and reduce costs by getting them to film some sequences themselves, instead of hiring a camera operator. On an observational film, for example, a self-shooting AP can pick up a sequence that might take half-a-day to film with a key interviewee, one that might prove too expensive to for a professional camera person to film, since most will not work for less than a full day's pay. On a decent budget you might also reserve a week for your researcher/AP to do a fact check during the closing stages of the edit.
- *Low budget films*: all research and assistant producer tasks will inevitably be undertaken by the film's producer/director.

46 – Production Manager (PM)

If you're working through an established independent production company, the PM is likely to be an employee. But many PMs work freelance – so you could hire one if you're running the project yourself.

- *Budgeted films*: it's a good use of your resources to take an experienced Production Manager onto the payroll during key stress periods on a film schedule: before any work begins to prepare a schedule and budget (half a day); during pre-production to organize research trips, plan the day-by-day film schedule, and contract staff and facility houses. How much time you'll need a PM depends on the complexity of your project, some films only need a day or two each week during pre-production – others might need a full-time PM. During production most budgeted films will have a PM on full-time to deal with the day-to-day stresses of a shoot. During the edit and post-production, a PM will normally only be on the payroll part-time to handle intermittent tasks (arranging filming that you need during the edit; obtaining transcripts for a late interview; organizing archive/stills; making payments – a PMs responsibility on a reasonably budgeted film).

- *Low budget films:* the producer is likely to take on this role. But there are some pressure points in a schedule where paying for a few hours of an experienced PM's time is money well spent. For example: half a day for advice on how to create a realistic schedule and budget; or a day with an experienced PM towards the end of pre-production to help devise a practical filming schedule. If you're working to a tight deadline or managing a complicated shoot involving lots of travel, all the logistical, financial and managerial tasks can rapidly soak up your energy – leaving you too drained to think creatively about the filming and editing. So don't take on too much. If needs be, persuade someone to help manage the production with you – even if they end up doing it for kudos and a credit alone.

47 – Fixer

On page 148 in Chapter 8 I explained the importance of working with a knowledgeable local fixer when filming abroad. Whatever budget you are on, my advice is *don't skimp* on a local fixer because they are, as their title suggests, someone who can not only fix things for you – but also get you out of a fix.

- *Budgeted and low budget films*: **you are likely to need this person during part of pre-production to find contributors, filming locations and arrange filming permissions; throughout production – accompanying you during the filming, and if needed, translating for you. And also for a day during your edit for fact checking.**

48 – Reporter

A reporter will be closely involved in the development of the film's narrative and need significant input during pre-production and a presence during production, the edit and post-production. For more on the reporter's role, see pages 65-69 in Chapter 3.

- *Budgeted films*: well-funded films will have a reporter on the payroll throughout the pre-production, production and editing. During the edit, you might wish to restrict a reporter's presence to the closing couple of weeks to attend viewings, draft out and rehearse commentaries and film final camera pieces. Plus a day and a half during final post-production to finalise the commentaries and record them to picture.
- *Low budget films*: you will have to limit a reporter's presence during pre-production to a regular advice session – perhaps a half day or one day a week – so that they can input suggestions, and critique the developing narrative. You'll have them on-stream during production only for as many days as are needed to film interviews and camera pieces. Then two or three days towards the end of the edit to view rough and fine cuts of the film and write commentaries. And finally half a day during final post to record them to picture.

49 – Archivist

An Archivist can be conducting research at any stage of your production up until near the end of the edit. There's more information on the issues you need to consider when using archive and stills in schedule 9 below.

- *Budgeted films:* most archivists are freelance and are usually willing to charge by the day. In return for their fee they add value to a film by suggesting clips that otherwise would never see the light of day – and by saving producers an awful lot of time and money by handling royalty issues and striking deals with copyright owners.
- *Low budget films:* the producer/director will be doing this research.

> An archive producer acts as your deal maker. If you know that more than one person has some material at $40/second, by the time we finish it will be down to under $20/second because I will be making a deal, saying: 'I can get this from various sources, but if I get it all from yourself, what's in it for me?' They will say: 'oh well, if you give us four minutes, we'll do a deal. Yes. Very much so'. For me deal-making is probably 60% of the job now. And also they are the ones who will say: 'Gerry here's a bit of archive – and you didn't clear it'. And if you did make a mistake, they would just say: 'oh it's slipped through your mind, Gerry'. You've dealt with these guys for so long they know to trust you. So trust is also a big thing as well.
>
> Gerry Healy, Film Archivist

50 – Production Accountant

- *Budgeted films:* on well budgeted film a production accountant sets up a dedicated bank account for the project and runs a cost manager to track spending. They issue regular reports, including a forecast of likely spending, which lets you respond to an overspend in one category, by using money from another to make up the deficit and keep the overall film solvent. At the end of production your accountant will produce a final cost report for your commissioner showing where the money's been spent and whether the production is over or under budget. Some American broadcasters also require what's called a 'general ledger', a print out of every item that's been spent. Accountants usually charge by the day – and how much time you need depends on the size and complexity of the project. A ball-park figure for factual films would be one day every two or four weeks during pre-production and editing/post-production; one day a week during production.
- *Low budget films:* you can dispense with an accountant if you are prepared to track your own costs as the project progresses. The risk is that you take on too much, fail to keep on top of your spending and find out when it's too late that you've gone way over budget. DIY accounting has its risks. You've also got to produce a proper cost report for a broadcaster or online platform at the end of production – and an accurate set of project accounts for the tax office at the end of the year. So don't take this on unless you are really convinced you have the ability and time to do it properly.

51 – National Insurance/Workplace Pension (UK) – Medicare/Social Security (US)

In the UK certain staff on a film production – broadly those with 'assistant' in their title (edit assistant, production assistant, camera assistant, assistant producer, etc.) can't be employed on a freelance basis. The tax office insists that such people are employed on a tax deductible contract.[1] Employing people on such contracts adds to your production costs because you, the employer, have to contribute to their National Insurance payments. The rate in 2020 was 13.8%.[2] UK employers also have to make a 3% contribution towards the workplace pension of such staff (unless they have opted out). So if you agree a fee of £200/day the real cost to your production could be £233.60. Employing staff on similar tax deductible contracts in America also adds to a production's costs – because employers are obliged to contribute to employees' social security and medicare payments – and also pay some local taxes which vary from state to state.

	SCHEDULE 3						
	OTHER STAFF	RATE	PRE	PROD'N	EDIT	POST	TOTAL
				DAYS			
52	PRESENTER	0	×	0	0	0	0
53	TRANSCRIPTION AND/ OR TRANSLATION	0	×	0	0	×	0
54	TRANSLATOR: EDIT SUITE	0	×	×	0	×	0
55	CONSULTANT	0	0	0	0	×	0
						Total:	0

Key

[shaded] Cells containing calculated totals [0] Cells requiring your input [×] Item not required

Figure 11.8

Schedule 3: Other Staff

These lines are for people who appear on your schedule for shorter periods but are not core members of the production team.

52 – Presenter

Not generally involved in creating the editorial content – so if you are using one, they will only need a day at the end of pre-production to get acquainted with the film. Whatever your budget, though, you will need enough time with your presenter during production to film interviews and PTCs; a day to put a 'personal gloss' on the style of the narration and to practice reading the commentaries to picture to make sure each one fits. If there are final camera pieces to film, you might also need an extra day during the edit, plus half a day to record the commentaries during final post-production.

53 – Transcription and/or Translation

I outlined the reason why you need transcripts when making longer films on pages 109–110 in Chapter 6.

- *Budgeted films:* you'll normally either be charged per 1,000 words of transcription/translation or per minute of interview time. Translation is much more expensive than transcription.
- *Low budget films*: I discuss ways of organizing transcription and translation for films being made to low budgets or tight deadlines on pages 174–175 in Chapter 9.

54 – Translator in the Edit Suite

When you've finished cutting a film that contains foreign language, you should always bring a translator into the edit suite to check your edits and your translations. This does not take very long – you might need to cost for half a day of a translator's time – but it will ensure that you don't make any unnecessary errors in your subtitles – or over-dubbing – and that the edits in interviews really are at the points you intend them to be.

55 – Consultant

Other key people involved on projects with reasonable budgets, are usually on the payroll for shorter periods of time. You might need a consultant, for example, on an historical or scientific film during pre-production and possibly also to check facts for the narration that you write towards the end of your offline. Such experts are usually not paid by the day – but are offered a set fee.

	SCHEDULE 4						
	PRODUCTION: CREW	RATE	PROD'N	EDIT	PROD'N	EDIT	TOTAL
			DAYS		OVERTIME HOURS		
56	CAMERA OPERATOR	0	0	0	×	×	0
57	CAMERA OPERATOR (OVERTIME)	0	×	×	0	0	0
58	SOUND RECORDIST	0	0	0	×	×	0
59	SOUND RECORDIST (OVERTIME)	0	×	×	0	0	0
						Total:	0

Key

☐ Cells containing calculated totals   0 Cells requiring your input   × Item not required

Figure 11.9

Schedule 4: Production Crew

56 – Camera Operator

A camera person's time is measured in days not weeks – even if your shoot extends to a week or more. Obviously the majority of a camera operator's work is done during production, when most of the filming is completed. But it is possible that you will need to film stand ups (PTC's) or, on investigative films, right-to-reply interviews or 'doorsteps' during your edit. More on PTC's on pages 65–69 in Chapter 3.

- *Budgeted films:* you have to decide whether to travel your camera operator with you with all the associated costs, or pick up a local crew in each location. That decision means balancing the extra cost of travelling with a camera person you know well, someone you can trust, who can create a style for your film, against using a local camera operator whose abilities might be a lesser-known quantity, but who won't rack up heavy travel and subsistence costs.

- *Low budget films:* a self-shooting PD is the most cost effective approach. So no need to fill in this line. The only extra costs to your budget then will be the hire of the camera kit. On a very low budget project, you are going to be self-shooting. But do you have the skills to do this? There's no point bringing back 20 hours of un-cuttable rushes to an edit. So be sure about your abilities as a camera operator, and as a film director, before deciding to shoot your own project. Chapters 3 and 4 tell you more about the skills you need to direct (and shoot) images and interviews.

57 – Camera Operator (Overtime)

Most camera operators will strike a 10 or 12 hour day deal with a production company. That means you pay for a day that lasts 10 or 12 hours from the time the camera person starts travelling to the location to the time he/she gets home again. Any time worked over these periods will incur an hourly overtime rate. If you are working with a camera operator, it's worth budgeting for a small amount of overtime (a few hours) because the unforeseen can sometimes make it very difficult to bring in a day's filming exactly on time.

58–59 – Sound Recordist and Sound Recordist (Overtime)

Many factual films are now shot without a sound recordist. But if you are working with one, exactly the same overtime principles apply as those outlined in line 57 above.

- *Budgeted films:* you might need a sound recordist for the odd day if you need to film a group discussion, for example, where you'll need a hand-held boom mic (a microphone attached on the end of a long pole) to effectively capture the sound of several people talking in different locations.
- *Low budget films:* if you have a group discussion to film, draft in some free help to operate the boom pole to keep costs down. If you are self-shooting, see pages 90–94 in Chapter 4 for more information on recording sound.

	SCHEDULE 5					
	PRODUCTION EQUIPMENT	RATE	PRE-PROD	PROD'N	EDIT	TOTAL
				DAYS	DAYS	
60	**CAMERA EQUIPMENT HIRE**	0	×	0	0	0
61	**SOUND EQUIPMENT HIRE**	0	×	0	0	0
62	**CONSUMABLES (i.e. BATTERIES, GAFFER TAPE)**	0	×	0	0	0
63	**LIGHTING EQUIPMENT**	0	×	0	0	0
64	**EXTRA LENSES**	0	×	0	0	0
65	**OTHER FILMING EQUIPMENT**	0	×	0	0	0
					Total:	**0**

Key

▨ Cells containing calculated totals   0 Cells requiring your input   × Item not required

Figure 11.10

Schedule 5: Production Equipment

60 – Camera Equipment Hire

If you're working with a camera operator you'll either hire their own camera equipment or rent it from an outside facilities company. Costs are calculated in days. Camera operators hiring their own kit usually don't offer a 'four days charged for seven days used' discount deal like equipment hire companies do – but if your schedule includes travel days where no filming is done, they'll often remove the kit charge on those days. Most camera operators are also open to negotiation over the daily cost of their kit – and the longer the shoot the better the discount you'll be able to negotiate.

- *Low budget films:* a self-shooting camera kit normally includes a tripod, batteries, carry cases, a battery charger, wet weather camera cover, flash cards. Consider the following when deciding what kit to hire:

The camera. Without training you won't be able to use a professional camera – instead aim for a high-end consumer model. Cameras are continually being updated so check with a facilities hire company to find out the range of cameras on the market suitable for a self-shooter.

The tripod. All tripods support the camera in a solid, static position. But not all tripods allow you to tilt the camera up and down or pan it left and right smoothly. This ability depends partly on the quality of the construction: heavier tripods are better at this than lighter ones because they are more stable and less likely to shift position as you move a heavy camera mounted on the top. It also rests on the construction of the movable part of the tripod head: controlling a smooth camera pan or tilt requires back pressure – otherwise, as you begin to move the camera, it will jolt out of its static position and then either judder or swing uncontrollably on its way to its destination. Cheaper tripods use friction to achieve back-pressure: as you tighten a screw the pressure increases. But it's very difficult to achieve smooth motion with friction operated tripods heads. Jagged, uneven moves are usually the norm. Smooth pans and tilts are possible with tripods that use fluid in the movable head to provide back-pressure. You can adjust the pressure to suit your needs. So if you want smooth camera pans and tilts, choose your tripod carefully – even if it costs a little more. A bad one can force you to shoot nothing but static compositions.

Camera cover. Always make sure the camera comes with a rain protector or you might find yourself paying for a costly repair if the kit is caught in a storm.

61 – Sound Equipment Hire

Sound kit hired from either a camera operator or sound recordist is budgeted in the same way as the camera gear: you pay a fee for each day you use the equipment and no fee on travel-only days. Your negotiation will be about the rate.

- *Low budget films:* if you're self-shooting and hiring from a facilities company you'll be negotiating over the number of days charged over your filming period – with four days charged over seven being the normal discount.

62 – Consumables

Anything used on the shoot that is not returnable at the end of the filming to your camera operator, sound recordist or a hire company. For example: batteries and gaffer tape.

63 – Lighting Equipment

Most documentary and current affairs shoots only need a basic lighting kit, sufficient for filming interviews in poorly lit rooms. But you might need more extensive lighting to raise the lighting level in a large room – filming a church service, for example, or in a school dining room. You'll find more information about lighting interviews on pages 84–89 in Chapter 4.

64 – Extra Lenses

The wide angle to telephoto zoom lens attached to professional or high end consumer cameras is sufficient for most documentaries and current affairs films. But some shots are beyond the ability of the standard zoom lens. Extreme telephoto images that provide a very narrow field of view and let you capture that huge image of the sun setting over the hills, need a long telephoto prime lens; very short focal length lenses can offer extreme wide-angle perspectives on the world; and macro lenses are required to capture close up images of small items like insects. If you do need extra lenses and are self-shooting, ensure that the camera comes with a replaceable – rather than a fixed – zoom lens. The effects you can achieve with different lenses are explained on pages 45–46 in Chapter 3, and page 90 in Chapter 4.

65 – Other Filming Equipment

A wide range of other filming kit can enhance the images you shoot. In Chapter 3 I discuss camera cranes, dollies, camera harnesses and aerial drones. There's a lot of other specialist kit for hire: car mounts that offer unusual perspectives on travelling vehicles; very small cameras to film in confined spaces or capture dramatic sequences like an armed police raid; and cameras disguised as shirt buttons or hidden in pens, cans of coke or inside a shoulder bag to catch those bad guys red handed. This kind of kit offers exciting perspectives on the world – but be aware that the costs can be high – and setup time can significantly impact on your schedule.

	SCHEDULE 6						
	EDITING: CREW	RATE	PROD'N	EDIT	PROD'N	EDIT	TOTAL
			WEEKS		DAYS		
66	**FILM EDITOR**	0	0	0	×	×	0
67	**EDITOR OVERTIME**	0	×	×	0	0	0
						Total:	**0**

Key

☐ Cells containing calculated totals | 0 | Cells requiring your input | × | Item not required

Figure 11.11

Schedule 6: Editing: Crew

66–67 – Film Editor and Editor Overtime

On a fast-turn-around film you might start editing before filming finishes – which is why there's a costing column during production for an editor in this category.

- *Budgeted films:* editors normally charge a weekly fee. When you are working towards a viewing, edits can become very pressured sometimes extending a normal working day well into the evening. Few editors are 9-to-5 jobs-worths and will put in the extra effort to make things work. But you don't want to exploit their goodwill either. So it's worth adding an overtime line to offer some compensation for unsocial late night working. One or two days is my suggestion – so in the overtime column, for two days, you'd put 0.4 (two days being 0.4 of a five day week)
- *Low budget films:* you can save money by doing the first part of the edit yourself – to produce a very rough cut of the film (see page 116 in Chapter 6) either on your own computer using a software package like iMovie (for Apple computers) or Adobe Premier Elements (for PCs) – or on professional editing software in a post-production suite. You're not actually editing the film. You are selecting the shots and interviews that you'd like a film editor to cut together, assembling them in a list along with all the images needed for each sequence. Then you'd hand the edit over to a professional editor. One downside of this is that, by limiting an editor's knowledge of the all material you've shot, you might limit their creative ability to make visual connections that add to the film. Filmmakers with significant experience of editing can, of course, opt to do the entire edit themselves. While neither of these approaches will shorten your overall schedule length, they will reduce costs by shortening the time that an editor is required at this stage of production.

	SCHEDULE 7					
	FLASH CARD STOCK	COST	PROD'N	EDIT	POST	TOTAL
			NUMBER	NUMBER	NUMBER	
68	**MEMORY CARDS/DISKS**	0	0	0	×	0
69	**HARD DRIVES**	0	0	0	×	0
					Total:	0

Key

⬜ Cells containing calculated totals | 0 | Cells requiring your input | × | Item not required

Figure 11.12

Schedule 7: Stock

Because this category handles the purchase of items, there is a 'cost per item' column – and the number of items needed for your project.

68 – Memory Cards/Disks

What you will need will be driven by the camera you decide to use. Most cameras now use flash cards – some still record onto disk. How many you need depends on whether you keep the rushes on the storage media at the end of each day's shoot – or, wipe and reuse the media after downloading the rushes to hard drives.

69 – Hard Drives

You need two hard drives to make safety copies of your rushes if you are re-using your flash cards. If not, one safety copy will suffice.

	SCHEDULE 8				
	EDITING AND POST-PRODUCTION	RATE	WEEKS	HOURS	TOTAL
70	**INGESTING AND TRANSCODING RUSHES**	0	×	0	0
71	**EDITING SUITE**	0	0	×	0
72	**TRACKLAYING**	0	×	0	0
73	**PICTURE CONFORM**	0	×	0	0
74	**GRADING**	0	×	0	0
75	**ONLINE**	0	×	0	0
76	**COMMENTARY RECORD**	0	×	0	0
77	**SOUND DUB**	0	×	0	0
78	**FINAL FILE PREP, QUALITY CONTROL AND UPLOAD**	0	×	0	0
79	**PREPARATION OF INTERNATIONAL VERSION**	0	×	0	0
				Total:	**0**

Key

[ ] Cells containing calculated totals   [0] Cells requiring your input   [×] Item not required

Figure 11.13

Schedule 8: Editing and Post-production

Most producers dry hire an offline editing suite and bring in their own film editor. But the dubbing mixer, online and grading editors – the key technical people who help you turn your edited film into a finished product – are covered by the hire charge of the post-production kit. So you simply allow the right number of hours for the final post-production technical processes in your budget. Although it's tempting to simply put the bottom-line total cost of editing and post-production into your budget, it is important to be clear about how long you have allowed to complete each of these processes. If you leave this vague, you are likely to run into heavy overtime costs. Schedule 8 has alternative ways of measuring the time because some aspects of post-production are measured in weeks (like your edit) while much of final post-production is timed in hours. The facility house that you've picked for the job will guide you on how much time you need to allow for each of these processes.

- *Low budget films:* if your budget is really limited, you can avoid most of the costs of final post by post-producing your film on the same computer on which you've cut the film together. First read the information in categories 70 to 79 below – then read on here. To post produce in the offline edit, you must use the original (rather than a degraded version) of the rushes during your edit. At the end of the offline, you extend your edit[3] to tracklay, record the final narration, mix the sound tracks together, adjust the quality and colour of the pictures, add graphics, subtitles, names and credits. Unless you're editing the film yourself at home, you'll be paying for an offline suite and an editor for this extra time – but it will be much, much cheaper than going down the professional post-production route.

So why, you might ask, bother with all that expensive post-production in the first place if you can simply do it for little cost in an offline computer? The reason is that the quality of your film suffers when you cut corners like this: the sound of your commentary will not be as good because it hasn't been recorded in a sound-proofed commentary suite; you have less flexibility to adjust the look of the images in your film; you won't be using a properly calibrated monitor so won't see the level of detail in the images possible on a monitor in a post-production suite; you don't have the technical kit to see whether the luminance and colour levels of your images are correct; and the ability to blur out faces varies with the software package being used, some are more sophisticated than others. You also can't generate a quality control report demonstrating that the sound and pictures comply with rigorous technical specification[4] that broadcasters and some online platforms insist upon. This might not matter on a YouTube film – but it will matter if you are delivering to the BBC, to a US broadcaster or to Amazon or Netflix. This process does have to be undertaken in a properly equipped post-production suite. Finally: the sound track requirements of some international versions can be complicated and are difficult to achieve in an offline suite.

70 – *Ingesting and/or Transcoding Rushes*

Before you can edit your rushes, they have to be downloaded onto the hard drive of the computer on which you'll be editing. This is called ingesting. It's a process that takes time and for which post-production houses charge an hourly fee. The editing software used in today's computers – Avid Media Composer, Final Cut Pro, Adobe Premiere, DaVinci Resolve for example – can ingest rushes shot by most digital cameras[5] without the need to convert them into another format. But if storage space on the edit computer is limited, you might need to transcode the rushes – removing information from them to reduce their file size and improve performance in the edit. It takes about 30 minutes to ingest each hour of rushes. Transcoding times depend on the quality of the original rushes – and can vary from 30 to 90 minutes for an hour of rushes.

71 – *Editing Suite*

Unless you ask your post-production suite to provide an offline editor to cut your film, this is the only 'dry hire' budget line in this category. If not, the cost of the editor is covered in lines 66–67 above. Most factual producers bring in an experienced freelance film editor to cut their projects.

72 – *Tracklaying*

More often than not in a film you are listening to more than one sound track at a time. There can be the natural sound of a demonstration, for example, overlaid with the sound of an interviewee speaking or a reporter's narration, plus a third sound track of music and sometimes a fourth of sound effects. All these tracks have eventually got to be mixed together at the right levels, but before that can happen, the different sounds have to be laid in the right places relative to each other: each different kind of sound (interviews, commentary, music, sound effects, etc.) has to be on a different track – with enough of a 'tail' at the start and end to allow for fading the sounds in and out. This is called track-laying.

73 – Picture Conform

Many factual films are still edited using images that have been degraded – to save on hard drive storage space or to improve the speed at which edit software operates. The pictures are viewable but have been transcoded to a lower quality format to produce smaller file sizes. So when you reach final post, each low quality image in your edit has to be replaced with its high quality original from the rushes. This is an automatic process. Your film editor supplies a list of in and out times for each shot that's used in the film and one by one, the originals are painted over the low quality, offline images.

74 – Grading

The process of adjusting the colour, brightness, hue and contrast of the images in your programme. You might need to correct under/over exposed shots or add a particular effect to a sequence – for example colourizing a dramatic reconstruction to make it stand out from the rest of your film. How long this takes depends on how fussy you are about the overall 'look' of your film.

Grading

Understand what you can achieve in the budget and time you've got available. If you are working with somebody that wants everything to be absolutely perfect – and I get that as a goal – you are going to go over budget. What usually happens is, you get too involved with the 1% increase in the black level, or a slight change in the gamma and then, when you watch it back on the run, you don't even notice that [change] was even there. It doesn't matter in the grand scheme of the story. So understand what you can achieve on your budget – and what the audience are going to notice.

Pixellating/Blurring Faces

What can take time is deciding how blurred you want it to be. It's a lot quicker if you just put a big blob on things because you don't have to worry too much about tracking it accurately. But somebody can think it doesn't look very nice if something is very blurred [and] want to minimize the amount of blur – because it takes away from the story-telling if stuff's got obvious blurs all over it. But the danger of that is that you then spend a lot of time squinting at it asking: 'would their mother recognize them?' That sort of question. And also: the tracking software works really well on nice tripod shots – but as soon as you go hand-held, undercover, which can be grainy, then the tracking software can have real issues and that's when it takes time because you're just doing things manually a lot of the time.

Peter Zacaroli, Managing Director, West Digital Post-Production

75 — Online

The final task in post-production — where you finish your film by adding graphics or other visual effects you might need; adding on-screen name captions, a film title, credits and a company/broadcaster/online platform logo at the end. The length of an online varies wildly with the complexity of the tasks. If you only need to add a few name captions and credits, it won't take very long. But if you need to blur out people's faces — the more faces, the longer the online's going to take (see the text box on the previous page).

76 — Commentary Record

Any commentary laid into a film during the offline will be a rough version, recorded on a lip mic in the edit suite. This narration is then replaced[6] with a high quality version recorded by a voice-over artist or your presenter/reporter in a sound proofed commentary booth. Whoever does the job reads each commentary link while watching the edited film - if a link doesn't quite fit, it can be subbed down on the spot to match the pictures.

77 — Sound Dub

The different kind of sounds in your film have now been laid out on different tracks, and your last sound task is the dub — also called the final mix: the process of mixing together all the sound tracks in your film at a pleasing level. It's no good putting out a film in which the commentary is swamped by the music. You'd lose intelligibility. It's equally no good putting out a film in which the commentary is so dominant that you can't hear the music track or the sound effects. You'd lose atmosphere. And you don't want to crash into an incoming music track — much better to gently fade the track in underneath an outgoing interview, for example. All these audio issues have to be ironed out in a sound mixing studio with a specialist dubbing mixer.

78 — Final File Prep, Quality Control and Upload

Post houses charge for combining the mixed sound track with the onlined pictures, undertaking the technical sound and picture quality control checks that broadcasters and some online platforms insist upon (read paragraph at top of page 224 plus the footnote), and uploading the final file to a broadcaster or online platform's website.

79 — Preparation of International Version

Films that have more than one source of funding — for example documentaries that are part funded by a foreign broadcaster, films for an online platform that need to be intelligible in different languages, or films that you wish to sell abroad — will need an additional final post-production process to prepare what's called an international version. This is a visually 'clean' copy of your film that has no captions, no subtitles, no credits and no opening and closing titles. You'll provide this information on paper to your co-producer or purchaser so they can add all this in local language themselves. You'll also have to provide a different sound track to the one that is prepared for your original film — one that at least permits the replacement of narration. The exact audio requirements of international broadcasters vary and you'd need to check individual needs.

	SCHEDULE 9					
	ARCHIVE, STILLS & MUSIC	RATE	NO.	HOURS	MINS	TOTAL
80	SEARCH FEES	0	×	0	×	0
81	VIEWING COSTS	0	×	0	×	0
82	DIGITISING FEES	0	×	0	0	0
83	ROYALTIES – ARCHIVE	0	×	×	0	0
84	ROYALTIES – STILLS	0	0	×	×	0
85	ROYALTY FREE ARCHIVE	0	0	×	×	0
86	ROYALTY FREE STILLS	0	0	×	×	0
87	MUSIC: ALLOW	0	0	×	×	0
					Total:	0

Key

☐ Cells containing calculated totals [0] Cells requiring your input [×] Item not required

Figure 11.14

Schedule 9: Archive, Stills and Music

Most archive footage and still images have now been digitized and put online – so getting hold of a viewing copy is normally a cost free process. You simply download a watermarked or low resolution version from the website of whatever library has the material you'd like. But calculating the cost of using archive material depends on whether the footage or stills originate from a royalty-based library source or a royalty free source. The fees charged by the former are more expensive and more complicated to calculate. Those charged by the latter are much simpler and cheaper.

Before using any images or filmed archive that have not been specially filmed for you it's prudent to carefully consider the costing issues listed in this schedule – whatever source you are obtaining them from. Failing to do this might open you to being sued after the film is shown.

The traditional libraries are clinging to the 30 second or 1 minute minimum [usage]. This method is being fractured by the new royalty-free archives as minimums will be increasingly difficult, if not impossible, to maintain. I was recently quoted a price of £3500.00 for a two second clip – because of the 1 minute minimum rules! This made it utterly impossible to accept. I got a better clip elsewhere for just $150.00. Unless it is impossible to avoid, no one will pay minimums for old archive. In my opinion, minimums days are numbered.

Gerry Healy, Film Archivist

80–82 – Search Fees, Viewing Costs and Digitizing Fees

You'll only be charged search fees if you need to ask a film archive to search out undigitized material. So if it's old film or tape footage you're interested in, you might need to obtain an estimate of the costs of their researcher digging out the material, viewing it on their equipment, and then giving you a digitized version.

83 – Royalties – Archive

Long-established archives like British Pathe, Movietone, APTN, the BBC as well as US networks like CBS, ABC, NBC, Fox, etc. charge a royalty fee for the use of their material. These are the fees that give you the right to use their footage in your film. They vary widely from library to library and from country to country. The cost that you put into this section can only be an estimate at the stage of preparing your budget as you're unlikely to know exactly what footage you'll need from which archive – never mind how much you'll use in your as yet unedited film. What you put in this spending category will ultimately restrict how much footage you can use – because you are unlikely to get a sympathetic hearing if you go back later on and ask for more money. So it's worth giving this section considerable thought as well as doing some costing research.

If you have an archive intensive film, and a reasonable budget, it is worth paying a specialist archive researcher who can help you find the footage and negotiate the rights clearances. You need to find out what clearances your commissioner requires before you can begin to estimate likely costs of using archive from copyrighted sources. With that information, you have to take the following seven decisions in calculating likely royalty fees.

How much footage will you use? Libraries usually quote the cost of using their material by the second. But many have a thirty second or even one minute minimum usage fee, with the cost accruing per second after the minimum is reached. Some archivists think the days of such minimum fees are numbered (see the text box on the previous page). The more footage you use from one library the better the deal you will be able to strike.

Where will the footage be shown? You will have to decide the territories for which you require clearance. In other words: where do you wish to screen their material? Clearly it will be cheaper to buy footage to show in one country – than it will to get clearance to show it in any country in the world. Royalty costs vary from country to country. The most expensive market is the US, so it is cheaper to request clearance to show the footage throughout the world if you exclude the US market – than if you include it. If you are using footage from an American archive the costs also tend to be higher. With many films now being placed on digital platforms, world clearance is now requested for archive used in most films.

In what medium will the footage be shown? Is it for internet use only? Or for internet and TV? Will it be used on a catch-up service and, if so, for how long? Or perhaps it's only for screening at a film festival? Or in cinemas? UK independent production companies that produce content for US-based TV or internet platforms like Netflix will normally clear archive for use in all media – either including theatrical (if the film is also being shown at film festivals or in cinemas) or excluding theatrical.

How long do you want to have the right to use the footage? Because many films end up on the internet, 'in perpetuity' (or unlimited) is the most common clearance that's requested. If a more limited period is required (five years, for example) and the archive will only grant a shorter licence (say, three years) you must make sure that the footage is at least clearable for the additional two years when the initial period expires, then flag this with your commissioner and come to some arrangement about how to manage the additional cost when the licence has to be renewed.

How many times will you screen the footage? If your film is being made for broadcast, how many times will it be shown? If it's for an online platform that places films online permanently, you'd request the use of the archive 'in perpetuity' (see above) and clear it for an indefinite number of screenings. Some traditional archives still insist on a limit to the number of screenings they will offer.

> Nothing is easier than to put something up on YouTube. Nothing more difficult than finding out who put it up there in the first place. So you can't just take something off Vimeo or YouTube, put it in your film and use it. You could be sued. Don't ever play fast and loose with it, it's just not worth it. You have to find someone who shot it and say: 'can we pay you for your clip'. That way you're covered. But you do not just use material in the hope that no-one sees it, especially nowadays when there are so many outlets.
>
> Gerry Healy, Film Archivist

YouTube and Vimeo footage. This is not copyright free, so using it without a licence from the rights holder is risky. The owner could object to its re-use and bring a damages claim against you. If you can't track down the owner, you can lower that risk, by keeping a paper trail of the steps you took to try and find them, and by setting aside a sum from your budget specifically to pay for any claim after the film has been shown. But this doesn't remove the risk and you could still end up paying significant damages in a legal dispute with the owner.

Underlying rights. Beware! Buying the use of the footage doesn't necessary buy all the rights to its use. You have to check if there are any underlying rights due: for example, payments to artists or musicians who appear in the clip, even when the clip is very old and tracking down every individual and negotiating a fee can be time consuming and costly in its own right even before you pay the fees. So it's best to avoid using clips involving dancers backed by a full-blown orchestra!

84 – Royalties – Stills

Deciding how much you need to pay for a copyrighted still image from a traditional, royalty based library is similar to the one described for archive. But you pay a 'flash' fee to use a still – that is, a royalty fee for each time you show the image in your film rather than a fee that increases as the length of time the image is on-screen increases. So if you show the still twice, you will normally pay twice – albeit you can get 50% reductions for second and subsequent usage. The other royalty issues (where will the image be shown? How many times will the film containing the image be screened? In what medium will it be used? And over what period do you want permission to use the image) are the same.

85–86 – Royalty Free Archive or Stills

These are a new breed of 'upstart' online libraries in America and Canada[7] plus a small number in the UK[8] that have dispensed with royalty fees and complicated licence agreements. Instead, for a set fee, you are given the right to use their footage worldwide, in perpetuity and

> The change in archive research has probably been greater in the last five years than it was in the last 50. It is becoming something akin to an 'Uberization' of the archive world. There are now so many, primarily United States, companies who are selling archive very, very inexpensively – almost akin to a Walmart style – in a way that's royalty free. You take it, you pay them, and it now belongs to yourself, not the company – because what they are selling is mostly, but not entirely, US public domain material. So in some respects film archive research has got much, much, simpler. The pitfall now, if you are a younger person, is to be very wary of copyright archive: the traditional archives are still operating on a royalty basis. And be aware that once you get a contract from certain companies you have to ensure that it covers everything you need.
>
> Gerry Healy, Film Archivist

are indemnified in the event of a legal claim for using the footage. Much of this is American public domain archive material – in other words footage that is no longer in copyright. Some is footage shot by amateurs or professionals and placed on these sites for re-sale. Fees are low: one site quotes between $105 and $350 for their clips, however you use them. Another varies the fee with the intended use of the footage: lowest prices on a personal website, more for corporate productions and highest rates for TV, feature film and advertising. But the fees are still much lower than those charged by traditional archives and there's no complicated clearances to worry about.

87 – Music

Only the best funded factual films have the budgets to pay for a specially written music track. Those that do usually negotiate a 'buy-out' deal with a musician – in which the musician agrees to relinquish any rights to further payments from future sales of the film in return for their fee.

Most documentaries and current affairs films use library music to complement their narratives. If you are commissioned by a broadcaster or online platform, you might be able to use library music without a cost to your film if the rights you wish to clear for a piece of music are in fact covered under the licence terms the broadcaster or platform has agreed with the relevant music library.[9] If the licence doesn't cover what you want to do with the music – you have to discuss purchasing a licence either with the library itself in the US, or via a collecting society like the PRS/MCPS[10] in the UK. You can obtain cheaper licences for films being made, for example, for festivals that can later be upgraded if your project does get commissioned.

	SCHEDULE 10						
	TRAVEL/ TRANSPORT	RATE	PREPROD	PROD'N	PREPROD	PROD	TOTAL
			NUMBER NEEDED	NUMBER NEEDED	DAYS NEEDED	DAYS NEEDED	
88	AIRFARES: RECCE	0	0	×	×	×	0
89	AIRFARES: FILMING	0	×	0	×	×	0
90	TAXIS: RECCE	0	0	×	×	×	0
91	TAXIS: FILMING	0	×	0	×	×	0
92	FREIGHT COSTS	0	×	0	×	×	0
93	AGENTS FEES AND CARNETS	0	×	0	×	×	0
94	GRATUITIES	0	0	0	×	×	0
95	VISAS AND FILMING PERMITS	0	0	0	×	×	0
96	VACCINATIONS AND ESSENTIAL MEDICATION	0	0	×	×	×	0
97	EXCESS BAGGAGE	0	×	0	×	×	0
98	CAR HIRE: RECCE	0	×	×	0	×	0

Figure 11.15

99	**CAR HIRE: FILMING**	0	×	×	×	0	0
100	**PARKING: RECCE**	0	×	×	0	×	0
101	**PARKING: FILMING**	0	×	×	×	0	0
						Total:	**0**

Key

☐ Cells containing calculated totals |0| Cells requiring your input |×| Item not required

Figure 11.15 Continued

Schedule 10: Travel/Transport

Some of these categories need little introduction – but one or two will not be obvious to newcomers to filming.

88–89 – Airfares

When estimating airfares it's worth remembering that a fare you see at the time of preparing your budget might have risen by the time you actually come to book it, especially if you're travelling during school holidays when airlines hike up their prices. So build a little slack into your cost estimate.

90–91 – Taxis

- *Low budget films:* taxis might seem like an unnecessary luxury, but there are situations where they might be the only option. On a foreign research trip, for example, if you're travelling light and are really pushed for cash, you can always take a bus to and from the airport. But on film trips, you can't expect people carrying heavy bags to do this. So you might have to cost for taxis instead – and do the same on the return trip. The costs can quickly escalate. You can't precisely estimate how many taxis you'll need – but on all but the smallest budgets it's prudent to cover the project for a certain number of cab fares.

92 – Freight Costs

Covering the cost of transporting items to and from a filming location. If you are on a tight deadline you might decide to send a hard drive with half your rushes back to base so that your editor can begin work before you finish the shoot.

93 – Agents Fees and Carnets

When you travel abroad with filming kit, customs officials in both your home country and the country you're visiting need to know that you are not using the excuse of filming to import or export goods on the quiet without paying tax. So you have to prove that the equipment you take out is exactly the same as the kit you bring back home with you. Carnets are used for this purpose in the 78 countries and regions that are members of the ATA carnet scheme[11] (ATA is an acronym, a combination of the French words 'Admission Temporaire' and the English 'Temporary Admission'). A carnet, then, is a temporary import/export document that lists all the technical items that you're going to be using on your shoot – and allows you to take them into a foreign country and bring them out again without paying any import duties. It's valid for 12 months. Carnets are prepared by official agents (an agent that's been approved by the customs authorities in your home country).

If you are travelling to a country that's not part of the carnet scheme, it's advisable to find an agent in the country you're visiting who understands the local import/export regulations to guide you through the bureaucracy and meet you at the airport to make sure all goes smoothly. Getting a crew into some non-carnet nations can be extremely difficult without such help.

94 – Gratuities

Simply getting things done in some parts of the world is much easier if you have some small change to pay tips to make your filming run smoothly. You might need a few pounds or dollars to give to a security guard to let you get that lovely sunset shot from the top of a building. Or as a thank-you to your driver for working a couple of extra hours when your shoot over-runs. But beware: this is *not* a green light to pay significant sums of money to bribe your way to a key interviewee or to get access to someone acting outside the law. You'll compromise the integrity of your film if you're seen to be buying a story.

95 – Visas and Filming Permits

Many countries require an entry visa and a filming permit before you can travel. This is simply a costing issue for factual films whose content raises no sensitivities with the government of the country in which they are being made. But producers of critical investigative films need to consider whether they can *honestly* fill out a visa application form or filming permit – including a description of the editorial content of the project – without being refused entry. Most democratic countries are used to critical journalism and won't try to prevent filmmakers from accessing their nation. But that's not the case everywhere and you will have to decide whether a more covert approach is appropriate. You might, for example, opt to travel in on a tourist visa and hire a local film crew or a local camera kit. The risks of doing this can be significant, so you must assess them responsibly – with expert and local advice, together with the agreement of your commissioner – prior to putting your plan into action.

96 – Vaccinations and Essential Medication

Anyone travelling on your behalf to a foreign country must be protected against serious local infections – both by being vaccinated and by taking prophylactic medicines on the trip to prevent illnesses like malaria. It's your responsibility to make sure your team know about medical risks and how to protect themselves against them. You also have to pay any costs. Check out the foreign travel section of your government's website for specific information about the risks in any country.[12] Your doctor is, of course, another useful source of advice on medical risks.

97 – Excess Baggage

It's very easy to get stung here for a lot of money if you are travelling abroad with a significant amount of filming equipment. Some airlines charge by the bag (so they allow you to take one bag in the hold and each excess bag is charged). Other airlines charge by the total weight of your bags – giving you an allowance of, say, 30 kilos, and charging for the rest by the kilo. So you need to find out the policy of the airline on which you are flying – and work out your likely excess baggage costs. The costs can be very steep – more than \$1,500 per trip if you are taking a lot of kit away. If the costs rise too high, then consider hiring your camera kit in the country in which you are filming.

98–99 – *Car Hire*

The standard insurance cover that vehicle hire companies offer when you hire a car covers you for third party damage (damage to other vehicles) and injury to other people. But it won't cover you for damage to the vehicle you have hired unless you take out an extra 'all risks' policy. This will increase your hire costs somewhat but is well worth the extra expense for the peace of mind it offers. The last thing you want on a tight budget is to find you've got a £500 bill to repair a dent in the back door.

100–101 – *Parking*

It's usually worth adding a small amount in here if you're going to be working in parking restricted cities.

	SCHEDULE 11						
	HOTEL AND LIVING EXPENSES	RATE	PRE-PROD	PROD'N	PRE-PROD	PROD'N	TOTAL
			NO OF PEOPLE		DAYS		
102	**ACCOMMMODATION: RECCE**	0	0	×	0	×	0
103	**ACCOMMODATION: FILMING**	0	×	0	×	0	0
104	**FOOD: RECCE**	0	0	×	0	×	0
105	**FOOD: FILMING**	0	×	0	×	0	0
106	**HOTEL PHONE**	0	0	0	×	×	0
107	**HOSPITALITY**	0	0	0	×	×	0
						Total:	**0**

Key

▨ Cells containing calculated totals | 0 | Cells requiring your input | × | Item not required

Figure 11.16

Schedule 11: Hotel and Living Expenses

102–107 – *Accommodation, Food, etc*

These lines are self-explanatory.

	SCHEDULE 12	COST	PERIOD REQUIRED			TOTAL
	LEGAL/ INSURANCE		**BEFORE PRODUCTION STARTS**	**ENTIRE PRODUCTION SCHEDULE**	**AFTER FILM IS AIRED**	
108	**PRODUCTION INSURANCE**	0	×	0	×	0
109	**FOREIGN STAFF ACCIDENT INSURANCE**	0	×	0	×	0
110	**E&O INSURANCE**	0	×	×	0	0
111	**LEGAL ADVICE (E&O COVER)**	0	×	×	0	0
112	**LEGAL ADVICE (CONTRACT)**	0	0	×	×	0
					Total:	0

Key

Cells containing calculated totals | 0 | Cells requiring your input | × | Item not required

Figure 11.17

Schedule 12: Legal/Insurance

The items in this schedule protect your team, your contributors, people you come across during your film trip, the equipment you hire and your rushes from the unforeseen. They also protect production companies from the costs of being sued before and after a film has been aired.

108 – Production Insurance

A production company that's commissioned and funded by a broadcaster or an online platform will have to sign a contract that commits it to taking out professional production insurance to cover against a range of risks. No commissioner wants to hand over a large sum of money only to find that all the hard drives containing your rushes have been stolen at the end of a shoot – and you have nothing to edit and no way of affording a re-shoot. Production insurance covers you against such a loss, and many other losses, by providing financial compensation to get you out of such a fix.

There are lots of insurers. While the insurance they offer is generally the same, different companies offer various enhancements to the cover and it's worth shopping around. The policies contain sections that are not likely to be relevant to most factual films (insuring animals used in filming, for example, cover for filming in planes or boats, insuring hired-in craning equipment). I've ignored these in what follows and give a brief overview of the key production and personal insurances that are likely to be pertinent to most factual films.

This overview is *not* a substitute for the policy wording itself. As ever with insurance policies: READ THE SMALL PRINT CAREFULLY to understand what's covered, what isn't covered and the compliance information to ensure you don't invalidate the policy simply through ignorance.

Cast cover. Insures the production against the additional costs of a key member of the team falling sick, having an accident, dying or suffering an unforeseen bereavement. Cast cover pays out for any extra costs incurred by having to delay the production – or reimburses you the money spent if you have to abandon the project. Key team members have to complete a statement of health declaration – or have a medical examination – and have this accepted by the insurers before they are covered for any risk other than an accident.

Film Union Travel Insurance. This offers financial compensation if any member of the production crew is injured, disabled or killed in an accident while working on the film. For normal activities, it applies anywhere in the world apart from the crew member's home territory. For hazardous activities agreed by the insurer, it applies anywhere in the world. FUTI usually covers medical and emergency travel expenses; loss of or damage to baggage, equipment and money; unavoidable changes, cancellations or delays to travel arrangements. It doesn't cover incidents caused by war/ terrorism. If you are travelling to a war zone or a country where terrorism is likely, you'll need to take out an extra accident policy tailored to such areas.

Media. Insurance that covers the production against the loss, damage or destruction of the rushes, sound track and archive footage. Insurers insist that you test the camera, lenses, storage media and sound equipment before the start of filming; that you check the quality of each day's filming as soon as possible after the shoot ends; and obtain the insurers' agreement to the back-up, storage and security arrangements you've put in place for the rushes.

Extra expense. Provides cover against any extra production costs as a result of damage to or destruction of a property being used by the production. It also insures the production against the breakdown of camera, sound and lighting equipment and portable generators that have been shown to be working before the start of work; against power failures and against strikes, bomb scares or civil protests preventing the production from entering a location.

Technical equipment. Covers the production for the cost of repairing or replacing camera, sound, lighting and other equipment that's lost or damaged. But not against unexplained or mysterious losses

Production office contents. Covers the physical loss of or damage to temporary office contents like computers, hired in for the production.

Money. Protects against the loss, theft or destruction of production money, unless left unattended in hotel rooms, unlocked offices or vehicles.

Terrorism. Covers the production if an act of terrorism damages property within their own country under the Media, Extra Expense, Technical Equipment, Production office Contents and Money sections of the policy. It also covers the production for extra expense caused by acts of Terrorism in the home nation that do not result in property damage – and for any loss caused by an act of terrorism in the UK that leads to illness or an injury in an individual insured under the cast cover section of the policy.

Public and product liability. Covers the production for its legal liability to pay compensation if someone not working on the film is injured or their property is damaged as a result of the production's negligence.

Employers Liability (UK)/Worker's Compensation (US). Covers the production's legal liability to pay compensation for an employee who is injured or contracts an illness as a result of the production's negligence while working on the film. In both the UK and US it is a legal requirement that employers obtain this kind of cover. If you are employing foreign nationals based in their own country, you may need to take out extra local liability cover.

Property of others. Covering the production's legal liability for any damage or loss of property owned by others that's being used in your production and is not covered by any other section of the insurance, so long as you have taken reasonable care of the property.

109 – Foreign Staff Accident Insurance

The cover offered by production insurance policies does not normally extend to people you employ who are foreign nationals. So if you are asking a fixer to work with you in another country, especially when working on difficult and potentially dangerous projects, you shouldn't forget to offer them some accident cover in case they get injured while working for you. You will have to take out a separate insurance policy to do this.

110 – E&O Insurance

E&O stands for 'Errors and Omissions' – and this is insurance cover that pays out if your film gets sued after it's been publicly screened. It covers the production against a range of legal risks including defamation, confidentiality breaches, copyright infringement, and privacy claims. If a production company is sued, defending an action can cost hundreds of thousands of dollars or more – and without insurance, the costs can quickly push your company into liquidation or you into bankruptcy. Most broadcasters insist that you get this cover in the contract you sign. And if you plan to distribute the film, E&O insurance will also be obligatory. An E&O policy covers a film for a certain number of years in the territory in which it is first broadcast. If the film is to be shown elsewhere, you either have to negotiate an extension or take out a new E&O to cover the countries in which it will be shown.

E&O Insurance

America

If you want your project broadcast and distributed, you need E&O cover. In my experience, networks and studios always require it. Ultimately what networks and studios are trying to do is eliminate risk. If you have a production agreement with any US network, they are almost categorically going to require that you indemnify them for everything. If there's a claim based on the broadcast, you're on the hook. And if you don't have E&O cover that could put you out of business because you are ultimately going to be paying to defend the claim. When we talk about considering legal risks and legal review, we can do everything in our power to ensure that we minimized the risks that, once this programme is broadcast, there should be no valid claim based on it. But what we can not ever do is guarantee there won't be any claims. People bring claims all the time that don't have a valid legal basis – especially in the US. They don't always go to court. They're not always formal complaints. But complaints have to be addressed and can be expensive and time consuming even if you ultimately 'win'. In most cases you're not going to recover the attorney's fees and all the other associated costs, and so having E&O in place just limits that liability to your deductible and you know, worst case scenario, you're probably not going out of business.

Mike Cleaver, US Media Attorney

Britain

Historically it was only used in certain types of projects but increasingly it has now become the norm – and the reason for that is it provides a level of protection for the filmmakers and their financiers in relation to any potential legal claim that may arise on the distribution of the film internationally. It is now considered to be best practice to acquire errors and omissions insurance – and in most contractual distribution arrangements, it is a mandatory requirement. So producers who feel they don't have the money to buy it, in many ways it's quite a simple answer: if you don't have it you would be unable to distribute your film. It protects the filmmakers from a variety of legal claims including defamation, confidentiality, certain types of copyright claims, privacy claims and it requires the film to effectively be vetted by a lawyer, either at the end of the film or during production, who then provides an opinion to the insurers saying: the film effectively is robust enough to defend claims internationally.

Prash Naik, UK Media Lawyer and Channel 4 TV General Counsel 2014–2017

111 – Legal Advice (E&O Insurance)

When you apply to an insurer for an E&O policy, the proposal form asks a lot of questions about the production company and the film. It also asks for the name, contacts and experience of the lawyer who will be checking your final film script for E&O purposes. You are asking an insurer to cover you in the event that your film is sued for libel. Inevitably, the insurer wants reassurance that all has been done to minimize this risk – so you have to budget for an experienced media lawyer to cast their eye over your script in advance of its first screening. Their advice might force you to make adjustments to your commentary or structure – so you should leave room for this at the end of your editing schedule.

112 – Legal Advice (Contract)

Some production companies pay a lawyer to advise on the contract offered to them by a broad-caster or online platform, to ensure that their rights in the film are protected and that what's formally being asked of them in the small print is reasonable. This can be money well spent because contractual language is complicated and without an experienced legal eye looking over the wording you might find yourself agreeing clauses that, later on, you will regret. Alternatively you might wish to add a clause to protect an interest that only an experienced media lawyer will be able to identify. And if your film has the potential of selling abroad, you are going to have to share some of the foreign sales proceeds with your commissioning department. But what that proportion is, and what can be allowable as the costs of such sales before any such split is made, is normally a matter of negotiation. With the internet and catch-up services, this whole area is very complex, and a knowledgeable media lawyer who's aware of industry norms can be invaluable.

	SCHEDULE 13						
	PRODUCTION OVERHEADS	RATE	PRE	PROD'N	EDIT	POST	TOTAL
			WEEKS OR NUMBER	WEEKS OR NUMBER	WEEKS OR NUMBER	WEEKS OR NUMBER	
113	**OFFICE RENT**	0	0	0	0	0	0
114	**PHONE**	0	0	0	0	0	0
115	**POST/ STATIONERY**	0	0	0	0	0	0
116	**COURIERS/ TAXIS: (OFFICE)**	0	0	0	0	0	0
						Total:	**0**

Key

  Cells containing calculated totals | 0 | Cells requiring your input

Figure 11.18

Schedule 13: Production Overheads

113 – Office Rent

If you are running your film production from home, you won't get a very sympathetic hearing from a cost controller if you add office rental into your budget. So you'll need to justify adding this line into your budget. And if you are in the fortunate position of running more than one project at a time from the same base, you might have to charge a fraction of the weekly office rent that you are paying. What is acceptable here also depends on the kind of budget you are being offered: very low budget productions are unlikely to be able to charge rent – and you might have no choice other than to run such a project from home or swallow the cost of rent.

114–115 – Phone, Stationery and Postage

You are going to have phone charges and stationery, postage costs to pay at your base and should estimate a likely amount during the different parts of the production. The phone costs are over and above those that your film crew will rack up while on location.

116 – Couriers/Taxis (Office)

The same applies to couriers and taxis needed at your base – or your post-production suite. The lower your budget – the less likely you are to be offered anything in this category.

Notes

1 Appendix 1 in the following guide lists the film production jobs the tax office recognizes as normally being self-employed. https://webarchive.nationalarchives.gov.uk/20140206155209/ www.hmrc.gov.uk/specialist/fi-notes-2012.pdf

2 In fact the 13.8% employers' contribution on PAYE staff is only paid on earnings above what's known as the 'secondary threshold' which in 2020 was £169 per week.

3 As a rough guide you might allow one day to post produce a 15 minute film – up to three days for a 50 minute film.

4 Anything delivered to broadcaster – and to some online platforms – has to have a sound and picture quality control report. This is generated automatically by putting the film through analytical software that delivers a verdict on whether the audio and video levels and various other technical specifications comply with established standards. The software on offline computers is not sophisticated enough to be able to achieve this.

5 Footage from some cameras will need conversion first – for example high spec cameras like the Arri Alexa that records images at a very high megabit rate, or 4K cameras that shoot in very high definition because their files are so large they'd unacceptably slow down performance during the edit.

6 Fast turn-around current affairs films sometimes use this guide narration in the final film.

7 Look at www.pond5.com; www.criticalpast.com; www.alamy.com; https://dissolve.com; https://vimeo.com/stock

8 Try http://footagefarm.co.uk/

9 These rights include the geographical area covered by the licence; the kind of programme you are making (e.g. a feature film? TV programmes? A corporate film, etc.); and where your programme is going to be shown (TV broadcast? An online platform?, etc.).

10 www.prsformusic.com. This is the website of the PRS (Performing Rights Society) and the MCPS (Mechanical Copyright Protection Society) which pay royalties to members for music used in TV films or radio shows, broadcast on TV or radio, performed in public, streamed, downloaded or copied onto CDs or DVDs.

11 More information on carnets can be found here: https://iccwbo.org/resources-for-business/ata-carnet/ata-carnet-country/

12 In the UK go to www.gov.uk/foreign-travel-advice – in the US see https://travel.state.gov/content/passports/en/country.html

Index